For the Love of His Own Creation

A Novel by Yeshua ben Yosef

Jane Gartshore

This novel is a work of fiction. Any names or characters, businesses or places, events or incidents, are used in a fictitious manner. Any resemblance to actual persons, living or dead, or actual events is purely coincidental.

Copyright © 2016 by Jane Gartshore. Canada. All rights reserved. No part of this book may be reproduced by any means without the prior written permission of the author, except for brief passages quoted in reviews.

The author may be contacted at: ForTheLoveNovel@gmail.com

ISBN: 978-1-365-43373-3

I dedicate my efforts to:

my mother, Hazel, who brought me into this world and continues to nurture and love me as I continue to grow

my father, Tom, who taught me to appreciate beauty in music, nature, literature, and art

and you, the reader—one of my many beautiful brothers and sisters in God's creation.

Jane Gartshore
August 2016

Contents

Acknowledgements iii

Preface v

Introduction 1

Chapter 1: The Final Day 3

Chapter 2: The Journey 7

Chapter 3: An Introduction 11

Chapter 4: The Past Revisited 19

Chapter 5: A Heart Awakened 25

Chapter 6: The Bond Forged 31

Chapter 7: Life Begun Anew 51

Chapter 8: The Oneness 57

Chapter 9: The Path Lit 63

Chapter 10: The Realm Beyond 71

Chapter 11: Into the Water 73

Chapter 12: The World Away 81

Chapter 13: Lost and Found 95

Chapter 14: Tanlar 109

Chapter 15: A Difficult Choice 115

Chapter 16: The Darkness 123

Chapter 17: The Great Truth 143

Chapter 18: Two Paths Diverge 151

Chapter 19: Borne into the Light 163

Chapter 20: A Summons 183

Chapter 21: The Effort to Save Halfene 189

Chapter 22: Truth and Prophecy 215

Chapter 23: The Wave 237

Chapter 24: The Paths Converge 269

Chapter 25: The Light 287

Epilogue 291

Pronunciation Guide 293

Acknowledgements

I would first like to acknowledge, with deep love and gratitude, my partner, Derek, and my children, Avery, Aeron, and Ember, for their patience and cooperation over the past year and a half as I prepared for and carried out this work.

To my beloved sisters and brothers in the Divine Love community: I thank you for your prayerful support of me and my family, for it has really helped. I would especially like to thank the following people for their moral support: Al, Jeanne, Judy, Betty, Terry, Helge, Hazel, Karen, Ellen, Jolene, Hal, Arie, and Marion. Geoff, I thank you for your publishing expertise and willingness to help. Eva, your last minute eagle-eyes were a blessing!

To my team of angels: I thank you for being by my side and at my call through all the ups and downs, tears, joy and frustration. I deeply appreciate the loving guidance, protection, and encouragement you give me.

To Yeshua: I thank you from the depths of my soul for your care of me during this amazing experience. I thank you for the opportunity to do this work; for the story, itself, which has touched my heart and inspired me; for the healings, guidance, and wisdom you have given me; for your patience with me when I have faltered. You have challenged me to grow more than I thought possible, and you have taught me, above all else, to seek first the Kingdom of God. I am humbled by your great love for your earthly brothers and sisters and by your willingness to see past our flaws, failures, and darkness to the light that shines within.

And lastly, to God: thank You for *everything*.

Preface

I did not write this book; I was its surrogate mother. The story came through me—channeled, via dictation—over a period of 6 months from early December, 2015 to early June, 2016. Its true author is the spirit who was known in his time on Earth as Yeshua ben Yosef—Jesus, son of Joseph, known to many as Jesus Christ. Although Yeshua inhabits the Celestial Kingdom and is very close to our Creator, he continues to lovingly involve himself in humanity's struggles and reaches out to individuals in many ways, through personal responses as well as through messages given through many mediums all over the world.

It was in May of 2015 that Yeshua (whom I usually call Jesus, out of habit) informed me that the project we would be doing together was a book; he did not mention that it would be a novel. When he did eventually break the news to me, I was surprised and wondered if I had heard him right! The idea of Jesus writing a novel, in spirit, seemed bizarre; teaching truths through parables while he was alive was one thing, but creating a few hundred pages of dramatic story with many well-developed characters was something entirely out of the ordinary. However, now that I have read the work many times through, I can see that this was a brilliant idea.

As the story unfolded I was challenged on many levels: physically, it was tiring fitting in this work with the busy schedule of motherhood—at times I would get up in the middle of the night to write; a level of spiritual commitment was required that I was not, at first, ready to give; and my faith was tested frequently. In the very beginning my ego got involved and I wanted to contribute my creative skills to the project—by suggesting different descriptive adjectives or sentence structures, for example. I got attached to the characters and didn't want anything bad to happen to them; it was difficult for me to get through the ugly and tragic parts of the story. I laugh now at my immaturity and ignorance and marvel at Yeshua's seemingly infinite patience. All of these challenges drove me deeper into prayer and so, with God's help, I was eventually able to complete the transcription and correction and proofreading of this amazing story.

I recorded this book with love, as it was written with love, about love. I hope you will open your heart and soul as you read it, that you may be touched and inspired by the messages within it. *God loves us.*

Jane Gartshore

For the Love of His Own Creation

Introduction

My brothers and sisters who read this book: to you I speak. This is a book that is not to be taken lightly. I have written it that you will learn from it. Please take to heart its message of love; you will need this love in the times to come, when your faith will determine the road that you must travel. Do not be afraid of darkness, but seek to know your God, and He will bring you into His light. I am the way, and I shall lead you. Peace be within you as you read. You are loved. I am your friend, your brother, and I walk with you.

Yeshua ben Yosef
August 11, 2016
Received by Jane Gartshore
British Columbia, Canada

Chapter 1

The Final Day

It was her love that called him that day, that drew him past the borders of what he then called home. His desire for freedom, which had always been the driving force within his being, fueled his escape. Freedom was something he had sought with desperation, and he had given up much convenience in its pursuit; because of this, he had little money and he ate simply. His endless wants were never met, but his basic needs were taken care of. His mother loved him. His father went away often. In his youth, his father had instructed him in the ways of their people, but those efforts were lost on him.

As puzzling as it was to him, there was no one to help him liberate himself from the confining existence in this small town. His cries were unheard; his mischief-making was to no avail. He was not wanted. Furthermore, the pace at which he carried out his duties as a citizen was far too slow.

The change came upon him rather suddenly. It *dawned* on him. He took it seriously and made the decision, in that one brief moment, to go forth alone, to do things his way, to neglect his duties completely, and to leave the only home he had ever known. Once he made the decision, time was short; there were no farewells, not even to his parents, whom he genuinely loved. He knew he would see them again some day, and for now that was enough.

Chapter 1

He packed what little he could collect in the span of a few short minutes, paused to look at his reflection in the only mirror in the house, and simply left. A smile spread across his face the moment he closed the door. He had no idea in which direction he was headed, but he yearned to take that first step.

Soon it became obvious that he should go west, in the direction of the mountains. He lifted his pack over his shoulder, took a brief look at his house, and headed off along a well-beaten path that meandered next to a row of uniform houses and exited the town at its most westerly gate.

There were many things in life for which this man was unprepared. One of them was this journey. He had a strong will, which drew him along the path, but there was little else to support him. His will was informed by something much deeper that he could not yet recognize: something foreign to him and, by nature, mysterious.

The sun was beginning to set behind the mountains ahead. He had gone this way many times before. The rough paths were well known to him—in daylight, at least. He had a resolved look in his eyes, a determination to face the fears of an unknown fate and to forge ahead, whatever the journey should present.

It was not long before the mountains rose up before him. They were tall, but still topped with green, despite the approaching winter. The air was chilly, and it occurred to him that he had not thought to bring his warmest cloak. He brushed away the thought and began to ascend, quickening his pace to keep warm. His pack was becoming heavier and pressed upon his neck. Once he attained a view of the valley below he laid the pack down with a loud thump and took a deep breath. There was not much to see. It was already quite dark, and there were no lights to be seen. He looked up. A few stars were visible in the clear sky, but the moon could not be found.

He lay for a while on a small blanket near a meagre fire that he had made from twigs. It provided little comfort, and again he lamented omitting to pack his warm cloak. He was not used to sleeping in discomfort, but he shrugged it off and allowed his thoughts to drift to better things. The excitement and anticipation he felt about the next leg of his journey kept him amused for hours until the sun broke through the small trees lining the path from where he had come. He was on his feet and striding down toward the valley by the time the early morning rays touched the place where he had rested. His boots left a mark that he had been there and then gone.

Chapter 2

The Journey

He made much progress the second day, which was, in fact, the first day of his life-begun-anew. Through the valley he went and on up the steep slope on the other side. Here the path was less obvious, and he faltered briefly, unsure of his direction. His inner compass was pointing him north now, and although the westward route appeared to be easier, he chose to turn to the right and forge ahead. His rations had dwindled drastically—another oversight—and he was feeling irritable. He was not one to skip meals.

Up to this point, Morok had not come across any other travelers, and he was enjoying the solitude. But lo and behold, he caught the sound of a conversation echoing nearby. His heart pounded in his chest as he darted, like a fugitive, behind the nearest rock. He crouched low, kept his breathing shallow, and froze until they were well past him and no longer visible. His unrest surprised him. What was he afraid of—that they would convince him to return home? Or that he would want to go back to the comforts that awaited him there?

No, he thought firmly to himself, *there is nothing for me there*. And with that decision, he started off again, wiping the sweat from his brow, and sped off up the trail.

The next day he was far removed from the territory he had been raised in. He had never traveled this far afield. It

Chapter 2

excited him and fueled his resolve to go beyond the confines of his old life. Leaving the mountains behind, he pursued a course northward through a dense evergreen forest that he had only heard about as a child. It led to the boundary of a neighboring country, one to which he felt he must go.

He was beginning to lose weight, having eaten the last of his food supply the previous day. He was on the move constantly, and even at night he made an attempt to cover some ground. The urgency he felt within to *be* somewhere kept him moving and kept him strong. He would not be deterred from his path.

As he was collecting water from a small stream he had come upon in the forest, it occurred to him that he had done so once before. *I must have dreamt this*, he reflected. He paused for a moment and strained to recall if that was true. Then he stood up, shrugging off the notion. But it disturbed him that he could not remember, for the feeling was strong that he had been there before.

When Morok was young he loved to walk among the trees. There was a forest to the east of the town that he frequented, searching for firewood and berries. Being in the company of trees was to him as pleasing as attending a gathering of people. And now he had that same distinct sense, that he was with a friendly group.

After two more full days of walking he decided to rest and to reevaluate his course. His energy was flagging, and physically he was tired. He felt a pang of homesickness, which he tried to ignore; it was probably just his empty stomach attempting to remind him of the bounty he had left behind. He looked about him, scanning the area for signs of food.

Back in the town the search party that had set out to find him the day after he disappeared returned wearily with little to report. Although his tracks had been easy to follow, there was no indication that this was an innocent trip into the mountains and back. He had left. And there was little they could do to foster his return. His parents were relieved—there had been no indication that he had been harmed. And although it concerned them that he had not told them he was going, they did feel, deep within themselves, that he would return some day. That gave them comfort. Morok's older sister, who had passed him on the trail without knowing it, scowled irritably. "Well, isn't that just like him, to rush off on a whim with nothing but the shirt on his back!" But she, too, knew that he was not gone forever. "I hope he will learn something useful on his journey," she added, glancing at the door.

"Be well, Morok!" the three chimed, in unison. It was a message of love, meant to reach his ears, wherever he may be.

Morok did feel something at that moment, but he brushed it off as meaningless. He decided to move on. He hoped to find something he could hunt for dinner. He needed food.

As luck would have it, food appeared soon after in the form of a small rabbit. It took a while for him to prepare and cook it, but the sustenance it provided was worth the effort. Morok smiled and felt a growing urge to seek somewhere inhabited, where meals were more readily available. He had not intended to be on his own for this long.

The following day the landscape changed again. Rolling hills were dotted with bare trees. He changed his course slightly to the east, as there were signs of civilization in that direction. He spotted a herd of cattle feeding on the bits of grass that strained to grow in the cold. He quickened his pace and was soon among the animals, enjoying the presence of sentient beings all around him. They were quite

Chapter 2

docile, and he was able to get close enough to benefit from the warmth of their hairy bodies. As he passed through to the hill bordering the field where they were grazing, he thought he heard his name called. He paused to listen but did not hear it again.

The days were noticeably shorter now, and the cold penetrated his body more deeply. He thought of spending the night among the cattle, where he could benefit from their body heat, but his drive to push ahead was strong, and he was determined to reach the town before dawn. Guided by starlight alone, it was not always easy to find a path, yet the terrain itself was not difficult. By the light of the breaking dawn he did indeed come upon what looked like a large town, perched on the edge of a river.

Chapter 3

An Introduction

With an excited gasp he scampered over a fallen log and broke into a run. There were some people about at this time—people not unlike himself, although dressed in slightly different garb, which was more appropriate for the climate. He smiled as he passed them, and they nodded back at him in greeting. *I wonder if they speak the same language*, he thought. He was soon answered: a young boy waved him over. He slowed his pace and walked up to the boy, displaying a gentle grin.

"Who are you?" asked the boy, in a familiar dialect.

"Morok of Gate-Town," he replied, and added, "Who are you?"

"Zev-ran, of Palador." The boy smiled. "Come!"

He led Morok along a wagon trail that stopped at what appeared to be the entrance to the town. Although the buildings here were not similar to those of Gate-Town, he felt strangely at home. Even the people seemed familiar to him. Everywhere he went with the boy they were greeted with smiling faces and an occasional invitation to stop and converse. He felt welcome.

The boy led him on to a small shop, where he was finally able to sit down in a chair. He sighed with relief and set down his pack. The boy, who was probably close to ten years old, invited him into the shop to meet his parents, the

Chapter 3

owners. Reluctant to get up, yet grateful for the boy's help, he entered the building and waited patiently while the boy described to his parents how he had found Morok while playing in the fields and how far Morok had journeyed to get there. Interested in getting to know him better, they offered him a chair, a bottle of wine, and some hot food. Morok was delighted.

The boy wished to please his new friend and kept offering him more helpings of food. The conversation was lively. Although the town was not isolated, visitors seldom came, and the ones that did come were mostly just passing through. The boy's parents asked Morok many questions about his life in that town where they had never been. Was it possible that they had relatives there? Was the journey to Palador difficult on foot? Morok responded to their questions, pleased at the attention he was getting. His belly was full, which it had not been in days, and this renewed his vigor.

After a while they were joined by Zev-ran's youngest sister, a little waif of a girl with bright eyes and keen observation. She said little, but watched the speakers as they rallied back and forth. Zev-ran, himself, lost interest after a while and retired upstairs to his sleeping quarters, where his play-things were kept. Morok could hear him chattering away to himself and occasionally singing. It was quite endearing.

The adults talked well into the night. Although they did not have a bed to offer Morok, he was content to be indoors, and the fire kept him warm all night. They brought him an extra blanket to cushion him from the hard wooden floor boards, and he slept soundly.

In the morning the conversations continued, but the topic changed to his current wishes and future plans. Might he stay in their town? But Morok had no answers at this time. His heart was silent, taking in the joy of their company and letting that gently feed his soul.

An Introduction

Zev-ran was at his side again that day, touring him through the streets, introducing him to his friends, neighbors, relatives, and various other townspeople. It seemed like he knew every person who lived there. What intrigued Morok the most about this place was the apparent lack of structure. There was a free flow. No one seemed to *have* to be anywhere at a certain time. There were not any placards displayed, as there were in Gate-Town, advising people of the various rules and regulations that one *should* adhere to. One could breathe easily here. There was also an openness, or even innocence, to the people, as if there were no secrets among them. He could look them in the eye. This place felt right.

Zev-ran led him up a small, south-facing hill and announced, "This is where we hold our marriage ceremonies." He paused and added, rather shyly, "Perhaps you will be married here some day." Morok did not reply right away, but absorbed the words quietly.

"I think I shall," he whispered.

The evening was uneventful. The previous night's conversation had left everyone with plenty of thoughts to mull over and not as many questions to ask. Morok helped to carry firewood and to clean up after the evening meal. There was no talk of him staying somewhere else, and he rested peacefully again by the fire.

The second morning of his stay in Palador the sun shone brightly. Frost glittered everywhere, and the town was bustling with people. He noticed, for the first time, the horses. Gate-Town, perhaps due to the lack of good pasture, had few. Here they were as commonplace as wrens, and very beautiful. The women here were beautiful too, but it was a different beauty than he was accustomed to, the kind that could not fade with age. It shone as brightly in the eldest elder as it did in the women of his own age. They were lights, every one of them. He thought of his sister, whom he greatly

Chapter 3

admired, but who always felt the need to hide herself beneath layers of paint. The faces were plain here, not painted, not bejeweled, yet they glowed.

Zev-ran led him to the outskirts of town that day so they could hike to a ridge that gave an expansive view of not only the town, but all of the surrounding geography as well. It was a quick climb for Morok, who was strengthened from his journey, and Zev-ran followed closely behind him, giving directions when asked.

The view was breathtaking. The river, which lay to the east, twisted and turned all the way to what looked like a distant sea, gray with storm clouds over it. He could see craft of various sizes making their way along the water, laden with goods and some, with animals. The vessels which had sails sped quickly along the water, while the movements of some of the smaller boats seemed almost imperceptible. Turning to the south he saw an expanse of fields, populated with livestock. It was here he had first met his young friend. Although it had only been a number of days ago, his feeling was that he had been in the boy's company a year already.

There were a few outbuildings, in various states of repair, at the base of the ridge, opposite to where they had ascended. He could not make out their purpose, so he questioned Zev-ran.

Zev-ran paused. "The small one is where we keep our loved ones who have gone before us."

"You don't bury them?" Morok inquired, puzzled.

"My parents told me that after the fire burns them up, we must put the ashes into the big bowl where the others are and mix them all together. It keeps them together on the other side of life, so that they can help each other out."

Morok did not know how to respond to this novel idea, and he merely lowered his head. Zev-ran was not offended by Morok's apparent discomfort but did not say more. He gestured to Morok to follow him to the highest

An Introduction

point of the ridge; there, they sat on a rock facing the afternoon sun. Zev-ran offered Morok some bread and butter and dried fruit, and they conversed casually until the darkening sky signaled their return to the town.

The evening was spent once more in quiet conversation, and Morok shared his deep gratitude for the kindness of his hosts and his young friend and tour guide.

The third day began more abruptly, as Zev-ran barged into the main room announcing excitedly, "Another visitor! Another visitor!"

Zev-ran's friend had brought over a man from a nearby town who had arrived during the night on horseback. Although he was a stranger, his town was not unknown to the family. He carried a funny-looking case with an inscription on it. Morok could not understand the text and turned to ask Zev-ran's father to read it for him, but before he could begin his request, the man came up to him with an outstretched hand and said, "I am Peter."

Morok smiled, stated his own name, and boldly inquired about what was in that case.

"I will show you," he replied, and proceeded to open the case. He gently removed a wooden instrument, brought it up to his shoulder, and began to play. His music entranced them, and he continued to play for many minutes before opening his eyes and gently replacing the violin in its case.

"I am a musician," he announced, "and I have come to entertain at your stage." He gave a little bow and smiled at the group, looking at each one in turn. "I'd best be on my way," he said gently, "for I have traveled far and have much need of rest." Zev-ran's friend exited the house, followed by the musician.

They had not gone far when a loud noise, accompanied by some hustle and bustle, shook up the street nearby. A cart had overturned and emptied its load onto the street. The musician rushed over to help, and he could see that indeed there was need of it: a small child lay trapped beneath a heavy box. He and the cart's owner pushed the box from its resting place atop the boy and rolled it off to the side. The boy's eyes were wide open with fright as he looked up at his father, but he seemed unhurt. He stood up, brushed himself off, and wobbled over to sit down on a small chair in front of the shop where they had crashed. After Peter helped the boy's father untangle his horse's harness and right the cart, they sat down with the boy. Zev-ran's friend had gone to get more help to clean up the mess and returned with a few townspeople.

Everywhere Peter went that day he was met with kindness. His guide and new-found friend, Olner, showed him a world he had scarcely known existed. It was a world of open doorways and helping hands, a place of honesty and truth. He fit right in.

His concert was scheduled for the following evening, and he took some time alone in the afternoon to practice. He was not alone for long, as the sound of his playing drew many curious listeners from their places of occupation to the little alcove where he was sitting. He wondered if they had ever heard this kind of music before. His town was well-populated with musicians, and he guessed that here he was a bit of an oddity—but a welcome one. They listened intently, and he played on. He chose melodies he had composed himself and was happy to see that they were well-received. He looked forward to entertaining a larger crowd.

Back at Zev-ran's home, Morok was reading a book about the experiences of one of the town's founding families. This story told of their adventures as they traveled from a city far away with little else but their skills and their desire for a better life. Morok could relate.

Day by day he was growing more accustomed to his new life. Zev-ran's parents offered him a permanent place in their home in exchange for help at their shop. They sold fish.

The fish were caught mainly by local fishermen who fished the sea at the mouth of the river. The fish were dried and then displayed in small wooden boxes in the shop's window.

Morok liked his job. He picked up the fish from the drying houses and packaged them into boxes. The boxes had to be made, and this was done in a shed behind the shop. Zev-ran assisted him. Fish was a favored food in this town; it was preferred over meat. The cows Morok had seen were used mainly for milking. Since he had arrived he had eaten fish prepared in seven different ways and a large amount of cheese. He drank milk and also a tea made from the leaves of an herb they called nanchun. It tasted sweet, and he liked it.

Winter was coming. More firewood was needed, and Morok was happy to assist. He felt differently about his duties here than those he had been assigned to in Gate-Town. There he was always reluctant to do anything that others required of him, for it took him away from his idle thoughts. But this was a whole new experience for him, this willingness to serve those with whom he shared his existence. He loved his new life.

Chapter 4
The Past Revisited

Morok was the happiest he had ever been. With Zev-ran at his side, providing him with much-needed companionship, he seldom felt lonely, and he was able to show the boy many things he had learned growing up in Gate-Town. Zev-ran, in turn, instructed him in the customs of Palador. Their time together was rich and varied. Some days they worked and some they spent climbing the hills overlooking the town.

Zev-ran taught him to ride a horse. He was timid at first but was soon encouraged by the horse's patience and calm. Zev-ran knew of Morok's hesitance around both horses and women, and he wished to help the young man overcome his fears. From his perspective there was nothing to be afraid of in either situation. The women of this town were friendly, and the horses were, for the most part, gentle. In Zev-ran's opinion, Morok should have both! To find him a horse would be easy. Finding Morok a wife was proving to be rather challenging. In this town the majority of the women were married already. The youngest ones, who had not yet been chosen as mates, still had their hearts set on marrying certain young men they had grown up with and considered to be loyal friends. Morok was now twenty-six years old and long past the age when most married here. Yet he was still young, in many respects, and would be desirable, had there been any older women available.

Chapter 4

Fortunately for Morok, spring brought new hope. With the arrival of warmer weather came an influx of vessels up the river, carrying goods from settlements across the sea. Typically much was traded at this time of year, and occasionally some families chose to stay and work in Palador. This particular year there were two families that stayed on, and one of them had four daughters.

Morok happened upon the group of young women one afternoon when he was waiting to help unload a fishing boat. He caught their attention with his singing—he had been singing an old tune from home as he paced back and forth by the river. His eyes were cast downward as he walked, and he did not catch the furtive glances of the young women who were crouched by the river's edge, washing their clothes. By the time he stopped singing, they were fully staring at him. It was then that he finally noticed and gave them his attention.

Morok was curious. Who were these young women and where had they come from? Surely they were not native to Palador. He was certain Zev-ran had already introduced him to every female in the town. Their dress was that of a colder climate, and they wore shawls that covered their heads. The colors were dark but their faces were bright and youthful. He walked up to them, overcoming what was holding his feet to the ground. He approached them with a quiet smile and introduced himself as Morok of Gate-Town. Although the name hardly fit him anymore, it was familiar and explained his origin to people he met. But he wished to be free of this link to his former residence, a man with no ties that bound him, but rather one who had the freedom to go beyond a name or a place. He deeply yearned for this. So when he gave the women his name it diminished him somewhat. He paused slightly, then added brightly, "And this is my new home. Welcome to Palador!"

The youngest of them blushed and looked at her sisters. "We have traveled far over the water and shall travel

The Past Revisited

yet further, yet we will stay awhile and are happy to become acquainted with the town and its customs."

Another added, "Please show us how to find our way back to the village."

They did not give him their names at this point, but they quietly packed up their clothing and followed his lead as he chose one of the two trails that led from the river's edge to the town's entrance on that side. Morok had to return quickly to where he had been waiting for the boat and promised to discourse with them again soon. They bid him farewell and headed off toward the rooming house where their family was staying.

The rest of the day was uneventful, and Morok found himself reflecting on his days in Palador. He had chosen to stay, to live his life among these exceedingly kind people whom he held in high esteem. He was happy and felt no urge to stray. He did not know why he had been drawn there so many months prior and, when he looked back, he felt rather shocked that he had abandoned his life in Gate-Town so easily. He thought of his parents and longed to see them. There was an empty place in his heart, and he wished for a deeper connection with his mother and father. He feared he had hurt them by leaving. He had not said good-bye, and he regretted that deeply.

The next day Morok spoke with Zev-ran's parents about the possibility of borrowing one of their horses to make a trip home to Gate-Town to visit his family. They consented and suggested that Zev-ran accompany him to gain knowledge of the surrounding area.

It was two weeks before they set out. There was much work to be done at the shop and neither could be spared until it was finished. But finally, the day arrived. They set out early, hoping to reach the mountains by nightfall. Morok had an air of nervous anticipation, and Zev-ran could see that this reunion was important to him. Morok said little during the

Chapter 4

early part of the journey; he seemed to be lost in thought. Zev-ran had endless questions about not only the lay of the land, but about what he would see and who he would meet in Gate-Town. He was excited, and his boyish enthusiasm pulled Morok out of his reverie. Morok was happy to answer his questions, and they forged ahead to the foot of the mountains.

The next morning they tackled the ascent on horseback. The animals had rested well and were sure-footed. Although the path was narrow, it did not pose a problem, and their journey was smooth. As they approached the outskirts of town that evening, Morok was seized with emotion and could barely contain the tears that threatened to escape the stronghold of his consciousness. He was home.

His reunion with his family was awkward. Although they were happy to see him, they had many questions about his departure that he simply could not answer, such as why had he gone. They wanted to know what he had been thinking and why did he not tell them he was leaving. He felt confused. What had caused him to uproot himself from one life and to plant himself in another one so foreign was something he could not understand and could not explain to them. He could not articulate that deep yearning for something greater in life that would never be found in Gate-Town.

Zev-ran stood quietly to the side and observed the family as they struggled to repair a rift that had been created by Morok's abrupt departure last fall. Zev-ran wished to help Morok regain his family's blessing somehow. He said to them, "I wish to console you on the loss of your son. And I come to thank you for this man who is now my brother."

Silence fell upon the room and everyone looked at the young boy. Morok put his hand on Zev-ran's shoulder. "And you are the brother I never had," he said kindly.

This was a side of Morok his family had not seen

before. They wondered what had happened to him that could have created a new man out of him. They invited Morok and their new friend to sit at the table and tell the whole story. Zev-ran was the one who did most of the talking. He paused on occasion to let Morok share his version of the events. The family was fascinated by the tale and expressed their joy that the adventure had turned out so well for their son. He had found his place, that was plain.

The horses were put up at a neighbor's stable and Morok and Zev-ran stayed in Morok's former bedroom, which had remained unused since his departure. In the morning they all visited some of Morok's friends, who had been concerned about his absence. They were relieved to find him well and also noticed a positive change in his demeanor. He was a new man. Everyone hoped he would stay and be a part of the community once again. But Morok was no longer a part of this world, the life he had left. He could not stay. Zev-ran encouraged him to stay for a week, to finish his business. Morok realized there had been much left undone at the time of his departure, and he desired to rectify things. He knew Zev-ran's parents would not be concerned for such an absence and would wait patiently for their boy's return.

The next week passed by quickly. They were kept busy with the chores that Morok's parents wanted them to accomplish. Morok's friends came to visit often, causing him to be away from Zev-ran more than Zev-ran would have liked; however, the children of Gate-Town were more than happy to have a new playmate, and they kept him well amused.

Gate-Town was different from Palador in many ways. Zev-ran felt the change of pace. Although he worked at home, it was a leisurely kind of process, one accomplished without pressure to succeed in each and every moment. He liked it that way. Here, even children younger than himself were burdened with chores. They were simple chores, suited to their age, but taken too seriously. Playtime was also

Chapter 4

limited, and the children seemed to be restricted in their friendships, with the adults dictating who could associate with whom. But Zev-ran shrugged it off and fit himself into the place they permitted him for the duration of his stay with Morok's family. He was able to show the children some of what he had learned in Palador, and they taught him some useful skills of their own.

Morok felt differently about his home than he had before escaping it. He saw a different side of it. Whereas before he was wrapped up in the duties and the schedules, fighting his urges to rebel, he now experienced the rhythm that such a structure created. He knew that he was just visiting and that the imposition on his time was temporary. His parents were pleased with his change in attitude and asked if he would stay longer. Although it hurt him to have to disappoint his family again, he was firm in his decision to leave. Palador called to him; *this* was no longer home.

The farewells were brief but heartfelt. His sister came to see them off and encouraged him to return again soon. He made no promises, but he extended an invitation for the family to visit him. He knew they would be welcomed in Palador.

The journey home—for he did feel that Palador was his home—took two days. They lingered in the mountains and rested from their labor before returning to the way of the town by the river.

Chapter 5

A Heart Awakened

Zev-ran was happy to see his parents and spent a lot of time in their company in the days that followed. Like a shadow, he went wherever they went. He had missed them dearly, and his sisters too. It seemed like he needed to be a child for a while before returning to the work he typically did for his parents.

Morok was relieved to get back to work, Palador-style. He did his work joyfully, reminding himself that this freedom was not found in every town.

The women he had met before he left Palador showed up once again. The warmer days caused them to shed their heavy clothing and head covers for garb that was more flattering. They wore their hair long, and their skirts just covered their knees. He was curious to know their names and more of their tale. The young one was again the one to speak.

"We are four sisters of Tanlar, a city by the sea. Our parents chose to travel a far distance to begin their lives again in a more peaceful place."

They were anxious to hear more about Morok's life and what had brought him to this place. They listened intently to his tale and wondered at that which he himself could not explain—the deep calling to go where he had never been before and to sever his ties with a way of living that did

Chapter 5

not complement who he was. He felt *right* here, that was all he could say. But they understood, because they felt it too. They felt blessed, but how or by whom they did not know.

It was a while before any of them spoke again. Finally, the oldest sister broke the silence of their pondering. "I don't know why I am here," she began, "but I can't seem to recall what it was like to be elsewhere. It's like my life before was a mere dream, and now I have awoken."

The third daughter chimed in, "I also feel this way."

They sat together for more than an hour, discussing their feelings about their new home, a home that had welcomed them already and had nourished their hearts. The youngest of the four sisters got Morok's attention with her colorful stories of their boat ride up river and the events surrounding their arrival at the eastern entrance to Palador. There they were greeted by a man who claimed to be the oldest person in Palador. He showed the family where they could stay and took them all over the town, just as Zev-ran had done upon Morok's arrival. In the city by the sea, where the sisters had come from, this would not have occurred. There, people kept to themselves and newcomers were left alone to find their own way among the masses of people living there.

There were a few things the sisters did not talk about. Morok never understood why their parents chose to leave the city, nor what their intentions were for their stay in Palador. But he did hope their stay would be an extended one, for he longed to spend more time in their presence. The youngest, whose name was Loobal, had an effect on him that he had not experienced with other women. Her openness and innocence were very attractive to him; he could ask her any question and she would respond with polite curiosity, always answering his queries with additional questions. She held his attention with her bright smile and voluminous laughter. The other sisters took notice of Morok's fascination with her, yet they were not visibly affected by it.

Loobal was twenty years old. She was glad to hear that he was not married. She had cried over the fact that none of them had yet found suitable mates. Her oldest sister, Marfal, was approaching thirty years old already. There had been little opportunity for them to meet eligible men in the city, for their work left them occupied day and night. They were seamstresses, like their mother, and could not afford the home they shared unless they all donated their earnings toward the expenses. It was a hard life, and there was little joy to reward them for their effort. Their life was simple and colorless. Their parents lived nearby and visited regularly but could not support them in creating a better life. When their father invited them to accompany him and their mother to search for a new life beyond the sea, they eagerly accepted the offer. They made arrangements for their possessions to be sold for enough money to contribute to the cost of the voyage and to their new life, wherever it should be.

Loobal looked at her sisters for approval while telling her story. She continued to tell Morok about their plans to find work in the town and hopefully stay there. He gave the women some suggestions for work and offered to help them, as he was more familiar to the townspeople.

When they finished their discussion the sisters took Morok to the house where they were staying, in order to introduce him to their parents. Ansera and Bekren were an interesting couple. They did not appear to be as old as the sisters said they were. The sisters told them that Morok said he could help them find work and that he, too, was a relative newcomer to the town. Morok told their parents about his trip back to his home town and how he found the routine there distasteful. The parents said they were happy to have discovered Palador but uncertain if they would stay on as citizens. They were tempted to go further up river to another place they had heard of, where some relatives lived. Their

Chapter 5

daughters expressed their preference to stay in Palador; however, they did not wish to oppose their parents and were uncomfortable with this turn of events. Morok left quickly so that the family could discuss their future.

The days passed and the season changed again, bringing longer days and more activities for Morok and Zev-ran. Morok was asked to help build a new addition onto the house, as Zev-ran's mother was expecting another baby. The work was completed in less than two weeks, thanks to the help they received from various neighbors.

Zev-ran's curious nature led him to ask Morok many questions, and one was about his interest in a certain young woman named Loobal. Morok was surprised that someone could have taken notice of his affection for this person he barely knew. He was growing very fond of her, and he visited the sisters often, inventing various reasons for these occasions. They were all good company for him, and he sought to help their family settle down in Palador; yet the parents were still resistant and planned to leave, come fall. They expected their daughters to accompany them on the voyage onward.

Morok was not discouraged. He felt that even if Ansera and Bekren did leave, their children would stay, in spite of the discord it could cause, and Loobal indicated as much. On one occasion when she and Morok were left alone together, she grabbed his hand and said, "We are going to stay, no matter what!"

At this point they had all found work—not as seamstresses but, nevertheless, work they could do, and they fit in happily. They had moved to a larger house that had been vacated when an older couple passed on. Zev-ran knew these people and was instrumental in making the arrangements with their kin for the rental of the home to Loobal's family. The sisters were fond of Zev-ran; they took it upon themselves to mother him when his own mother became too busy to tend to him after the new baby had arrived.

Chapter 6

The Bond Forged

It was fall. After a few months of debating, the sisters' parents made the choice to stay in Palador. Loobal was overjoyed. They purchased a small farm at the edge of town and brought the family there. They had achieved success in building up a business of their own and could foresee a prosperous future.

Morok assisted the sisters in relocating their belongings and some furniture to the farm, and he brought them a gift to welcome them to the new home.

The next day he was there again, helping to repair a fence which had fallen down over the years and had never been fixed by the previous owners. Loobal's parents were grateful and asked him to stay for dinner that night.

They spoke of many things that evening, and the daughters' future was one topic of intense focus. They were concerned that their daughters were getting old and would not be having families of their own. Loobal answered their questions.

"We have worked for years, Papa, and that has been our existence. We have had no time to find husbands or even to think of having children."

Bekren stared at her remorsefully but said nothing.

It was her mother who answered, after a long pause. "There is still time, my dear." She looked fondly at each

Chapter 6

daughter in turn. "I have hope for all of you."

The oldest daughter, Marfal, was not convinced and said to her, "I know that you want only the best for us, but I don't believe this is probable in my case. I have waited too long."

"Now Marfal," she replied, "you would make someone very happy. You are kind and loving. We could find someone for you, I'm sure of it." She looked to the second oldest daughter. "Halfene, my dear, you were never one to give up easily." And then she turned to Morok. "How about you, dear, have you ever been intended to someone?"

Morok coughed. "I had never thought of settling down until I moved to this beautiful place. But I don't want to make plans just yet, I..." he trailed off. Loobal was looking at him intently. "I must go." He looked at Ansera and said, "Thank you for the meal." Then he got up abruptly, nodded to them, and left.

"Mother, I think you frightened him with your question," said Loobal, bothered. She began to gather the plates and then disappeared into the kitchen. Her sisters followed, to comfort her. They assured her that he would be back.

The following day Morok did appear back at the farm. He did not apologize for his abrupt departure the night before but simply asked if they needed any more work done, as he was happy to oblige.

Bekren showed him an old well behind the house. "There were two wells on this farm," he said. "This one was not used for many years, but I think we can get it going if we try."

The men worked together all day digging deep in that cold, damp hole. It was unpleasant, but it did give them the opportunity for some conversation. Morok wondered if the conversation was going to turn to the daughters' future again, but it did not, sparing Morok the awkward discussion.

The Bond Forged

They mainly spoke of work and politics, two topics which did not interest Morok—although he feigned enthusiasm, in order to be polite. Bekren did not notice his disinterest and engaged him in a lively conversation that continued until evening.

Morok chose not to stay for dinner, although he was invited. He excused himself and returned quickly home, preferring to spend the evening in the company of Zev-ran, who always made him feel at ease. The two had become close friends, despite the gap in age, and Morok was now considered to be a member of the family. He had his own room, and he contributed much to the family business, in return for their kindness.

Zev-ran's family was growing and it was a bustling household. His two younger sisters, Aplan and Cerba, were elegant and sprightly. The new baby, a big boy, was healthy and loud. It seemed that there were children everywhere. Morok took this in stride and helped wherever he could. Although he did not have any experience caring for children, as he was the youngest in his own family, he managed to be of assistance, and the children loved him as a brother. He was called upon often to tell them stories and sing with them, for he had some talent.

In the days that followed his last trip to the farm, he avoided the four sisters and their parents but still thought of Loobal. He wished to see her but did not want to answer any more questions. Although he thought of marriage, he was not sure he was ready to make that commitment.

Loobal's perspective was different. She liked Morok, but she did not want to pursue a marriage with him lest her older sisters become jealous. Surely they should be the first to get married. She hid her feelings from them and instead pretended to be interested in caring for the horses. Marfal saw past this façade. She saw Loobal as being the only one of them who had a chance at finding a love-mate in this place,

Chapter 6

and she wanted to give Loobal her full support.

"Why won't you just tell Morok how you feel about him?" she asked Loobal one evening, when they were alone.

"Oh, no, I—I couldn't," Loobal stammered. "I'm not the one who should be pursuing a husband."

"Perhaps not," Marfal replied, "but I can tell that he loves you, and you know it would make our parents so happy to see one of us engaged."

Loobal thought for a moment as she stared out the barn window. When she turned back to her sister there was a small smile on her face. "I do like him very much."

Marfal gave her a hug and said, "Don't let him get away then."

The weather turned cold the next week, and there was some urgency in the town to finish harvesting the crops. It was tradition in Palador that everyone who was able helped. Morok abandoned his job at the shop and joined a number of men who were cutting hay in the outskirts of town. It was hard work but allowed him to get to know some men who were close to his age. One man, named Samso, he found easy to befriend. They had similar views on life, and although Samso's experience was limited to life in Palador, they had much to talk about.

At the end of the day, Morok decided to go to the farm. He was inspired by his new friend's description of his own family life, a happy one with wife and children, and he wished to talk with Loobal. He left the fields and headed back into town on horseback, tired from his work but invigorated by the thought of seeing her. She was not home when he arrived, but Marfal directed him to a building where Loobal had gathered with some other women to sew. He met her there as she was leaving, her arms stacked with cloth. He dismounted the horse and came to her, meeting her curious glance.

"Loobal, should I walk you home?" he asked quietly.

"Thank you, Morok, I would like that," she answered him. They said little at first, walking side by side with horse in tow. It was dark, but the way was not far, and the path to the farm was well lit by the lantern she carried. They walked further, slowing their steps to prolong their time together, for they knew that once they arrived home the others would have much to say.

Loobal was nervous. She wanted to connect with Morok on a deeper level but did not know how. Morok, however, was feeling brave that night, encouraged by his friend's tale, and he took it upon himself to take that first step in the direction of the life he wished to create.

"Loobal—" he began, turning to her, "please accept my apology for the other night. I did not want to leave, but I could not stay and have that conversation with your mother." He paused and looked in her eyes. "I really do care for you, you know."

"I...share these feelings," she replied, smiling at him. They walked in silence for a moment, being at a loss for words to express the emotions that were trying to surface in them both.

It was Loobal who spoke first. "Remember the day we first met?" she inquired.

"By the river. You were washing clothes."

"When I laid eyes on you a strange feeling came over me, and for a moment I could not breathe. I remembered you."

"But how?" he asked. "We had never met."

"It was a dream I once had, as a young girl. I never forgot it. I'm sure it was you."

Morok was nonplussed, yet intrigued. "Tell me more," he encouraged her.

"Well, it was only one dream, long ago," she began, "but its effects lingered. It was a happy dream. You stepped out of a cloud and said to me, 'Come with me, my love.' And

Chapter 6

I, who was with my sisters by a river, took your hand and felt the most amazing sense of love and happiness. There was not much more to it than that. When I awoke I felt happy. I never forgot it." A tear fell from her eye, which she quickly wiped away. He brushed her cheek with his hand, gently. It moved him to see her this way. He paused and looked her in the eye.

"Loobal, I love you. I really do. Let us begin anew, as husband and wife."

"Oh, Morok," she returned, "who can say what the future will bring us? But I will live it with you."

They walked over to a place where they could comfortably sit on the ground and sat close together, ignoring the chill of the night. With his arm around Loobal's waist, he drew her close and looked to the sky, bright with stars.

"I knew there was a reason I came here—to Palador," he started. "Something drew me here. I never understood the pull, why I left home so easily. Can you believe it?" he asked.

She said nothing, but held his hand and joined his gaze.

"And here you are, with me, after this long journey we've each taken to get here. I cry for the beauty of it! Loobal, a great life awaits us, together." He held her close and then whispered, "I want you to know that I am here with you for a reason, and whatever that reason may be, I will uphold it. You are my wife, Loobal, and I shall hold you in my heart, always. Let us be joined in marriage, for everyone to see, and let us live a full life here in this place that we love."

Loobal put her head on his shoulder and laughed. "And to think I would have found you a partner in one of my older sisters, just to keep the peace in my family. No, you are for me, and me alone. I knew it all along. Yes, Morok," she affirmed, "I shall marry you. Gladly." She took his hand and placed it gently upon her heart. "And you live here now."

The two smiled at each other and locked their gazes

The Bond Forged

for a moment. And then, feeling the cold of the night, they brushed themselves off and continued on to the farm, which was not far off. They lingered at the door awhile, reveling in the glow of the happiness that was bursting from their hearts.

It was not long before they announced their engagement to Loobal's family. The family was not surprised, and everyone was overjoyed with the news. The couple did not want to wait until spring for the ceremony, which was always held outdoors in Palador, but were willing to risk snow just so they could be together as soon as possible.

Fortunately, the sisters were as excited as Loobal and Morok were, and they set to work immediately with the plans for the celebration. They began to sew a long gown for Loobal. It was green and decorated with beads. Unfortunately, she would need to cover it with a heavy cloak for the ceremony. Her hair was to be adorned with ribbons, and they chose two green ones and five purple ones for the weave.

The month passed quickly. At Zev-ran's house the mood was uplifted as well, and his mother began preparing food for a number of guests that would be invited there after the ceremony. Of course, everyone in the town would be present with them on the hill to witness their union. Zev-ran had mixed feelings about this. Although he was happy for his friend, he knew it meant the end of their days together. His father consoled him, seeing his upset, and suggested they spend more time together in the coming days. Zev-ran, who did not normally receive much attention from his father—not for lack of kindness in the man, but because he was usually occupied with work or with the other children—was relieved to have a chance to be alone with him.

When the weather changed and brought a winter storm upon the town, so did their plans. Morok was called to help dig a trench to allow passage to the river, and this took

Chapter 6

several days, with many people assisting. But the sun was shining the day they climbed the hill to be wed. Loobal rode up on one of the horses, as was customary, and only dismounted once everyone had arrived and formed a circle around them. Beyond their vision, but real nevertheless, an angel of the Realm of Light descended upon them to bless the young couple as they held each other's hands and said the wedding prayer. The townspeople held their hands extended as they looked to the sky and recited a prayer of gratitude. Loobal was radiant in the light of the heavens that streamed down upon them.

The winter sun did not linger long upon the hill, and it was soon time to return to the town. The people cheered as the couple departed first, astride Loobal's horse. Then came the throng, filing down the path, chattering happily.

Back at Zev-ran's house there were many guests. They filled the hallways and rooms alike. Sulfan, Zev-ran's mother, had made a variety of dishes, hot and cold, to satisfy everyone's hunger. Zev-ran's siblings and a few neighbors' children brought the food into the rooms on trays and filled everyone's glass. Next there was singing, and space was created in the main room for the young couple to perform a dance. They clapped, stomped, and bowed, and Morok spun Loobal in a circle. Loobal was giddy with laughter and danced about as best as she could, falling on occasion, but always caught by Morok. The ribbons in her hair fanned out behind her as she swung around, and her green dress, which was almost the color of her eyes, flowed like ripples on the sea.

Loobal's sisters took turns dancing with her next, performing intricate steps that were traditional in Tanlar. They received much applause and continued until they were out of breath. Morok then took his new wife to the table so they could eat, as they had been so busy talking with everyone that they had hardly taken a bite.

It was apparent to Morok that he and Loobal were

well-received by the townspeople and had much support and many well-wishes for their new life together. A smile spread across his face that he could not contain. The only thing missing in this beautiful celebration was his own family, but he did not feel upset at that moment. He knew that he would visit Gate-Town again—someday—and bring his lovely wife to meet them.

Loobal could not have been happier. The look of sheer joy on her parents' faces was a great gift to her. They kept telling her how happy they were for her and how they adored Morok and accepted him as their son. When the party died down they took Morok and Loobal aside and demanded to know why they had been so secretive about their relationship. The couple had little to say about it, only that they could not have told them what they were not yet aware of themselves.

"We were the same way," Ansera admitted. "Your father and I did not realize we were in love until someone else pointed it out to us!" She laughed and patted Morok on his cheek. "With you two it was pretty obvious there was something going on."

The conversation ended abruptly when Zev-ran rushed in and gave Morok a big hug. Morok squeezed him hard and then gave him to Loobal, for she had become very fond of the boy also. She hugged him and kissed his cheek and whispered quietly to him, "I know you are a little bit sad, Zev-ran, because your life is changing. But you will still be able to see us often, and I will make sure that Morok always has time for adventures with you."

He smiled and looked up at Morok. "I like her," he said. They all laughed.

"And so do I," Morok returned.

It was past midnight when the last of the guests left the house and Zev-ran and his sisters retired upstairs to their sleeping quarters. Morok and Loobal said goodnight to

Chapter 6

Sulfan, who was cleaning up, and expressed their gratitude for all the work she had done.

"It was my pleasure," she said, and gave them each a hug. Morok led Loobal to his room, so happy to have time alone with her at last. They fell into kisses the moment the door was closed, and they were not seen again until late the next morning.

It was a bright day and the house still held a lingering air of happiness from the previous night's revelry. Morok and Loobal joined the family for a late breakfast and then set out to the farm to spend time with Loobal's family. There was talk of building an addition onto the house there so that Morok and Loobal would have a place to be together, but the couple had other ideas.

"There is a cabin for rent by the river which I feel is a suitable place for us to start our life together," Morok told them.

"It is quite nice," added Loobal. "We looked at it last week."

"Whatever you think is best," Bekren asserted. "It is time for you to make your own decisions now."

Ansera put her arm around her husband. "We will miss you."

"I will visit every day," assured Loobal.

"You say that now," Halfene kidded her, "but in no time you will have forgotten us."

"Okay, well, maybe not *every* day," Loobal returned, smiling.

The couple walked over to a neighbor's home later that day to borrow more horses for the move. They did not have much to move but wished to do it quickly. Zev-ran's parents as well as Loobal's had given them a number of household items, bought as well as home-made, to furnish their new home, wherever it may be. Morok had secretly arranged to rent the cabin the day they had viewed it, but they had not told anyone until after the wedding.

It was a day or so before they were fully settled in. They were exhausted from the busy-ness of it all and from their late nights getting to know one another better. The two were inseparable, like any couple in love, and when they were not planning their future, they were celebrating the present, with as much affection and love as they could possibly lavish on each other. The days went by quickly in a whirlwind of newlywed bliss. Morok was excused from work at the shop while they got settled. It was not a busy time of year, as the fish were already mostly packaged for sale, and the new catches would not be coming in until spring.

Morok could not believe how easy it was to be with Loobal. He had feared marriage, to some extent, as he supposed it would limit the freedom he valued so strongly. Yet now he felt more free than he ever had. He felt as though he could do or become anything he wanted. And Loobal, who had never known any kind of life aside from one lived with three older sisters whom she was obliged to obey and follow, felt free to take her own lead.

Their time passed in a manner that was satisfying to both of them, and they got to know many things about each other. Most of the time their hearts were as one, united in a beautiful bond of love like neither had ever experienced before. At times, however, their patience with each other grew thin. They never fought, but they did disagree about certain things, like what they should do for a more permanent home. Loobal was content to stay at the cabin. It was quaint and warm, and in a good location.

"We'll never find something better," she warned.

Morok wouldn't listen. "Once we have a house of our own we can start a family. This place is too small!"

"But Morok," she countered, "there's no rush. We have time to plan our little family. I don't wish to start until we are ready."

Chapter 6

Morok sighed. "All right, then. I suppose I am getting ahead of myself."

Loobal was logical and Morok loved her for that. It tempered his restless idealism.

Zev-ran often appeared at the cabin, but his parents were concerned that he was spending too much time there and not allowing the young couple their privacy; so he began spending more time with his parents, and they were happy with that.

"You are growing up, Zev-ran," said his mother. "Soon you will be asked to aid your father in the shop."

Zev-ran held his mother's hand. "I will love that, Mama," he told her.

"Okay then," she said. "I will tell your father that you are ready to start your new job." Zev-ran smiled and gave her a big hug. "I love you, my son," she said.

When it was time for Zev-ran to begin his new job, his father brought him to the front of the house, where the fish store was located. In the past, Zev-ran had spent most of his time helping Morok package the fish in the back shed. Now his father wanted him to sell them. Zev-ran was perfect for the job. As friendly as he was, he brought love to every interaction with his customers, who were really his neighbors and friends. He would talk about the weather and the latest happenings in and around the town. It was a hub of news in that room. And Fordon was now free to spend more time with his wife and younger children, which was a great help to Sulfan. He had never really enjoyed selling the fish, being a rather shy man who liked to keep to himself. His own father had passed the shop to him, and it was his duty to keep it going.

For Zev-ran, this offered a rare opportunity to try out his entrepreneurial skills. He had some innovative ideas about how to run the shop: he saw where his father could improve the business. He asked his customers many questions about their likes and dislikes, noting them carefully until he got an overall sense of what was needed. He came up with an idea to change the flavor of the fish by varying the type of salt used on them and by adding seasonings. His father went along with his idea and let him experiment. The results were surprising. Fordon preferred the new flavors and began packaging these specialty fish in a unique way. When word got out, many people flocked to the shop to try them. Fordon made a lot of money, and the customers were happy to have something different to eat for dinner.

Although Morok had been absent from the business for a while, he was called back to help keep up with the demand for the new product. He was happy to continue working in the back, doing the packaging, as—like Fordon—he was not particularly outgoing. The time spent away from Loobal was a welcome change, for although they were very much in love, they had hardly left each other's side since the wedding.

Loobal missed Morok when he was at work, and she decided to find some work of her own to occupy her time. She found it at a home with young children where both of the parents went off to work in the fields, preparing the ground for the spring planting. This was enjoyable to her. There were two girls and a boy, all close in age and full of mischief. She kept them busy playing games and walked them all over town, stopping to meet other children along the way. Loobal had a way with children, and these three were keen to have her look after them. The parents decided to give Loobal an ongoing job as caregiver, at least until the fall harvest was over and they could be home. She did not work every day, as there were times when only one parent tended the fields; this was fine, as she did miss her sisters and wanted to see them more often. They too had work, but not so much of it that they had no time for her. In Palador nobody worked too hard.

Chapter 6

Now the days were full, and Morok and Loobal longed to spend more time together. They cherished their evenings at home, cooking together and talking about all that had passed that day in their jobs and interactions with people. They entertained guests on occasion, mainly Loobal's family. Morok had grown close with them and was just as happy to have them visit as his wife was. The sisters did not have much news. None of them had been introduced to available men, and they were rather disheartened. They were not jealous of their little sister, so happily married, but yearned to have such an experience themselves. Meanwhile, their joy came from their days together at the farm and in the town, relaxing and shopping, meeting other young women, and making new friends. There was a sewing guild that they all joined, and this activity brought them a feeling of satisfaction that their work as seamstresses in Tanlar never had.

The sisters found that once Loobal had moved out of the farm their time became more focussed on doing what they could to please their parents. They all missed Loobal, and there was an emptiness where her bright presence had been. This caused Bekren and Ansera distress, despite their great support of Loobal's marriage. Therefore, the daughters tried to fill that hole with activities that suited their parents' interests and to join them at meals if Loobal was missing.

One day when they were discussing whose turn it was to look after their parents, Loobal appeared at the door. She had left work early that day and wished to speak with her siblings. They told her of the burden that was theirs since she had moved away. Loobal was shocked, as this was an effect she had not foreseen, and she promised that she would visit more often. She joined them for dinner that evening, and Morok, having missed her at home, went to the farm to see if she was there. He was welcomed by all, and the evening was a joyful one. Bekren and Loobal talked about ways in which they could stay better connected, as he missed her deeply. It was decided, after much thought, that Loobal and Morok would come to the farm twice a week to share a meal with the family, and the family would also meet at Loobal's cabin for a weekly visit. This arrangement was congenial to everyone, and the couple left satisfied, knowing all was well.

The next time they got a chance to be with the family there was a different mood in the house. Bekren was unusually quiet, and Loobal sensed that he did not want to tell them something. When they left he held on to his wife for a long time.

Soon after that it became obvious to everyone that Bekren was ill. He had stopped working and was not able to do much except lie and rest. His voice had become hollow and faint, and his eyes were dim. It seemed like he was wilting. The girls were very worried and hovered about him like bees, seeking to tend to his every need. Ansera was uncommunicative. She watched them but did not speak. Loobal was distressed, and Morok did not know how to comfort her.

Bekren beckoned to him one evening and croaked out, "My dear Loobal—take good care of her, will you?"

Morok was alarmed. "Bekren, why do you ask this? Are you leaving us?"

Bekren struggled to pull Morok close and whispered, "I am not long for this world, Morok. Take care of them." He smiled weakly. "It will be okay. My love is with them always, and I will see them again one day."

He said no more but closed his eyes for a spell. Morok sat beside him and patted his hand. When the women returned to the room they were speaking once more. Bekren was looking up at Morok, smiling.

Morok and Loobal left shortly thereafter. On the way home Morok broke the silence. "Your father will be leaving us, Loobal."

She looked down. "I know it," she said quietly. "I can

Chapter 6

see he is ready."

Morok grasped her close as they rode slowly back to the cabin, winding through the narrow streets of the town.

In the morning word came that Bekren had passed on in the night. Loobal was shocked. "But I didn't say my last good-byes to him!" She cried bitterly and held on to Morok, soaking his shirt with her tears. "My Papa!" she wailed.

Morok could not comfort her; he was mourning the loss himself. He held Loobal as tightly as he could and rocked her gently as his own tears fell upon her. They stayed that way a long time, and then they went to the bed and sat down.

"My dear," he said finally, "I think we should move back to the farm. At least until your mother is settled."

"Okay," she said simply. "Let us go there now, for I must be with my sisters."

They packed some clothing and took the horse back to the farm, stopping briefly along the way to alert Zev-ran's family and Loobal's employers to the news so that they would not be expected at work for a while.

The farm house was awash with sorrow, and Loobal began to cry again as soon as she crossed the threshold. "Mama!" she shrieked, and ran to her mother, embracing her fiercely. Her sisters joined them and continued to mourn loudly. Morok stood aside, allowing them space to express their grief.

Bekren's body had not yet been moved from the house, and Morok took one last look at the old man. He had never seen the death of a person, and he wondered at this strange transformation. What was now missing? The man lay there, yet he was not present. Where was he? His skin was cold and artificial.

Loobal approached but then turned away from the body, burying her face in Morok's chest. "I can't bear to look at him thus," she cried.

"Then say your farewell to the man he was, not this shadow that lies before you," Morok suggested.

He led her out of the room and into the kitchen where her mother and sisters were sitting. Loobal shook her head sadly and sat down with them. "What are we to do?" she asked her mother.

"We will wait for the men who will carry him to the pyre for us. Then we will gather on the hill and watch as his body is returned to the earth. His ashes we will collect and bring to the burial house for a ceremony. And then we will move on with our lives."

Ansera's heart was broken, that was plain to see. Her husband gone so suddenly, she seemed empty and worn out. Loobal gave her a hug. "We are going to stay with you, Mama, Morok and I," she said.

Ansera sighed. "I was hoping you would."

It was not until the next day that the pyre was ready to be ignited. This allowed the women some time to prepare for it emotionally. It was a difficult time. They were not used to making any sort of decisions without Bekren's involvement, and the idea of having to make arrangements for the future without his wisdom was daunting. Morok was little comfort to them at this point. They were mired in memories and deep grief, for which there seemed no antidote.

The procession up to the ridge that day was sombre. This was not an event attended by all of the townspeople, as the wedding had been; only those close to the deceased made the climb. As Bekren had been relatively new to the town, the gathering drew few people: only his family and a few close neighbors. This caused his daughters all the more grief, as they wondered who was going to remember their wonderful father. It was a cold day and they shuddered under cloudy skies upon that ridge where Zev-ran had brought Morok hiking so long ago. The pyre was lit and the fire

Chapter 6

blazed; it erased all traces of the husband and father who had been such an important part of their lives.

They returned home at nightfall for a simple meal and a solemn sleep, and climbed the ridge again the next day, with tear-stained faces, to collect the ashes. The bulk of them were left on the hill, to be scattered by the wind, but they carried a container-full to the place below where the symbolic mixing would occur. It did not matter that Bekren was new to the town, for here all lives were cherished.

The door to the small building that held the ashes of everyone's ancestors was stuck fast, and Morok struggled to open it for them. When they entered the room they were overcome with a sense of peace and well-being that they had not felt since before Bekren had left them. He was there. All of them knew it. His presence was strong, and it gave them comfort, like he was there to say the good-byes he had missed. Ansera gently poured the ashes into a deep bowl that stood on a large pedestal at one end of the room and stirred them in. They bowed their heads and silently prayed for Bekren's peace and happiness in his new existence. His presence was joined by that of many others of that unknown place, and the room was lit up with their joy. Tears were replaced with wondrous smiles and laughter in those present, and they were lifted into a state of grace and acceptance; it was a gift to all of them. It was this feeling of warmth and well-being that they carried with them beyond the burial house, up over the ridge, and back to the farm. Their energy renewed, the women cooked a large meal for those who had attended, and the farm rang with laughter that night as Bekren's life was celebrated and mirthful stories were told.

The days that followed ushered in a period of adjustment. Morok and Loobal remained at the farm, as promised, and Morok was a great help in taking care of many duties that Bekren had let slip over the course of his short illness. Ansera was fragile, weeping openly and often, and her girls did what they could to run the household without her participation. As a group they decided that they would sell the farm and find a smaller place in the town to rent while important decisions were being made about everyone's future. Ansera was not even sure if she wanted to stay on in Palador, as she believed she could find her sister if she travelled on a ways. The girls opposed this plan; they sensed their mother was only trying to escape a life she had planned to share with her husband.

Chapter 7

Life Begun Anew

At Ansera's request, all of Bekren's belongings were kept as they had been when he was alive. She was clinging to the illusion that he was still there or that he would be returning. The girls were alarmed. Although they, too, wished for his return, they knew it would not occur.

Morok took over the role of man of the house as best as he could. He worked hard on the farm, and he continued his job at Zev-ran's. There was hesitation to move from the farm just yet, as Ansera was so unsettled. She now seemed resistant to selling the place, as had been decided by the lot of them; she did not want her life to change.

Spring came like a breath of fresh air into the town: the sight and scent of flowers lifted everyone's spirits, and the longer days drew them out of their homes and into the streets. The girls took turns looking after their mother so that each was able to return to work. Loobal was glad to be with the children again, as they brought her joy, taking her mind away from sad thoughts about her father. Halfene began a small business of her own, selling bunches of flowers in the main square of the town. Marfal was asked to prepare some clothes for export, and she enlisted her sister Serbrena to help with the beadwork. It was a busy time for all, but all the comings and goings enlivened their home. The girls took turns cooking, cleaning, and tending to the few animals they

Chapter 7

had kept. They had cows to milk, and the horses they rode whenever they were going somewhere in the town that was too far to walk or if they had a heavy load to carry.

Morok and Loobal did return to the cabin eventually, having been reassured by Loobal's sisters that they could get by without her. The couple kept up their duties at the farm but enjoyed their nights together—a return to some semblance of normalcy as a married couple.

As the days wore on, Loobal began to notice changes within her body. It was not a surprise to Morok when she finally approached him with this news. "I feel that I am with child, my dear," she told him.

"Ha ha!" he exclaimed joyfully. "I had a feeling it was so!" They embraced and twirled around the room, giggling with glee.

"This will cheer my mother up," said Loobal.

And it did. The news sparked a change in Ansera's outlook. It was like she woke up from a deep sleep. She busied herself with running the household once again, which lifted a rather large burden from the shoulders of her overworked daughters.

Loobal's sisters took it upon themselves to create more opportunities for social engagements in their lives. The first step was for the three of them to join a choir. Their voices were beautiful, and they harmonized especially well with one another. Naturally they were welcomed by the choir, whose membership had dwindled over the past year for various reasons. There were men as well as women in the choir, and this afforded them a welcome opportunity to get to know some potential mates. Halfene was particularly bold and did not hesitate to introduce herself personally to all of the men on the first evening they joined the group for practice. She was charming and easy to like. Marfal, the kindest of the three, was a little bit shy, and it took her some time to feel comfortable engaging them in conversation.

Serbrena was a different sort of woman altogether. The most beautiful of the sisters, she drew attention wherever she went; yet she did not seem to notice it. In fact, she was quite inept, socially, and gave the air of being terribly lost in a world of her own creation. She was often seen talking to herself and drawing little pictures on whatever materials she could find. Still, it was endearing.

Not surprisingly, Halfene was the first to secure an eligible man. His name was Dentino, and he had lived in Palador all of his life. Dentino caught Halfene's attention by spontaneously serenading her one night at choir practice. He chose a funny tune that caused her fits of giggles. At the end of it she joined him, in harmony. He walked her back to the farm that night, and they talked continually the whole way, on such topics as her past in Tanlar, his parents and the merchandise they sold, and what he liked to do for fun in the summertime. They did not have much in common, but that made them all the more interesting to one another. Dentino asked Halfene if he could spend some time with her when she wasn't working, and Halfene suggested they meet the next rainy day, as she did not ever sell flowers in the rain. The next day it poured, and Dentino showed up on Halfene's doorstep before noon. Their plan was to make a picnic and then hike to a forested area where they could eat under the cover of the trees. It was a soggy endeavor nonetheless, but their laughter rang through the woods, and when they returned later that day, one could see that a romance was blossoming. In Ansera's eyes, they were a good match, and she was happy to see that Halfene now had a hope of marriage, where at one time it seemed like all of her daughters would grow old alone. Ansera thought now that it would be she herself who was destined for that outcome.

Things at the farm were going well in spite of Ansera's occasional relapses. Her daughters handled her gently at those times, knowing she would pull herself out of it if she

Chapter 7

felt their love and compassion. She was still raw from the sudden loss of Bekren, who had been her husband as well as her best friend, and her nerves were testy. She would tremble at times but brushed it off as fatigue. Her daughters knew better, and they comforted her by talking about their fondest memories of their beloved father. They missed him too but knew that he was not far way. Sometimes as they were falling asleep at night, when their minds were at rest between waking and dreaming, they would feel his presence. Just as he had done when they were younger, he would tell them he loved them. Ansera could feel him too but was too heartbroken to respond. She wanted him to appear in the flesh, but of course he could not.

The late spring brought beautiful weather, and the accompanying joy in the townspeople was palpable. Songs were aplenty. The choir performed its first concert of the year at a small outdoor venue and drew a large crowd. Among the listeners was the violinist, Peter, who had returned to the town that week for a visit, but not to play. He was struck by the beauty of the music and its singers, and after the show he went up to them and proposed a collaboration of sorts for the future, where he would accompany them on violin. They were open-minded and suggested he join them at their next practice.

Loobal was growing slowly into a mother. It was not just her body that was changing, but her way of being in the world. She looked at things differently. A great compassion grew within her, compelling her to attend to little things that she would have once overlooked, such as the need of a flower to have soil brushed off of it so it could right itself and turn toward the sun. The life within her caused her to be more attuned to the life around her. Colors seemed more vibrant, scents more potent, and sounds more elaborate and meaningful in their construction. She could feel subtle things, like the will of the bees to do their work and the joy of the horses to serve. She could almost hear their thoughts and would catch herself talking back to them. Morok found this quite amusing.

Loobal was brightened by the pregnancy. She had always been beautiful, in Morok's eyes, but now heads were turning toward her wherever she went. Her presence could not go by unnoticed. Although Morok did not understand what was happening to his wife, he felt a change in himself as well. Something had started to awaken within him. A memory? No, it was deeper. It was who he was. He began to *know* himself. And soon he became drawn to seek out the one who had eluded him his entire life: God.

Chapter 8

The Oneness

Morok was indeed a changed man. It astounded him that he had been so blind and deaf to a reality that was interwoven with all those things he could touch and feel and experience—yet were virtually lifeless without this intricate web of light and color and passion that supported it all. He could see it now; it was so beautiful it took his breath away. The feelings that began to arise in him were overwhelming.

He closed his eyes in humble prayer, and he began to pour out, in gratitude, a lifetime's worth of sincere appreciation for all of the opportunities he had been given; and for the path and the calling that had led him to this town, to his dear wife, and now to their child. He cried out sincere apologies for the life he had lived in ignorance and apathy before this moment and for the thought that he was not worthy of this goodness. Morok knew, deep within himself, that God loved him more than he could fathom.

Loobal knew that a shift had occurred within Morok. She could see it when she looked into his eyes. It helped her to see past her little life to a vast universe filled with beauty beyond her imagination. Their relationship grew deeper, as it was based on a bond of love and trust that was strengthened by their new-found awareness of their connection to all things.

The baby was growing, and Loobal felt his presence.

Chapter 8

She knew it would be a boy and so did Morok. Their new outlook on life had changed their perception of parenthood as well: it was an honor to give this child life, and they were both humbled by the opportunity.

Peter stayed in the town longer than he had planned. Something kept him rooted there, and he let go of his plan to leave. The choir had responded positively to his suggestion of a collaborative effort, and he began to join them at practice. At first he only quietly supported the melodies with his violin; later he created contrast and harmonies that complemented the singers in an innovative way. They were pleasantly surprised, and it inspired their singing to reach new levels.

Peter's interest in the choir went beyond his love of music. There was one particular woman whose voice and demeanor drew his attention in a way he had not experienced before: the lovely Marfal. Her beauty went beyond her dark eyes and long red hair. It was her kindness that shone so brightly, in his mind. She was ever smiling. Her smiles, so innocent and love-filled, melted people, disarmed them. One could walk into the room, disgruntled and objectionable, and all it would take would be a look from Marfal, and the attitude would immediately alter itself to something more pleasant and congenial! How could one so unassuming hold so much power?

He was nervous to approach her, to make her acquaintance. Although it was easy to see that she was open and accepting of everyone, he still felt somehow inferior, that he was unworthy of her attention. This caused him to reflect on his life and to wonder why he felt this way about himself.

Peter was a solitary man. He preferred the company of his violin to the company of others, for he was quite shy. He had been one of those children who retired to his room to play alone rather than venture out into the neighborhood to seek a playmate. Girls had always frightened him. It was no surprise, then, that at age forty he was unmarried. His focus was his music, and the rewards of this concentrated effort were that his performances were attended by many and that his reputation had grown beyond the town whence he came. He was thus encouraged to travel. This was his second time in Palador, the town closest to where he was born. The people here did not produce much in the way of music—few were trained to play instruments—but they were good listeners. His last performance in Palador had earned him many invitations from individuals to stay with them at their homes or to come over for a meal. It brought him out of his shell, to be received so warmly. But Marfal he could not approach.

It was her sister, Halfene, who extended an invitation, one day at choir practice, for him to visit them at their farm. The next day he arrived for dinner and was met at the front door by none other than the lovely Marfal. She welcomed him with a broad smile that left him momentarily breathless. He gathered himself together quickly and entered the home, thanking them for inviting him. Ansera had been curious to meet this man whom her daughters had told her much about.

"Welcome, Peter." She greeted him with an open smile and extended her hand to him. "Do join us at the table."

The meal was delicious and the conversation revolved around the choir and an upcoming performance, the first one to showcase his accompaniment. He caught Marfal staring at him a few times and nearly choked on his fish soup. Halfene giggled but was quickly silenced by a meaningful glance from her mother.

Peter stared for a moment at his bowl and then smiled, finally laughing at himself.

"Lovely soup," he directed at Ansera.

"I'm glad it meets your approval, Peter," she replied, smiling back at him.

Halfene cut in, "Well, Peter, all of us are glad to make your acquaintance. Some of us even more so." She looked

Chapter 8

directly at Marfal, who blushed.

Peter was flustered. He was not used to being in the presence of so many women at once. He felt rather like a trapped animal and sought a quick escape.

Ansera picked up on his discomfort, and she was reminded of the night she had pressured Morok to answer a question that had obviously made him feel uncomfortable. She had learned her lesson that day, and she did not want a repeat.

"Peter," she began, "please tell us about your home town. We are curious to know more about how others live in this area, as we come from yonder sea."

The change in topic put Peter at ease, and he began to describe Portshead, the place where he was born and still inhabited.

"It is larger than Palador, with many more people. I am so glad to have found Palador, having been once invited to play my music here by one who visited Portshead and saw me perform there. I am tired of that place, and I do find this town more to my liking. It suits my quiet nature." He paused for a moment. He was not used to talking so much about himself, but it was clear that the women were interested in hearing more.

"There is always music going on in Portshead. Some of the best instruments are, in fact, made there. I did not make my violin, but I learned to play at an early age. My father was also a musician, and he was supportive of my lessons. Sadly, he is no longer with us. My mother and sister live together in the home I grew up in."

"We lost our father too," said Marfal quietly. "Just this winter. He died quite suddenly."

They all bowed their heads for a moment, pausing to respect their departed loved ones.

By the end of the evening they were all at ease with each other and chatting freely about all sorts of things. Peter was almost reluctant to leave. But he thanked them profusely and bade them farewell, noting that he would see them soon at choir practice. His walk alone back to the house where he was staying was pleasant, and his thoughts circled about along the way, centering themselves always upon the lovely Marfal.

A change was occurring in the town, and Loobal and Morok began to perceive its subtle nature. Unbeknownst to them, a shift which had taken place at a higher energetic level had filtered down to their material realm. What was now different about the world? Morok sought to grasp it. He discussed it with Loobal. It was difficult to express in words that which he was perceiving, but she understood.

"I thought it was the baby," she mused. "I thought perhaps he was changing us." She paused, a far away look in her eyes. "But this is bigger than us, our little family," she continued, "and I have a feeling something profound is occurring that has never happened before."

Morok took her hand gently. "I can feel God, Loobal," he whispered, "everywhere." He looked at Loobal. There was a tear in her eye.

"I know," she said.

They sat in silence. It was all they could do in that sea of oneness that they found themselves in.

Chapter 9

The Path Lit

In the morning Loobal and Morok sought out the one person in Palador who, they deemed, would have the answers to difficult questions. A wizened old man, Geminus the Seer looked as though he had been around long before the town had been founded. He wore a dark cloak and clasped a walking stick and did naught but wander the streets of the town, chanting songs that the people never recognized, but which made them feel at ease. He was short in stature and often overlooked by people who were not paying attention as they went about their business in the town; yet for those of a more spiritual nature, who reflected on life rather than strove to direct the outcome of their affairs, he was quite noticeable. To those people he would beckon, and he would draw them into conversation. He had spoken with Loobal once before, shortly after she had become aware of her pregnancy. "With child you are," he had said, and she had asked, dumbfounded, "How did you guess?" He replied that such things were visible to those who could see and that it was never a matter of guesswork. He had laughed and reassured her that all would be well with her pregnancy and that the baby was a boy. She had not said much but thanked him awkwardly and went on her way. It was one of her friends from the sewing guild who explained to her who he was and told her he could be trusted for wisdom and advice.

Chapter 9

"He knows what many do not," said her friend.

So off they went that morning in search of Geminus the Seer, and soon they found him wandering behind the butcher shop, talking to a small dog that was there begging for scraps.

"Geminus," Morok called, to get his attention.

He turned and grinned widely when he recognized Loobal.

"Geminus, may we speak with you?" asked Morok softly.

"But of course, young man," Geminus replied, righting himself with the help of his cane. He continued to stare at Loobal.

"The child within you grows strong!" he exclaimed, opening his eyes wide. Although he looked comical, his demeanor was serious.

"What is it you wish to discuss?" he inquired.

"Well," Morok began slowly, "we've been noticing some changes and wondered if you perhaps could tell us what is happening."

"I can," he stated simply. "Please sit down."

There was nowhere in particular to sit, so they lowered themselves to the ground, which was dry but dusty.

"Long ago," he began, "God made this world that you see." He moved his arm in a wide arc, gesturing to the earth, the sky and all around them. He paused, as if making sure they followed his idea.

"He made it, but it had a life of its own. He liked His creation, for it was beautiful...but it did not reflect the highest part of Himself, the true *gem* of His being. So he made people, and He put them into His world, giving them permission to do as they liked within this creation. And for a time all was well. But that was long ago," he added quickly.

"Eventually," he continued, "things got a little complicated here and a little unsavory. There were fights and conquests; there was destruction and despotism. What was once pure began to look ugly. And it got uglier still.

"Now God had made a promise to let people do what they wanted to do, and He could not, in all fairness, take away that privilege. So He let them be. But He had another plan. And this plan took a really, really, really long time to carry out. That is why the world has for so long suffered in this state of darkness and disarray. But now it is time for what has been designated by God to happen, and change is occurring rapidly. This is what you are experiencing."

Loobal looked puzzled. "Geminus, I don't understand. What is this darkness you describe?" she asked bluntly.

He laughed, tilting his head backwards. He then looked at Morok, who was just as perplexed as his wife.

"You two live in a place that is virtually untouched by that which plagues the rest of this world. Yet you can still feel the difference when the darkness begins to lift from it. For some people, in some places, all they know is suffering and despair. They cry in their misery. They shake with fear. They trust no one. It is a suffocating blanket of illness and treachery that lies upon them, snuffing out all hope of a better future. Yet—" and he paused, gazing intently at both of the wide-eyed seekers—"it is changing. Now. Forever and for good. Because. God. Wills. It." he finished emphatically.

"How do you know this?" asked Morok, incredulously.

"I have seen it," Geminus said simply. "There is much about this world that you don't know," he added; "your lives are sheltered in this little oasis here."

"Have you been here long, Geminus?" Loobal asked.

"Long enough to know that this is the only place I want to be," he answered quickly. "I have travelled far in my many years. I have seen much. It has aged me, what I have seen. It has grieved me, what I have lost, for I have lost much. When you are as old as I am you will see what I have seen." He stopped talking and began to pet the dog, who continued

Chapter 9

to loiter behind the shop.

"What is God's will for us, do you know?" asked Morok.

Geminus looked up at them again. "To show the way—the right way—to live."

"And how do we know what the right way to live is?"

Geminus laughed. "Ask God."

Morok and Loobal looked at each other, then back at Geminus.

"Uh...thank you," Loobal faltered.

Geminus laughed again. "Good luck."

Morok led Loobal back toward the center of the town, with Geminus' laughter echoing behind them. They did not speak until they reached Zev-ran's shop, where they had intended to go next.

"Well!" huffed Loobal emphatically. She did not know what else to say. But Zev-ran had spotted them through the shop window and rushed out the door, enthusiastically greeting them before they had a chance to reflect further on their bizarre conversation with Geminus.

Zev-ran was eager to share with them all that had transpired in his life since he had last seen them. Morok had moved on to different work and was no longer working with Zev-ran's father, so the boy rarely saw him. They had grown apart somewhat over the previous months but still maintained a brotherly bond that would always persist. They listened to Zev-ran's animated stories with amused grins on their faces and laughed with him. He talked excitedly for almost an hour, until a flock of customers arrived and he had to excuse himself to tend to them. Morok and Loobal took that opportunity to return to the cabin, where they could finally discuss Geminus' advice to them.

They sat in silence for a while before attempting to put into words all of their feelings about what the old man's words had awoken in them.

Loobal was the first to speak. "God wants us to be ourselves. This I know. He has put within us a desire to seek Him and to know ourselves." Loobal smiled at Morok affectionately. "I am happy, Morok. I remember another dream I had when younger, although not as young as I was when I dreamt of you. I was standing in a field, a vast expanse of green grass and small flowers. The sky was endless. I was alone at first but then joined by two others, neither of whom I recognized as having met in my life. They came up to me. One was a man and one a woman, although they did not really look like people, and they said to me, 'We have come to bring you some information that will help you. You are destined to become a leader of many at a time when the Light will return to the earth. We are here to prepare you. We are your guides on the other side.'

"I remember that I had many questions and that we talked for what seemed like a long time. But unfortunately, I do not remember what was said. It is hazy. I never believed it, so the memory of it was pushed aside. But now, back it comes."

Morok looked at her for a moment, then began to describe his own perceptions on the matter. "Loobal, I have given this much thought since I started feeling God's presence. What we must do is ask God for direction in our lives and follow it day by day. Why don't we do that now?" he suggested.

There was an awkward pause as they both attempted to settle into a state of receptivity in which they could connect deeply to God beyond the entanglement of thoughts that had been stirred up by the day's happenings.

Morok began: "My God, I seek your presence. I ask for You to be with us, my wife and I, as we try to know You and understand what it is You will for us to do in our lives from this day forth. We are happy to do as You ask us, knowing that You are wise and all-loving."

Chapter 9

For a moment nothing happened. They sat with their eyes closed and their hands held tight to one another. They waited patiently, beginning to relax into a feeling of peacefulness that was brought on not only by their desire to be this way but was also encouraged by some benevolent force outside of themselves that seemed to be present with them in the room.

Loobal felt herself drifting deeper into a state of oneness with Morok and with the angelic presence there.

Morok was drifting away. He could not even feel the room, but he experienced a lifting of his being to a higher realm, a place of light which was brighter than anything he could imagine. And there, God spoke to him.

"My dear son," came the words, not from anyone he could see, but felt as a message that filled his consciousness, "you are beloved and blessed, as is your precious wife. I have called you. You are bearers of wisdom for your people. You will hear Me and know My will and share it with those who will listen."

Morok was held in that space of light for a time. He silently absorbed the words of his Creator and received a blessing that filled his entire being with warmth. He felt elated.

Loobal, on the other hand, had a different experience. To her it felt as if there were beings of light surrounding her, healing both her and her unborn son. She became very relaxed and sleepy, and she almost slumped down in her chair, but for the grip Morok had on her hands. When they awoke—for it did seem like a sleep—they stared at each other with eyes wide. A smile slowly spread across Morok's face. "He spoke to me, Loobal."

She listened attentively as Morok repeated God's words to her.

"So we must make time to listen," she concluded, "and simply trust that He will tell us what we need to know and what to do."

"Yes," agreed Morok. He took a deep breath and exhaled slowly. He could still feel the warmth of the love he had received. He reached out his hand and touched Loobal's cheek. His hand was tingling with heat. She placed her hand on top of his.

"I can feel that!" she exclaimed. "Your hand was never like this before."

Morok drew her close. "I believe I have received a gift," he mused.

"And I have received a healing," Loobal told him, "and so has our son."

"Let us give thanks for these blessings," suggested Morok, and they prayed together in silence.

Chapter 10

The Realm Beyond

It was dark when they finished their discussion and began to prepare their evening meal. Loobal was tired but uplifted by all that had transpired that day, and she sang a tune while she cooked. Morok was pensive but also felt uplifted and inspired. In his earlier years he had been a daydreamer with little ambition and little ability to focus. Now he felt a clarity and a purpose that he foresaw leading him onward to the realization of a great work, designed and directed by his all-powerful, all-knowing, ever-loving God.

When they sat down to eat that night, a strange thing happened. The food they had prepared did not appeal to either of them. It was lifeless, and they could not stomach it. They ate in silence, slowly nibbling the food. Finally, Loobal pushed her plate away. "I can't eat this, Morok."

He began to laugh. "Neither can I."

They put the food away and sat down on the bed. The candle on the window ledge glowed gently, bringing a peaceful mood to the room.

Morok turned to Loobal and said, "Let me call upon the presence of our dear Father once more, and then we shall sleep."

He closed his eyes and began to pray aloud, invoking the Heavenly presence. Loobal felt her heart opening with a rush of love toward her husband, her son, and God. Again,

Chapter 10

the presence of angels was detectable in the room. Morok could barely stay awake, he was so powerfully overcome by the energies in the room which were pulling at him, lifting him up and beyond that which he identified as his *self*. All around him colors were swirling, a myriad of rainbows, moving in and out of him in a lulling pattern. Loobal was also pulled out of herself into a higher state of consciousness, one that she had never experienced before. The two met in a powerful union, soul to soul, awakened in that state, seeing each other as their truest selves. It was breathtaking. They both shuddered in the physical while still maintaining their embrace in higher consciousness. Loobal felt that she had gone beyond herself, expanding into the oneness that *is*. At this time they both heard a voice that was beyond them and at the exact same time within them, and it shook them to their core.

The voice said, "My children, I am with you. I have called you. Together you will go forth into the world and do great things for Me. I ask you to listen and to trust. My angels will guide you. You will be told what to do. You are loved, and I am with you always."

The feeling of this love bubbled up within them, a golden fountain of unimaginable beauty that filled them with pure, ecstatic joy. And as the sensation subsided they became aware that they were surrounded by many angels in this place of light and beauty. The angels were beaming love at them too. Morok and Loobal soaked it in, this new crescendo of overpowering goodness. And then the angelic presence slowly faded away, leaving the two speechless as their eyes fluttered open and they felt, once again, to be inhabiting physical bodies in a small cabin in a town called Palador.

Chapter 11
Into the Water

It was twilight the following evening. Peter was walking along the road between Palador and Portshead, a road barely used but strangely well kept. He had not brought a horse this trip as the weather permitted the longer journey on foot. Although he was reluctant to depart from Palador, he knew he must go home to settle his affairs if he was to return to Palador for an extended visit. Deep down he was hoping that he would be able to reside there permanently. His collaboration with the choir was becoming a successful venture, and their upcoming performance was highly anticipated by the townspeople. But beyond music, which had been his great love, it was the love of a woman that he now sought. And that woman was, of course, the lovely Marfal.

Peter knew she was interested in him. He had witnessed her blushing when he had looked at her. But he had no idea how to proceed. He was tongue-tied and flustered in her presence. Despite his age, he lacked any kind of experience in the art of romance. He felt clumsy and awkward. Yet he was not willing to give up. His desire for a relationship with her was so strong that he surmised that it could overcome his ineptitude. And with this in mind he hastened home to inform his mother and his sister that he would be leaving his home town for good.

Chapter 11

Back at the farm, things were in an uproar. Halfene's new companion, Dentino, had forgotten to close the latch on one of the gates, and a number of pigs had made their way into Ansera's vegetable garden, trampling much of what she had planted there. The girls' attempts to capture the stray animals made a comical scene, and Dentino experienced the wrath of one irate mother-to-be. He sheepishly left the farm house, promising Ansera that he would return the next day to salvage what plants he could and to start some new ones. He would have helped capture the pigs, were it not for an injury he had recently sustained, from falling off a horse, that had left him with a pronounced limp and an inability to do much lifting.

There was a moment of confusion as the pig that Marfal was attempting to capture darted under Halfene's skirt, knocking her over. Marfal scrambled to help her sister to her feet, but the pig was weighing down the fabric of her skirt, and she could not be moved. Serbrena, normally quiet and reserved, burst into a fit of laughter that spread to both sisters. Soon all three were on the ground, collapsing in their uncontrollable giggles, and the pigs, four in total, wriggled away again, exiting the garden at a quick trot and heading for the farm house. Ansera, quite overwhelmed at this point, quickly went inside and shut the door.

It was Morok who eventually came to the rescue. He and Loobal had appeared for an unexpected visit and came upon the scene of three mud-splattered sisters heading back to the house to wash up, while four wayward pigs wandered the yard, searching for something to eat.

It did not take Morok long to coax the pigs back into their enclosure, bribing them with bowls of supper scraps.

When Loobal's sisters were once again clean, the family gathered in the kitchen for a light meal. Before they

Into the Water

ate, Morok took it upon himself to ask a blessing for the food they were about to consume. The sisters paused and allowed him his prayer, closing their eyes in respectful silence.

When he was finished he took a deep breath and addressed the women: "For too long I have lived my life without the gratitude I should have felt toward God for all that He has provided me with, in His grace and love. I wish to change my life and truly live in harmony with Him."

Loobal, at his side, added, "I too must change my ways. God has asked us—Morok and me—to do His will, and we shall."

Halfene and Marfal stared at their youngest sister and her husband with jaws dropped. Ansera looked at them curiously, and Serbrena just smiled quietly, unsure what to think about this new revelation.

Halfene was the first to speak. She always had something to say. "Well," she began, eyeing them curiously, "I don't know what has happened to you two since we last saw you, but I would certainly like to know! Please do share your story."

So Morok, aided by Loobal—who interjected frequently—told their story of what had happened the day before and the days that led up to that. The group listened attentively, but the expression on their faces showed that they held some doubts. When they were finished talking no one had much to say. Such things were not within their realm of experience, and thus they could not *know* it to be true. So Loobal and Morok left that night somewhat disheartened at the response to their tale, but they vowed to each other to go home and pray about it.

When they had left the farm house, and the sisters were helping Ansera with the last of the dishes, Serbrena surprised them by announcing that she, too, had been touched by God. It was when she was young and alone at work one day. While staring at a dress she was still working

Chapter 11

on at the end of a long day and lamenting, to herself, the futility of this life of endless toil and no creativity, she suddenly felt a hand upon her shoulder. It had not felt exactly like someone's hand, but that was the way she described it to herself at the time. It was a soft touch and warm with a kindness like her mother's had been when she was a baby. She saw no one there, but the feeling lingered, and it gave her hope that things would get better. She was able to finish her job that evening and to return the next morning feeling at peace.

"Do you really think that was God?" asked Halfene.

"Well, maybe an angel." Serbrena shrugged. "But it made me feel that there *was* a God."

"I miss Papa," said Marfal. "He would have some answers for us."

"Do you think Papa's an angel?" asked Serbrena innocently.

Ansera looked thoughtful. "I don't think so, my dear. He always told me he'd be going to live with the angels one day, though. Remember the day we collected his ashes? I was sure he was there with us. And many angels too. It felt so peaceful and loving in that little building over the hill."

"I could almost see him in that room," said Serbrena. "And he's been to visit us since, I know he has," she added.

"It's not the same," declared Halfene. "I wish I could give him a real hug."

"I'll give you a real hug," said Marfal and squeezed her tightly. Halfene laughed.

They left the conversation at that and went off to bed, to dream about angels and pigs and dear Bekren, whom they all missed deeply.

Halfene dreamt that Dentino had come to tell her that the pigs had escaped again, but this time there were twenty-five of them. They were in the house, upstairs and down. He could not help her but simply stood by as she chased them out the door, their little feet leaving muddy tracks everywhere.

Serbrena dreamt she was in a boat, drifting out to sea. Her father was with her. The water was calm, and she was not afraid. Although she had no oars with which to row or any means of steering, she was able to lie back and feel the rhythm of the gentle waves beneath as they guided the boat to a far-off shore. She asked her father where they were going. He said nothing but smiled calmly at her and turned to face the bow. When she awoke the next morning she was in a peaceful mood.

The town was quiet for the next few days. Nothing out of the ordinary seemed to be happening within its friendly borders. However, by the end of the week the weather turned foul, and an unpleasant smell was in the air.

Something is not right, thought Loobal, as she hung out the wash. The air smelled of smoke—but not of the wood fires she was accustomed to. It disturbed her so much that she went indoors to escape its stench. Morok was working and not expected home until evening. She decided to sit awhile in prayer and seek answers from above.

It was difficult for her to reach that expansive sensation of going beyond herself and connecting with the oneness of creation. Instead of feeling a blissful peace, she was keenly aware of a disturbance around her. She felt fear and anguish; panic. It was unexpected and made her feel uneasy and afraid. She began to pray fervently for understanding and insight, that she might know why this was happening and what she should do about it.

The answer was immediate: "Find Morok."

Covering her face with a kerchief, she ran out of the cabin. She had to find him. The sky was becoming dark, and a light film of grit was descending upon Palador. She hurried through the streets to where he said he would be—helping one of his friends repair a fence.

Chapter 11

As she ran she saw many people in the streets shouting and pointing up at the sky. Debris was falling now, and the wind blew mightily. Loobal ducked out of the way as a large piece of wood flew toward her. She was close to where Morok should have been, and she began to call out his name, terrified of what was happening.

"Morok, where are you?!"

Suddenly he appeared, breathless, around the corner of the building beside which she was trying to take shelter. He grabbed her and pulled her inside the door.

"Stay here!" he yelled. "I have to get Gartener out—he's pinned under the fence."

He left before she could say anything. She poked her head out the doorway, trying to follow him with her eyes, but it was dark and he had already disappeared.

The chaos continued. Although most of the people had by now taken shelter indoors, there were various animals running loose, wild with fear; and the sound of the raging wind was exceeded only by that of falling items crashing against the buildings. Loobal slumped to the floor. What was happening? Where were her sisters, her mother? Were they okay? What was taking Morok so long? She needed him desperately. She turned to prayer, at a loss for what to do. The answer was forthcoming: "Go! Leave the town as quickly as you can. Go by the river."

Although her first instinct was to remain frozen to the spot, helpless, a surge of energy from within drove her to her feet and out the door. With wild desperation she screamed for Morok once more, bracing herself against the relentless wind. For a moment she could not hear nor see anything; then, out of the darkness he appeared, carrying his lifeless friend over his shoulder. He laid the man down inside the building where Loobal had been and turned to her.

"Run!" he screamed. He took her hand and nearly dragged her along the street, sprinting toward the edge of town that led back to their cabin and the riverbank.

There was a wooden boat tied to a stake at the water's edge. It thrashed against the bank, pummeled by the waves. Morok grabbed on to the side of the boat to steady it and tipped his wife in.

"Hold on tight!" he yelled as he cut the boat loose and jumped in beside her. The river was frothing and the current was quick. There was nothing they could do but hold on for their lives. Behind them the storm raged over their beautiful town, threatening to destroy everything they held dear. As they approached the first bend in the river, they turned to get one last look at Palador as it disappeared behind a cloud of dust. Tears streamed down Loobal's cheeks, and Morok held on to her tightly as the wild river carried them away.

Chapter 12

The World Away

Peter opened his eyes. He blinked slowly in the yellow half-light and strained to look around. He was lying in the dirt beneath a bench. His body hurt all over. The ground, which was layered with a thin film of dust, appeared ghostly. He rose slowly to his feet, shuddering in shock. How long had he been lying there? He strained to remember what had happened. Was it an explosion? The wind had shaken everything. He had quickly taken cover under this bench outside of his family home. Something had hit his head. He was a little dizzy and rather confused. He knew he was back in Portshead; he remembered having arrived the night before and having been warmly welcomed by his mother, who made him a late supper—but the town was now barely recognizable. Where was everybody? What time was it? It must be day, but he could not locate the sun. He inched his way slowly through the haze, toward the door of the house, coughing from the dust. Inside the house it was dark and dusty. But he was welcomed by the sound of his mother's voice—weak, yet alive—coming from the kitchen. He found her lying on the floor, smiling up at him.

"Peter," she beamed, "you are okay! I was so worried."

He crouched down and propped her up to a sitting position. "I'm okay," he confirmed. "And you?"

Chapter 12

"I am a little sore. This was not a comfortable place to sleep. But no worse for the wear, really."

She smiled again and patted him on the arm. "Where is your sister?"

"I didn't see her, Mama."

A look of concern crossed her face.

"She wasn't here when I arrived last night, remember?" he said. "I think you said that she was visiting friends."

"Oh, that's right. I do hope she is not hurt."

The wreckage in Portshead was extensive. Peter searched all over but could not find Meana. There were few people around to ask. Although some had fled during the night, it seemed that most of the townspeople had perished in the storm. An unpleasant feeling arose in the pit of Peter's stomach. He continued his search, but it was to no avail. *I will continue in the morning,* he thought. *I must look after Mama.*

He returned to the house and found his mother sweeping the floors. She had not left the building, nor had she bothered to look through the window. She looked sad.

"She's gone, isn't she?" she said.

"I don't know, Mama. I can't find her," Peter said gently. "It's awful out there." He could not say more. It would break her heart. "Get some rest, Mama. I'll clean up."

She slowly shuffled off to her room, silent with the shock. Peter started to sweep but then set down the broom, shaking his head. He knew they would have to leave. He decided to pack what food he could find and a few useful items that were easy to carry. He did not know where they should go, but he knew there was only one place he wanted to be: Palador.

<hr>

The dust had settled on Palador. It was a ghostly scene. The town was unrecognizable. There were few signs of life in and about it. Farther away, to the north, there was a black cloud on the horizon. The storm had left; its wake of destruction lay behind it.

Marfal sat at the edge of the woods. She was conscious, but barely so. She could not move her right arm. Her sisters, who had been with her, were nowhere to be seen. She was in shock. She looked up at the broken trees. Her head hurt.

To her left was a large boulder, covered in moss. She felt an urge to crawl behind it. Using her left elbow to prop herself up, she slowly dragged herself to the far side of the huge rock. What she saw there devastated her: it was Serbrena, beautiful, sweet Serbrena, lying dead.

Marfal wept openly, her voice creaky. Her tears made rivers on the dusty map that was her face. But the sound of her crying drew to her a miracle: Halfene was alive.

"Mmarfal!" came the shout from a small indentation in a nearby rock face.

"Here!" she yelled back hoarsely.

Halfene appeared to be unhurt. She was covered in dirt and her dress was badly torn, yet she walked without limping. She approached Marfal cautiously, stepping over the many fallen branches along the way. When she saw Serbrena, she shrieked in horror and collapsed to her knees, hovering over the lifeless body.

Marfal crawled closer and hugged Halfene. They held each other and cried together, their tears falling sadly upon their beloved sister.

When they released their embrace, Halfene looked hard at Marfal. "We must gather ourselves together. I will help you. And we shall look for other survivors. There is nothing we can do for her."

The severity of the situation was clear to Marfal, and she nodded to Halfene.

"We will do what must be done. I wish to look for

Chapter 12

Mama."

"She wasn't with us when we hid here, Marfal. She couldn't keep up."

"We left her?! I cannot remember what happened."

"We had no choice."

There was a long silence. Marfal burst into tears, her resolve failing in her despair.

Halfene grabbed her arm gently, helping her to her feet.

"We must be strong, Marfal," she encouraged. "We are alive, and that is a gift. I'm going back to the farm."

It was difficult to find the path through the woods due to the accumulation of debris and broken trees. The light was dim. They moved slowly, stopping frequently so that Marfal could rest. Her arm had regained some sensation, but it was weak, and she held it to her chest.

Eventually, they came upon some landmarks they recognized, but the farm was destroyed. The buildings—including the house—had been reduced to rubble. Ansera could not be found.

"She's with Papa," whispered Halfene. "I know it."

Marfal smiled weakly through a new gush of tears. "She's happy then. She missed him so much."

They sat for a while, catching their breath, trying to somehow make sense of how their lives could have been altered so drastically in just one day.

Finally, thirst drove them to seek out water. The well that Bekren and Morok had resurrected was still working, and they pumped up a few buckets-full to drink and to wash the dust from their hair and faces.

Refreshed, they ventured forth into town—or what had been the town. The scene was heartbreaking, and they almost gave up in despair, but for some glimmer of hope that was given them: there were a few people yet alive.

They found one woman lying beneath a store-front

awning that had collapsed. She was crying out for help, and they were able to free her. She was not someone they knew, but they held her nonetheless, took her hand, and helped her to locate her son, who was indoors. He was barely alive, yet hope was not lost. His mother knew well the ways of healing and was sure she could take care of him, if they could help her find some necessary items and herbs.

Once they had done this they set out on their next mission: to find Dentino. Halfene was truly in love with him, and although she dared not hope he was still alive, she went straight to his house. Miraculously, the building was still standing, although it was piled high with debris. She found the door and pushed hard to wedge it open.

Dentino sat in the center of what used to be his living room. He looked up when she barged through. For a moment his stare was blank, as if he did not recognize her; he seemed to be in shock. But when she whispered his name, he snapped awake, leapt up, and ran to her. The two embraced passionately, overwhelmed with emotion.

Marfal had followed her sister into the house but now backed away to allow them a more private reunion. She was happy for them; it was truly a miracle that both had survived. But her own heart ached sadly for a man she never got the chance to be with. He had left Palador earlier for his home town. Although he had told her choir it would be a brief trip and that he would soon return, she had no hope for that now. There was not much to return to.

Peter shook with fatigue as he helped his mother out of the house. Laden with supplies and belongings for the two of them, he was hoping to find a horse or a mule to ease his burden and carry them back to Palador.

They did eventually find a horse, after walking to what had been the southernmost entrance to the town. The horse

Chapter 12

was obviously frightened. Peter recognized the animal and called it by name, calmly approaching it with an outstretched hand. It came to him, perhaps relieved to connect with someone familiar. It had no harness or saddle, but Peter, a confident rider, was willing to go without. He hoisted his mother onto its withers and climbed on after her, carefully balancing their belongings behind himself. The horse did not object. They wished to proceed along the south road, which lay just ahead. It was difficult going because they had no means to steer the horse, yet they managed to make their way nonetheless, slowly wandering from their devastated community to an untold future ahead.

───

Back in Palador the search for Loobal was underway. Marfal, followed by Halfene and Dentino, made her way to the cabin by the river. The cabin was flattened, fallen upon itself. They circled the rubble and called out many times for Loobal and Morok, but it was to no avail. There were no indications that anyone was alive there.

Marfal was at a loss. Exhausted, she sat down. "I wish I was dead."

Halfene said nothing. She was staring at the river, her hand resting on Dentino's arm.

Her eyes suddenly narrowed, as if she was attempting to focus on something far, far away. "They left..." she said slowly.

"Who?" asked Marfal, briefly looking up at her sister.

"Loobal and Morok," Halfene answered quickly. "I have the strongest feeling that they went to the river."

"To the river? Then where?" asked Marfal.

Halfene was mulling something over in her mind. "I think they escaped. I see a boat."

Marfal was skeptical. Halfene was a very intelligent girl, but she did not possess the gift of second sight.

Halfene knew that Marfal doubted her. But the impressions were strong, and she felt that they must be true. She looked at the river once more, then she turned to Marfal. "I must follow it, Marfal—the river," she stated bluntly. "To see if I can find them." She paused. "Perhaps there is something they understand that we do not, and I must find out. Will you join me on this quest, Dentino?"

His stare was intense. "I never want to be parted from you again."

"Marfal?" she asked.

Marfal looked out at the river, then back at Halfene and Dentino. "I cannot join you," she lamented. "I must find Mama."

"But you'll be all alone!" wailed Halfene.

Marfal said nothing. Her mind was made up.

The couple decided to rest for the night among the ruins of Palador and then gather what they could for their journey in the morning. It was cold, and the three huddled together for warmth. They were put to sleep through sheer exhaustion, and although the ground was hard, they managed to sleep through until dawn.

While they slept the landscape of the town continued to change. The wind picked up again during the night, stirring the layer of dust upon the devastated town and bringing a few more precariously-standing buildings to the ground.

In the morning a ray of hope burst through the clouds, lifting the spirits of those left alive in the town.

It was difficult for Marfal to say good-bye to her sister. As the eldest, she had always been the one responsible for caring for the other three when they were young. How could she let Halfene go off on a journey like this one, with no destination and no assurance of ever finding their sister?

Dentino promised Marfal that he would take good care of her little sister.

"I'm not so little," argued Halfene, "and it will be *me*

Chapter 12

taking care of *you*."

Dentino laughed. "I am in pretty rough shape, aren't I?" He was still limping due to his riding accident.

"We shall look after each other," concluded Halfene.

She turned to Marfal. "We will come back. Whether or not we find them."

Marfal took a deep breath. "All right, Halfene. I will do what I can here and await your return. Please take care, and do come back soon."

The sisters embraced, trying not to cry. Then they parted ways, Halfene running off with Dentino to quickly prepare for a potentially long journey on foot, and Marfal slowly turning back toward the farm, knowing what she must do but unsure of her strength.

When she arrived back at the farm, she was met with a conundrum. So much had shifted with the night's wind that she was unsure which path would take her to the woods where Serbrena lay. She had hoped to retrace her steps back to the body and to search for her mother along the way.

She wandered aimlessly for a while through the wreckage of the farm buildings, gathering useful items that were not broken. When she came upon a shovel that had been her father's, the tears welled up again, and she sat down. This was not going to be easy. Furthermore, it had begun to rain. A light rain, it was; still, it added to her worries. She resolved to search the woods.

It was not hard to find Serbrena's body, as she recognized the boulder there. She tripped on a fallen branch as she approached the site, and stopped to examine her bruised ankle. She did not want to get up again. Having had to face her father's death was hard enough—an old man who had been ill—but this was unbearable. Serbrena had been such a light in her life, always a joy to be around. And there she was, dead in the forest, cold and lifeless and broken like a doll. It was all she could do to push herself up and continue on to the place where Serbrena lay. Yet she knew she must. She could not leave her lying thus; it was unthinkable.

Marfal decided to move the body. She carried her as best as she could to the top of the hill by the woods. She knew it would be impossible to build a decent pyre on her own, especially in the rain. But try she must. In the end she gave up, exhausted. There was nothing she could do but leave the body there and return to the farm to spend the night. She hoped to make some kind of shelter from the rain before it got dark.

The next day there was sun, and her resolve strengthened. She returned to the hill-top and completed her beloved sister's funeral pyre. When she was finally able to push the body on top of it, she broke down once again, sobbing relentlessly. She prayed for her sister's happiness in the heavens, and she said good-bye. She felt truly alone.

It was difficult to get the fire started with such damp wood, but in the end it burned brightly. She watched for what seemed like hours, mesmerized by the flames and lost in her own sorrow.

And then she remembered her mother. Marfal had been so consumed by Serbrena's death that she had completely forgotten to continue the search for their mother. She ran down the hill, leaving the fire to burn itself out, and began scouring the woods and the fields beyond the farm for any sign of her mother. Eventually, she realized she had not eaten and had hardly drank anything in days, so she paused her search in order to find sustenance.

The farm house pantry was inaccessible, but she was able to get into the kitchen through a broken window. It pained her to be inside the house—a place where her family had all been together happily, until recently. She found some bread and ate hungrily. It was enough to give a little strength to her weakened body.

She set out toward the woods again, examining the

Chapter 12

ground closely. The further Marfal wandered, the more unsure she felt of her direction. The ground was bumpy. She went on unsteadily, her footsteps faltering. There were few indications that anyone had been there. But as she neared the edge of the woods, her attention was drawn to a distant shed. It stood next to the fence that ran between the woods and the edge of the field. Alongside the shed grew a thick layer of vines. They almost obscured the door, which was open. It was the door that caught Marfal's attention, for in that small crack she caught a glimpse of something red.

As she approached the shed her stomach knotted. She was sure that the red object was her mother's shawl. She held her breath and shut her eyes, hesitating to go further; but when she looked in the shed, her mother was not there. She picked up the shawl, gently, and stood quietly while fresh tears welled up.

Her mother's body was behind the shed. Marfal knelt down beside it and gently touched her mother's face. She burst into loud sobs. "Mama! Not you, too! I can't bear this..." she trailed off, feeling broken inside. There was a moment of silence as Marfal simply sat, unable to fathom how everything she loved could have left her in such a short period of time. It was in that moment of silence that she detected the very faintest whisper from the still body beside her. Looking now at her mother's lips she could see that they moved.

"Mama!" she yelled. "You're alive?" But there was no response. Marfal quickly draped the red shawl over her mother's body and rubbed her back, hoping to miraculously coax her back to life. "Mama, speak to me," she persisted, holding the old woman's cold hand in her own.

But the light had gone from her. It was plain to see. There was nothing for Marfal to do; no hope that Ansera could be brought back.

Marfal was crushed. It descended upon her like a load

of rocks, that had she left Serbrena in the woods and went searching for her mother instead, she may have been able to save her. The thought of her mother suffering here alone broke her already-wounded heart.

It was with great heaviness and despair that she walked back into the ruined town that evening. Ansera was much heavier than Serbrena, and there was no way that Marfal, weak from grief and hunger as she was, could have moved her. She felt utterly spent. And she had no place to go, no arms to seek comfort in. She cried miserably, pitifully, and collapsed onto the street, her head buried in her hands.

The road was dark as Peter and his mother rode to Palador. They were numb and tired and sat astride the horse as if in a daze, a dream. But the horse was faithful and sure-footed and seemed to know where it was going.

As the dawn broke they made their way into the dust-covered town. The scene was similar to that in Portshead: rubble interspersed with stable structures. The few people that they saw greeted them somberly. Though Peter was compassionate at heart, he was not inclined to carry on a conversation. He had one goal in mind, and that was to find Marfal. His mother did not know his intention but clung to the horse and to a hope of safety and comfort. They walked on, the horse stumbling occasionally on a rock or loose board. Peter would have bypassed Marfal completely if it had not been for one of those occasions. He dismounted to check the horse's hoof and there she was, in a crumpled heap. She lay still except for a fine tremor, from cold or perhaps from shock. He whispered her name, not believing his eyes—that this was the lovely Marfal.

"Peter, help me down," his mother called to him. He quickly went to the horse's side and lifted his mother gently to the ground. She accompanied Peter as he returned to help

Chapter 12

Marfal, and together they rolled Marfal onto her back. She appeared to be awake, yet she was unable to grasp what was happening. Her eyes were unfocussed and expressionless.

Peter gently brushed her hair from her face and called her name softly. "Marfal—it's Peter, from the choir."

She blinked her eyes a few times but did not say anything.

Peter's mother stood up and went to the horse to fetch their pack. She took out a small flask of water and offered it to Marfal.

"Pour a bit on her lips," Peter suggested. This seemed to bring some life to Marfal, and she focussed her gaze on her two helpers.

"Marfal!" Peter called again.

This time she looked at him directly. Her eyes widened and she let out a small gasp.

Peter's mother lifted the flask to her mouth, and this time she drank a tiny sip.

"Let us help her up," Alemara suggested, and she and Peter slowly pulled Marfal into a sitting position. However, she began to slump, and they realized she was not yet strong enough to sit on her own. So Peter held her, and once again his mother attempted to give her some water.

It was a slow process. She was not very alert and would barely open her mouth to receive the drink. But they knew they must persist. Eventually, a man came by and offered them a place to lie her down in his house, which was remarkably intact. He helped them carry her there, and his wife gave both of them chairs to sit on.

When they perceived that Marfal was asleep, Peter and his mother brought out what little food they had, to share it with the kind couple. But there was food in the house, and their offering was not needed. At first they ate in silence, reluctant to begin a conversation that would surely lead to those dark and depressing events that had brought them together. Yet when the wife finally broke the silence, she asked Peter if he was the violinist who had joined the town choir.

"Why, yes," he answered, pleasantly surprised at her query.

"Have you got your violin with you?" she asked.

"I do." Tired as he was, Peter got up and fetched the case from among his meagre belongings. Looking lovingly at Marfal, he opened it, took out the instrument, and began to play.

The tune evoked a feeling of loss and sadness, such as he felt at that moment—as he could feel in the air from all of the people of those ruined towns. Yet there was also a note of hope. He looked at his mother, smiling up at him, and a teardrop fell from his eye. She was alive, after all. He looked at the couple seated before him, holding hands as they gently moved to the music. And then he looked at Marfal, so still, yet not lost to him. To her he played, and the tune swelled with a great crescendo of emotion that surged from his heart to the bow and into the strings. Her eyelids fluttered as if she were lost in a dream.

When the music stopped, Alemara went to Marfal's bedside and spoke to her quietly. She took her hand and stroked it, saying, "You are safe now, dear lady; we are here and will take care of you."

Once Alemara was satisfied that Marfal was resting peacefully, she returned to the group to discuss what to do. They talked for a long time, telling their stories of the past few days' occurrences and comparing the situation in Palador to that in Portshead. No one could determine the cause of such destruction, nor did they know if any other towns had been affected. And no one knew what to do.

The husband said, "I have lived in this town my entire life—in this house, in fact. It has always been peaceful here, and we have never experienced any serious problems, aside

Chapter 12

from a short drought ten years ago. I can't imagine how we could repair this much damage and return to our normal ways."

His wife began to cry. "I can't bear to leave the house. I'm afraid to see what's outside."

Peter looked at his feet for a moment, unsure of what to say. He took a deep breath and began: "I know this is very hard for you. It is a tremendous shock, what has happened—for all of us. But we can't hide away and pretend it will get fixed on its own. That will be our death. There are people outside who need help—your friends and neighbors. And the dead must be taken care of too. We must have food to eat and clean water."

He paused and looked at his mother. "Mama," he said, "you need to rest. I will go outside and see what needs to be done."

"I will go with you," the husband offered, encouraged by Peter's words.

The wife sighed. "All right," she said. "I will look after this woman you brought to us, and you—" she indicated Alemara— "may sleep on my bed."

It was not long before Alemara was asleep and Peter and his new companion were out the door, ready to face the new world.

Chapter 13
Lost and Found

When Halfene and Dentino began their journey, they had no clear idea of where they were headed. There was no consistent path along the riverbank, merely some wagon trails that paralleled the course of the river a ways and then veered off. These roads were easy to follow, but otherwise the journey was full of obstacles. And for Dentino, this was a serious strain on his injured leg. But Halfene, headstrong as she was, would not turn back. It appeared that where they were headed was not so badly damaged by the storm. The grass was green, unlike the dust-laden fields of Palador, and there was a sweet scent in the air. Halfene felt encouraged.

There were no signs of Loobal and Morok, however. Halfene was not even sure what to look for. The vision she had been given at the riverbank by their cabin had been so clear and strong that she thought she would be led right to the lost couple. She had no further insights since leaving the town, and now it seemed like they were just going, rather than going somewhere. There was little to guide them but the river itself. Racing along its course, it called to them to hurry their pace; but as keen as Halfene was, in spirit, to pursue it, they could not keep up.

Coming to a fork in the road, Dentino laid down the pack he was carrying and turned to face Halfene. "For two days we've walked, my dear," he said wearily. "I cannot

Chapter 13

continue like this. It seems futile." He took her hand. "Return with me to Palador. I know it is bleak, for much of what we held dear has been destroyed. Yet I feel we can rebuild our lives. I wish for us to be together. Forever."

Halfene smiled at his honest proposal. Then she turned to the rushing river. It was difficult to choose.

She looked Dentino straight in the eye. "I choose you," she said fervently. "However," she was compelled to add, "I would like to continue our search for my sister. There is something that she and Morok know that God has told them, and I want to know it too!"

Dentino shook his head. He seemed to be weighing things in his mind. In the end Halfene's insistence won, and he agreed to go on. They chose the path that hugged the river and slowly followed it onward, their fatigue showing.

When Morok and Loobal left Palador, it was with terror in their hearts. It was a journey over which they had no control. The river was relentless as it surged forth to the open sea, and the boat was tossed mightily. It seemed that by God's grace they stayed afloat. There was nothing to do upon that boat but to pray. They were too frightened to move, lest they upset its balance, and there was no food or drink. So pray they did. They prayed aloud and silently. They prayed through their tears. They prayed for Palador and for those whom they had left behind, and they prayed that they would survive this storm. For a while it seemed like they were praying into the wind, that no one would hear their pleas. But God answered them. And His answer came not in words, but in a feeling of pure peace that descended upon them like a warm blanket on a cold night. The feeling was so overwhelming that they actually fell asleep, and the boat carried them on to an unknown, yet trusted, fate.

Their journey was a long one; for several days they

drifted until the river had calmed enough for them to steer the boat toward dry land.

They were exhausted. Morok was concerned for the baby; Loobal had not eaten since the day they left Palador.

Upon reaching the shore he carefully removed his wife from the boat, carried her to a soft place, upon which she could lie, and set out to find food and water. They were in an uninhabited area, not far from the mouth of the river. He could see the great gray sea expanding out to the horizon. It was beautiful but uninviting. He shuddered and returned to his search.

Loobal was moaning. Morok ran to her side and lay down. He caressed her cheek tenderly; she was cold.

"Morok," she said quietly, "where are we?"

"Near the end of the river," he replied.

"Then we are near my home," she said softly.

"Tanlar?"

"It is not so far, by boat."

"Could we walk?" he asked hopefully.

"No. It would take us many days. Morok, I don't feel strong enough for such a journey. We have suffered much already."

Morok sighed. He did not want to go *anywhere* by boat.

"Then let us stay here and gather our strength," he said finally. "We need to eat and rest."

He gave her a hug then was back on his feet. "I will fetch some water from the river; you rest."

He carried the water to her in his hands, a sight that drew laughter from her despite her weariness. She asked him for more, and he ran back to the water's edge.

"What a good husband you are!"

He laughed. "And now to find food."

He was gone for a while and did not return empty-handed. "Some roots for you, my dear," he

Chapter 13

announced, "and I shall eat moss."

They had barely finished their meal when Loobal said, "Morok, I'm worried about the others." She was remembering the scene when they had left. "How could anyone have survived that?"

Morok sat in silence, contemplating. "Loobal, we are alive because God brought us out of there...perhaps they were spared too."

"But how will we know?" she cried.

"We must pray," Morok decided. "That is all we have left. We must ask to know God's will for us and for those we care about."

As they sat together on the grass, in that wild place, and closed their eyes to pray, a shaft of sunlight broke through the clouds and illuminated their little circle, warming their cold, tired bodies.

Morok began: "Dear Father, our beloved Creator, I come to you with thanks for the life You have blessed us with, and it is our desire to know Your will for us." Morok paused. He did not know what to say. He was overwhelmed with emotion—fear for the future, worry about Loobal, joy for the baby that would soon be joining them, sadness for the loss of his home, and deep gratitude to God for sparing their lives when others had died.

Loobal was equally perplexed; her worries were for the baby and for her family back in Palador.

But their hearts were sincere, and their prayers did reach their Father above, and He spoke to them: "My children, do not cry for your losses. My work is being done upon this world. And you worry, for your lives have changed, and you do not know where to go. Do not be afraid. You are in My care. Go to Tanlar. The way will be shown."

Morok fell into a deep state of bliss and was transported far away. He no longer felt tired or hungry but was enlivened by the powerful energies accompanying him.

Lost and Found

He was told many things by a group of angels that he was taken to meet, and upon returning to his material surroundings, he had a clear impression of what he was to do.

He was not able to describe to his wife everything that he had seen. He had been shown many things of the future as well as of their past, but the worst of it was what they had shown him of the present, the state of affairs back in Palador.

Morok was heartbroken. How could he tell his beloved wife that her mother and sister had been killed? He had seen Zev-ran's death as well. He wept openly. Loobal tried to comfort him, but that only made his sorrow worse. How could he tell her?

She was insistent. She knew he must have seen something horrible. "Morok, you must tell me," she whispered. "I can't let you bear this alone."

But silent he remained.

Finally she asked what he had seen of their future.

"I see us in Tanlar," he said. "We are surrounded by a gathering of friendly people. The baby is fine. It is a boy. I don't see Palador in our future."

"But my family!" Loobal protested. "Surely they are with us?"

Morok shook his head sadly. "I do not see them joining us, Loobal. This path is for us alone."

"But I never got to say good-bye!" she wailed. Morok held her tightly, her face against his chest.

"I can't bear it either," he said. "Loobal, we can't let this destroy us. You know we will see them all again one day."

"In the Realm of Light?"

He nodded.

Loobal was inconsolable. "But that could be years from now—when we are old and withered."

He held her in silence, too fragile to answer.

Chapter 13

"Do you want to know what I saw?" she asked.

"Yes," he said, happy with the change of subject.

"I saw the moon and it was orange. It lit up the sky, but not in the same way it does here. It was eerie, what I saw." She shuddered and paused for a moment, recalling the vision. "I saw black clouds and falling stars. Not shooting off to the side, but falling straight upon the earth. The land was burning. And then it went black. Everything. But a voice told me, 'Be not afraid. This is the end before the beginning. Go forth in faith, for new life awaits.'" She looked at Morok. "What do you think this means?"

His expression was sombre. "That the worst is ahead of us." He looked at her intently. "Loobal, I have hope, you know. There is a reason for all of this. We *will* be guided. Please do not lose faith."

He took a deep breath, for he knew what he must divulge to her. "Loobal," he began gently, "it was your mother I saw, and Serbrena. They died in the storm."

Loobal gasped and began to cry.

"What about Halfene and Marfal?"

"I saw them not."

Loobal hugged him tighter, clinging to a hope that he had some better news for her. "Maybe they got away?" she suggested.

Morok shook his head. "I was not shown. I saw many deaths. Zev-ran is also gone." He hung his head. "That boy meant more to me than anyone. He was the best friend I'd ever had—" he smiled weakly— "until you."

"Oh, Morok," she lamented, "this breaks my heart, all of it. How will I go on, knowing of the devastation we left behind? We could have helped, had we stayed."

"We could have died, had we stayed," Morok said quickly. "This is our path, Loobal, and ours alone. We must walk it without fear and without regret."

She sighed deeply. "If it weren't for God I would feel

so lost."

"So would I," he agreed.

They decided to rest for the night and begin their journey to Tanlar in the morning. It was cold, but they managed to keep each other warm and fell asleep in a close embrace.

The next day they were faced with a dilemma—should they go on foot or risk the trip by sea? Loobal, who was beginning to show her pregnancy, preferred to sit in the boat, but Morok was concerned that they would not make it there alive.

In the end they agreed to take the long, cautious journey by land. Morok promised to carry Loobal if she got tired.

They had nothing to pack so they were soon off, following the river to its mouth at the great gray sea.

It was not long before they reached the place, and they stopped to stare at the breathtaking view. The water seemed to stretch on forever, although they did catch a glimpse of a far away shore to the east. The water was calm, and Morok almost regretted his decision to go on foot; however, his memories of the trip along the river came rushing back to him, and he turned to his wife and said, "Let us move on."

They walked for an hour before stopping to rest. It was a sunny day, and mild, and would have been the perfect weather for such a hike if their spirits had not been so deeply dampened by the tragedy and terror of recent events.

There was nothing to eat for lunch; they drank water from a stream, which was a small tributary of the river, and lay down in the lush grass. They were content to just lie, resting their tired bodies. And then Morok's stomach grumbled.

"I'm hungry, Loobal."

"I am too," she admitted. "Do you know how to fish,

Chapter 13

Morok? I never learned."

"No," he replied. "But that won't stop me from trying." He leapt to his feet and walked over to the stream, inspecting it to see if there were any fish. He was not disappointed. It took him a while to figure out how he could possibly trap one; eventually, he took off his shirt and used it as a net. His catch was small, but he was ravenous and would have accepted much less. They made a fire and cooked it on a stick, sharing the tasty treat equally with each other.

The next leg of their journey was more difficult, terrain-wise, but their spirits were uplifted by their meal, and they were keen to cover more ground before dark. Fortunately, fresh water was plentiful in the area, and they drank often. They saw many animals along the way but none that seemed predatory. Morok felt at ease; he thought that their journey would not be impossible after all.

They came upon a sheltered area in a rock face, and here they decided to make a bed for the night, using soft branches. Loobal was tired and wanted to eat something more, so she sent Morok off in search of food. He returned with some young shoots of an edible plant, which they ate raw with relish.

Sleep came quickly to both of them. Their dreams were long and confusing. Morok dreamt that he was flying over water, searching for a place to land. There were no solid surfaces to be seen anywhere. Finally he spotted a level area that resembled the top of a building. He stepped onto it and found himself inside another building, which was on a mountain top. Inside this building was a dog. The dog said to him, "You have come too far and must go back." He left the building and suddenly fell from a high cliff, landing perfectly, below. It was then an angel appeared, dressed in white. "Come," the angel said, beckoning him to a cave at the foot of the cliff. "It is here you must go." He walked inside, finding himself in a dark, but comfortable, place, with many people in it. They asked him his name and he looked at them, surprised. "I am Morok; I have come to teach you." The group greeted him happily and invited him to join their circle.

It was then that Morok woke up.

Loobal, too, dreamt that she was flying over water. The sea was endless, as though the land had all vanished. She dropped down to get a closer look. Beneath the waves she could see trees and buildings and many people. They were waving to her frantically. She skirted the edges of the underwater town but could not seem to submerge herself to appease their cries. Hovering above the scene, she called to God, "Show me the way and I will go." A voice said to her, "You cannot help them, they are gone. Come with us." She saw a swarm of bees approaching. *Why, there must be land!* she thought. She followed the bees as they passed her by, and sure enough, she could see land. It must have been the top of a mountain, for it was jagged rock, covered with snow. She alighted gently on the ground and turned around to face a giant eagle that had been sitting there, watching her. "I am here to warn you," the eagle said, showing its talons. "There is a fierce storm on the way." She looked to the west and could see a belt of enormous dark clouds with a blanket of rain streaming from them. The eagle picked her up and carried her northward. When she awoke she had tears in her eyes.

Neither of them felt rested from this sleep, and their walk that morning was a dreary one. They discussed their dreams, which both could recall vividly, and speculated as to their meanings.

"I think the world is in danger," said Loobal.

"I think we are in danger," said Morok. "Let us pray. Perhaps we will get some guidance."

They paused on the rough trail they were following and sat down side by side on a large rock. Loobal began: "Dear Father, Blessed One who made us, we call on You for

Chapter 13

Your guidance and comfort. We are confused, Father, and wish to understand what our dreams have shown us, and what it is that You wish us to do. We love You and seek Your peace, Your presence. Please help us."

They closed their eyes and waited; and help did come, in the form of an angel. He sat with them: they could feel his glorious presence. They felt at ease and began to let go of their worries. The angel said, "There is much to tell and much to hear, if you are willing to listen."

They nodded.

"I have come with tidings from our Father, who wishes that both of you should grow in His light, becoming the happy souls you were meant to be. Yes, there is a time of hardship upon this world, and it *must* be so. We ask that you hold strongly to your faith, for you will be challenged by these coming events, just as you have been challenged by what has recently come to pass. Be wary of the desire to stray from your path, to seek comfort and the gratification of the flesh, for this may lead you into danger at a time when it is vital for you to follow the will of God. Be strong, and know that your needs will be met, and you will be kept safe in the arms of the Lord if you but listen and follow. He means for you to be well and to carry His truth to the many darkened souls who are *not* listening nor following the way of truth and light. If you follow your guidance you will be taken, in time, to a place that *is* safe and new and bright, that holds the hope for the future of your people. We ask you to listen and to pray often; to follow the path of light and truth that is laid out before you. Be good to yourselves and love your God, for He loves you and will carry you onward to better days."

The angel then gave them each a blessing, which they felt deeply, and then he disappeared.

Morok and Loobal sat in silence, absorbing his words. At last they opened their eyes, gave each other a hug, and resumed their journey.

Lunch that day was simple: bird's eggs cooked with insects and leaves. They rested for a while after, enjoying the fire even though the weather was indeed mild. They spoke a bit of the angel's advice and decided to pray once again, entreating God for His wisdom and grace upon their journey. They received no verbal reply, but experienced a rush of warmth and goodness that spread from their heads to their feet. Loobal felt the baby move. She was overcome with love for him and for God, who had blessed her with such a gift. She wept joyfully and hugged her husband, for whom she was also grateful.

They began a slow ascent up a steeper ridge in the afternoon, and by nightfall they had made camp—again, simply a bed—at the summit. The night was peaceful with few stars. The clouds gently enfolded them, and their sleep was profound.

In the days that followed there were more signs that they were fast approaching a civilized area. The paths they encountered were wider and well-trodden. Loobal was relieved to have even ground to walk upon.

They stumbled upon an old building, which looked deserted; as it was raining that day, they decided to stay there awhile. There were two chairs and some books, welcome comforts for two weary travelers.

Food continued to be scarce and wild. Morok became adept at catching fish—when he could find a decent stream. Otherwise, they ate plants and, once, a young hare. Loobal had lost weight but overall seemed fit. Morok was always hungry, and this made him rather cross at times, yet he was encouraged by his wife's bravery and tried to keep up a cheery disposition for her sake.

They did not stay long in that little shack, for they felt a constant urge to hasten their journey to Tanlar. It was a rather ominous feeling, like there was something behind them, yet they did not expect to find much joy once they had

Chapter 13

reached their destination—the angel's words had warned them of such.

It was at dawn the following day that they became instantly aware of a darkness about. Holding their breath in fear, they watched quietly while two men passed them where they lay and continued off down the trail. The men were tall and carried weapons. When they were certain the men were well past and could not hear them, they got up from their bed and hastened on their way. They held hands as they walked, finding comfort in their union.

Loobal thought the men were guards of the city, but she was puzzled that they were this far out. "Usually they tend the gates and outer walls," she told Morok.

The terrain was beginning to look familiar to Loobal, who had spent most of her life in this area.

"When I was a girl we would hike these hills and down to the sea." She paused, her heart aching. "Morok, I miss them so much!"

"I miss our family too, Loobal. I wish we were back at the farm house right now, laughing around the supper table."

She looked at him sadly. "Will we ever see them again?" Morok did not answer.

They found a spot that afternoon that was well-hidden in the trees and served perfectly as a camp from which to explore the area before they made their final trek down to Tanlar. The city was visible from atop this particular hill, and they examined it cautiously from their distant vantage point. Loobal showed Morok where she used to live and where they went to market to sell some of the clothing that she and her sisters made. Thinking of her dear sisters brought tears to her eyes once again, and she had to turn away from the view.

"Life was so simple then, Morok. I hated working—I always wanted to play instead—but now I would give anything to be back there, sewing with them, living with my parents in our old home..." she trailed off wistfully. Morok had nothing to say to her but stroked her hair. He understood. He missed his own parents. He did not think of them often now, as caught up as he was in his new life with Loobal, but he did wish that he could see them again.

That night, as they sat down to pray, a thought came to him. He wondered what would happen if they did indeed follow God's will to the end—would there be a happy life awaiting them? Would they be reunited with their loved ones? The hope of this welled in his chest. He closed his eyes and began: "Dear Father, our beloved Creator, we seek Your counsel and to be close to You. Our love for You is strong and pure, and we wish to remain in Your grace always. Please guide our steps as we return to Loobal's birthplace, for we know not what awaits us there. I ask You, Father, to watch over us and keep us in Your care, to protect our baby as he grows inside his mother. May we always walk in truth and light. We thank You, Father, for all You have given us this day and forever."

They sat there for a long while, quietly communing with Him. They heard no words but could feel His great presence enveloping them, and the love that filled them was immense, powerful. Loobal shook from the intensity of it.

"I am healed, Morok," she said afterwards. "All of that pain I was feeling, that aching for the loss of my family—it is gone!" She was actually smiling, something Morok rarely saw these days.

"I'm at peace, Morok," she continued. "I feel light and free and almost—" she grasped for the proper word—"elated."

Morok smiled back at her. Her joy was palpable and contagious.

"We are on the right path, Loobal. I know it." He put his arm around her and gave her a kiss. "You are beautiful," he said.

They walked toward the center of the hill, where they

had the best view of Tanlar, below. There was a darkness to the city, a shadow cast by the clouds above.

"I'm not afraid of it now," Morok said solemnly. "We shall go tomorrow. Let us rest and gather our strength."

They spent the rest of the day sitting quietly and taking brief trips into the surrounding woods to gather food. They encountered no people, but they did hear voices, at one point, coming from a trail below. Loobal was curious to find out who they were, but Morok held her back. "Let us stay hidden for now," he advised.

The next day it rained hard, and they chose to stay sheltered in the trees and wait until the storm passed to make their descent. Loobal was restless, anticipating what would happen when they arrived in Tanlar. "I wonder if I will see anyone I know?" she mused. "I haven't been gone that long, really."

They sat and discussed their plan. "We will seek shelter and food," Morok reiterated, "and then try to discover why God has brought us here."

"I am a little worried," Loobal admitted. "It was a hard life there," she said. "People were not as friendly as they are in Palador. And there is competition, always competition. What one gains, another loses."

"That is not the way of God, Loobal," Morok stated humbly.

"I know it," affirmed Loobal. "We must take care not to fall into that way of being. Or—as the angel told us—we will be in danger."

"We will keep up our relationship with God, and He will show us the way through this."

Before they fell asleep that night, listening to the soft fall of rain, they said a prayer of thanks to God and asked that they be clearly guided on the next leg of their journey.

Chapter 14

Tanlar

When the dawn broke they had a clear sense that this was to be the start of their journey down to Tanlar. They felt brave, encouraged by a deep knowing that God would be with them, every step.

The trek was not difficult; they found a well-used trail that was not too steep, and it was a mere hour before they were standing at the main gate of the city.

The gate was open; Loobal assured Morok that this was normal during the day and that anyone could pass freely in or out.

They walked through the gate slowly, taking in their surroundings. It soon became clear to them that *they* were drawing attention: the people passing by them were stopping to stare and whisper. Loobal became very self-conscious, and she took Morok into a sheltered area of a nearby building.

"It's our dress," she said in a hushed tone. "I was so caught up in our plans that I overlooked the fact that we look absolutely dreadful."

Morok looked down at his hands, his clothes. He was quite dirty; his shirt was stained and ripped, his pants had the remnants of days of muddy hikes upon them, and his shoes were well worn. Loobal's dress was covered in mud, her hair was tangled, her shoes were falling apart, and she lacked the customary scarf that the women here wore upon their head.

Chapter 14

There was nothing they could do but ignore the curious citizens and continue on.

Loobal had it in her mind that they should first seek the counsel of one of the town elders, who resided in a large building near the water. They would explain the situation—the destruction of Palador and their abrupt flight from the storm—and ask for help and advice.

They meandered through the town slowly, taking in its intricate architecture and vast walls. To Loobal, it was quite familiar, and she felt at home there once again. But for Morok, a stranger, the city was unlike anything he had ever imagined. So many people in such a small place, dogs running loose everywhere, buildings as tall as trees...it was overwhelming for him, and he felt small, insignificant. The people were not friendly, as Loobal had warned him. They would not meet his gaze but looked down or to the side of him. He was beginning to feel hungry once again and urged Loobal to find them some food.

"We will have to beg," she told him. "Here it seems there is never enough to go around, and the food is not shared as it is in Palador. Some go without while others feast. We worked hard, my sisters and I, and we managed to earn enough money to get by. But I have seen people die of starvation in these streets while others looked on."

They turned down an alley-way and, by chance, spotted a man who was taking garbage out of the back of a shop. There were a few dogs lingering hungrily by the door, and he shooed them away harshly.

Morok approached him timidly. "Could you share some food with us, kind man?"

The man stopped what he was doing and looked at them blankly. "What food?" he bellowed. "I have none for you." He turned away and went back inside the shop.

Morok was shocked. No one had ever spoken to him in this way. Loobal took his hand and led him away, determined to have better luck somewhere else.

He tried asking a few more people for food but always received the same answer: "We haven't got enough."

Discouraged, they continued on toward the house of the elder. Loobal rapped hesitantly on his door, and there they waited, humbled, for their last chance at a meal and some comfort.

It was a while before their knock was answered. An old woman finally opened the door, and after looking at them up and down with an amused grin, she bade them enter. They took off their shoes at the door, as was customary, and followed the woman down a lengthy hallway, which was decorated with tapestries depicting men in battle. At the end of the hallway was a large room, and here it was that they were introduced to Gotsro, the elder. He did not recognize Loobal, for they had met only once, when she was a child; but when she mentioned the name of her father, the man's eyes lit up and he said, "Ah yes, Bekren, a good man. We had some dealings together a few years ago. Where is he now, for I heard he left town?"

Loobal looked down. She did not want to bring up any more tragedy.

"He died last year. He was ill."

The man looked at her, puzzled. "Why have you come to me?"

Loobal did not know where to start and said as much. Gotsro seemed rather impatient, like he had better things to do, so she wanted her story to be concise.

"Well, we moved to a town far up the river—its name is Palador—and all was well until very recently when a great storm hit and destroyed the town. We, my husband and I, managed to escape by boat and came here. We have nothing. I do not know if my family survived. We are here to ask for your help. We would like to get some food and a place to stay and some clean clothes. We have no money to pay but could

Chapter 14

work in exchange for your kindness. I am a seamstress and Morok has many talents which could be put to use. Please help us."

Gotsro looked at his female companion and said, "Fetch them what they need. They may sleep in the servants' quarters. I will put them to work tomorrow."

They thanked the man graciously then waited in the room while the old woman made arrangements for their care. After a time she brought in a plate of food for each of them—some bread and cheese and a few pieces of dried fruit. They ate ravenously. When they were finished she took the plates and offered them water to drink. They thanked her, and she smiled back at them kindly. It took a while for her to get clothes and shoes that would fit the two of them, but eventually she did so, and she also brought a bucket of warm water for them to wash with. She gave them some privacy in a curtained-off area of the room that was used for private conversations and then left to prepare their bed.

It was such a joy to sleep indoors, on a bed, that both Loobal and Morok were able to let go of some of the anxiety that they felt about being in a stranger's house. The servants who shared the room were hostile, in subtle ways, but kept to themselves. People came and went in this place, and they were used to the change, as much as they detested it. Before falling asleep Loobal said a silent prayer of thanks to God for the bounty they had received that day and prayed for all of her family and friends back home, whom she missed dearly.

The next week was spent acclimatizing to their new surroundings at the elder's mansion. They, along with the other servants, did laundry and maintained the grounds, cleaned and washed, cooked and swept. There was plenty of work to go around, as Gotsro was continually entertaining guests and holding meetings. The house was always full of people. Loobal and Morok found themselves swimming in a sea of ungodly behavior. There was always fighting going on—shouting matches or, occasionally, a fistfight. Alcohol, which was consumed in modest amounts in Palador and Gate-Town, flowed in abundance here, although the servants were forbidden to drink it. Morok overheard many lies told by men who pledged to trust one another, in business or battle, as it were. And Loobal was the target of many lustful glances, although her growing belly deterred the unwanted advances. Morok kept a close watch over her.

The servants with whom they shared their sleeping quarters were unfriendly, at best, but the couple began to notice a change in them as their time together increased. At prayer time, which was every evening before bed, Morok and Loobal would sit down together on the bed, close their eyes, and pray aloud for many things, one of which was always the well-being of their coworkers. At first the others ignored them. They would play their card games or sing lewd songs, their voices loudly marring the beauty of the prayers. But one night they set down their cards and actually listened. They watched the couple, sitting there in their innocence and humility, and although they could not hear every word said, they certainly felt something unusual. It was peace. In that noisy house of anger and treachery, they felt peace. They slept soundly that night.

Chapter 15
A Difficult Choice

A week after they began their journey along the river, Halfene and Dentino were at their wits' end. They had been fighting for days over whether or not to end their search, and Dentino's injuries were getting worse. But they were at a stalemate. As much as Dentino would have liked to turn back, he refused to leave Halfene, whom he considered to be his wife. He loved her desperately. Halfene was more determined than ever to find Loobal and Morok; it seemed the further they went—finding nothing—the more certain she was that they would come across a clue around the next bend in the river. It was illogical, and Dentino could see that she was obsessed with the mission.

"This is folly, Halfene!" he shouted at her, almost in tears. "We are going to die out here!"

She said nothing.

"What are you afraid of finding back home that drives you so far away?"

She stomped her foot indignantly. "I'm not running away!" But there was fear in her eyes, the fear to admit that he was right.

Dentino had learned that reasoning with Halfene was like trying to reason with a wild animal. He tried another tactic. "Halfene, you don't realize how much pain I'm in. I can't keep up with you. I fear that if I don't take care of my

Chapter 15

leg soon, I will be lame for life. You don't want that, do you?"

He caught her attention with that.

"Let me look at it," she said quickly. He took off his pants and sat down, wincing.

"Why, it's swollen from hip to foot!" she exclaimed. "Why didn't you tell me?!"

Dentino said nothing.

She sat down beside him and began tearing her kerchief into pieces. Once she was finished, she submerged them briefly in the cool water of the river and returned to lay them on top of his leg. "That's all I've got, my love," she said sadly. "No medicine, no bandages. How am I to take care of you?" She sounded anxious.

"You can start by letting me rest."

That made her cry. "Oh, how horrible I've been to you!"

He smiled weakly. "It's my fault too. I shouldn't have let you have your way."

She sighed, frowning. "I guess our quest is over then," she lamented.

"I can't go on, Halfene, I really can't. I'm not even sure I can make it back home."

They sat together silently, mulling over their problem. Dentino felt extremely vulnerable. He was weak, crippled, in pain, and hungry. There was no way for him to help Halfene find food, and he realized that he was putting her life at risk by keeping her with him. Dentino also grieved the fact that he was not able to help her find Loobal. He knew how much that meant to her, how desperate she was to succeed in her mission. She had left Marfal to do this; to come back to Palador without the lost couple would be devastating for Marfal as well as for Halfene.

Halfene was losing strength. Normally bold and vivacious, she was now beginning to see her own weaknesses, how her stubbornness could cause difficulties and pain for herself. She wanted to help Dentino—he was her first love—but she did not think she could.

It was Dentino who said, finally, what both were thinking. "Halfene, go and get help for me. Go as fast as you can. Bring a horse. It's the only way. I can't walk, and you can't stay with me here."

"I know, my love. I'm just so frightened to leave you here alone." She looked at him softly, her heart reaching out to his.

"Halfene—" he paused, smiling, as she touched his face— "I want you to know that I love you as much as it is possible to love. I will survive. I have water here, and if you can forage some food before you leave, I will also have sustenance. There is shelter in the trees. Leave me the blanket, if you would. I trust that you have the energy to keep going and will be able to protect yourself from the elements. I wish that things were different, that I could be the strong one. Alas, I must accept this, what is, and hope that the day will come when I am strong enough to be there for *you*."

Halfene put her arms around his neck and hugged him tightly for a long while. She was reluctant to let go but realized she must find him food quickly and be on her way.

She located some early berries and picked the lot of them. Then she gathered all the edible roots and shoots she could find and a large pile of sticks for making fire. She gave him what little illuminant they had left, ensuring him that she would find a way to keep warm at night.

Their parting was traumatic for both of them. Tears spilled from their eyes as they shared their last kiss and whispered "I love you" and "be strong."

Halfene hurried away, following the trail they had taken to get there the day before. She glanced back only once. Dentino was staring at her, a look of fear on his face.

Chapter 15

It took Marfal several days to fully regain conscious awareness of her surroundings. She was lost in a dream world, living a different life than the one she had left and the one she would awaken to. She saw her mother there, in that place of mystery. Her mother was well, and told her that she need not worry about them—herself and Serbrena. Serbrena looked radiant, all aglow with love and beauty. She said nothing, but smiled at Marfal and then vanished into a white mist. Marfal tried to follow her but could not see where she went.

"You cannot go with her," her mother told her. "It's not your time. I will wait for you and watch over you and your sisters."

She sat with her mother, looking out over a sparkling blue sea.

"You couldn't have saved me," her mother said. "I wasn't meant to survive. Treasure your life, Marfal. It is a gift. And be brave. There are difficult times ahead for you." She looked away for a moment.

And then Marfal asked the question that had been puzzling her for a long time. "Mama," she said, "where is Papa?"

Her mother turned back to her and smiled. "He is here. Would you like to see him?"

"Oh, yes!" Marfal exclaimed brightly.

The mists into which Serbrena had disappeared now parted, and there stood Bekren, gloriously rotund and healthy, much different than he had appeared before his untimely death.

"Marfal," he greeted her, with arms open. "I have missed you."

She ran to him and embraced him, tears of joy flowing from her eyes. It felt so good to be safe in her father's arms,

A Difficult Choice

after all that had transpired in those horrible days of Palador's ruin. She clung to him while her mother looked on, smiling. There was a moment of silence while Marfal composed herself, and then Bekren invited her to sit down, that they might talk awhile. He asked her how she was doing.

"Papa, the things which have occurred—you wouldn't believe! Everything is gone! The farm—" she looked at her mother. "I can't go back there. I can't live my life without you, and her, and Serbrena. I just can't."

"But what of your other sisters, my dear?" he asked. "Surely you would go back for them?"

Marfal could not answer.

"I think you will find that things are not as hopeless as you anticipate," Bekren suggested. "Now you can't stay with us forever. Rest awhile in this place, and then we will say our good-byes."

Marfal nodded reluctantly and climbed into her father's arms as she did when she was young. She closed her eyes and went to sleep.

Peter was fetching water from a neighbor's well when he heard his mother calling to him, "She's awake!"

He rushed back to the house, bucket splashing. When he reached Marfal's bedside she turned to face him, wide-eyed and peaceful.

"Hello, Peter," she whispered, smiling.

Peter took her hand gently in his.

"I am so glad you survived, Marfal. I was really worried."

"Where am I?" she asked, looking around the unfamiliar room.

"In the house of Mortin and Saminelle, a kind couple who took us in after we found you lying in the street three days ago. You were unconscious and very cold. My mother

Chapter 15

has been tending to you, along with Saminelle."

"May I see her," she asked, "your mother?"

Peter beckoned to his mother to join them.

"Thank you," Marfal said to her. "I am so lucky to have been saved. What is your name?"

"I am Alemara," she said warmly.

"Would you like some food?" Peter asked Marfal. "We have been trying to feed you, but not much went in."

"You must be starving, my dear," said his mother. "I will get you some broth." She left them, and Peter leaned in closer. He could contain himself no longer.

"Marfal, I must confess that I came here looking for you. You have been in my thoughts since I left Palador. When Portshead was also destroyed, I could not stay there. I was compelled to come back here, to seek your company. I did not know that Palador had suffered the same fate as Portshead. It was quite a shock to me."

Marfal blinked, trying to take in all that he was saying. "You came here for *me*?" she asked.

He gave her an enormous smile. "For you," he confirmed.

It took a moment for the significance of his words to sink in. "You mean, you want to be with me?" she asked, still thinking it was too good to believe.

"I do," he replied. "I love you, Marfal. I have for a long time."

To hear such great news amid so much tragedy and despair was confusing to her, and her emotions were in turmoil. She began to cry.

Peter did not know what to do. It was not the response he had hoped for, yet he understood that she had suffered greatly and would need some time to think things over.

He stood up to walk away, to give her some room, but her grip on his hand prevented his departure.

"Peter," she said, "I love you too."

Peter nearly cried for joy. Hearing those words was the best moment of his life. He kissed her beautiful lips and wiped away her tears.

When Alemara arrived with the bowl of broth, the two were smiling at each other lovingly.

Chapter 16
The Darkness

Morok was in a tizzy. The elder had left him with so much work to do that he barely saw his wife for a moment that day. He rushed about, tending to the garden, then fixing the roof, washing the wagon, then feeding the horses and cleaning their stable. He was exhausted by suppertime, and still there was no sign of Loobal. Benshed, one of the other servants, said Loobal had been sent into town to buy food for the next day's celebration. It unnerved Morok that his wife would be walking alone in such a treacherous place, but Loobal did return within the hour and seemed none the worse for the excursion.

The days passed quickly, and summer was upon them. The city bustled with people going to and from the market and to and from the sea. Visitors and traders poured in from other places, and Gotsro's home was home to many. The servants were grumpier than ever, finding every job distasteful and too much for them. Morok was often allotted the chores that no one else wanted to do.

Loobal's experience at the mansion was different. Because of her condition, she was usually given the lighter chores, such as cooking and washing up. Her chores were interspersed with rest. She was not allowed to leave the mansion except on duty, however, and this troubled her. Although she had worked hard during her youth in Tanlar,

Chapter 16

she had always had the freedom to do as she pleased when finished.

She discussed this with Morok one night; they needed to make a plan for their future.

"We can't stay here, Morok," she whispered intently to him. "And I am most certainly not going to have our baby in these conditions. There is evil in this house."

"I know it," he said quietly, glancing about to see if anyone was listening.

"Morok, I would like to pray about this," Loobal requested.

"All right. Let us do that," he agreed.

Loobal took it upon herself to begin: "My beloved Heavenly Father, Who loves us beyond our ability to understand, please be with us now. Draw us close to Your heavenly bosom, that we may be nourished in this time of darkness. We wish to know Your will for us, Your desire for our lives, that we may fulfill this desire and live in eternal harmony with You. Please show us the way to rise above the conditions of this city and this household and how to bring Your peace into its midst, that all may benefit from Your heavenly presence. I ask for a blessing upon our son as he grows and upon me as I prepare to nurture him. Give us the strength to endure our life here and to thrive in spite of the limitations that are imposed upon us. I am Your loving child, and I will follow Your will to the end of my days."

There was a pause as Morok opened his eyes to check the room again, and then he, too, offered a prayer: "My beloved Father who reigns above, I call to You to save us from this place in which we have landed ourselves. Please guide us to a safe haven of freedom and love where we can truly live in accordance to *Your* laws and be the people that You created us to be. Your will be done."

They waited in silence and felt that familiar pull, that longing of their souls to be with God in all His grace and beauty, His perfection and stillness and goodness. They opened themselves with faith and trust, reaching higher up into the Heavens with their longings, and felt the warmth and purity of God's response. He had no words for them, but gave them a vision. They saw a dark cloud over Tanlar, a threatening storm. In the cloud were warriors battling to the death. Drops of blood fell as rain over the city. Down in the street below they saw themselves, Loobal still with child, standing strong amid a great crowd of people. The people were frightened, cowering from the battle above, but as Morok and Loobal reached out to them, in love and peace, they slowly began to stand united, holding strong together. They began to pray together. The cloud lifted from the town, and the bloodshed ceased. A glow of golden light emanated from the city itself, and the buildings were encased in jewels.

The vision evaporated as quickly as it had come, and the couple was greeted by an angel, the one who had sat with them on the rock. He said to them: "This, my children, is to be your destiny, your mission."

Morok and Loobal listened intently, determined to hear and understand his words.

"You must go from this house. Leave tomorrow. Take nothing but your clothes. Gotsro will try to keep you in his employ and refuse to pay you if you leave, but do not submit. You are needed elsewhere. Go to the house of the tailor on Malend Street, and there you may seek refuge, for he is a good man."

The angel then blessed them and left.

They were flabbergasted. Although they were keen to leave Gotsro's house, neither of them relished the thought of communicating this intention to him. They had worked for their keep and for the clothes and other personal items they had been given, and had been promised money, in addition, for their labor. He was a cruel man—this they had witnessed on numerous occasions. His promises were not always kept.

Chapter 16

And the two of them had become valuable assets to his household.

Morok held Loobal tightly. She was whimpering in nervous anticipation of what was to come.

He summoned his courage and said to her, "I will go and tell him tonight. You gather our belongings. We will leave in the morning."

Gotsro, as predicted, was not in a pleasant mood once he had heard Morok's plan. "And what makes you think you can just leave like that, without even a day's notice for me to hire other servants to replace you and your wife?" he growled.

But Morok was steadfast. Remembering the angel's words, he said, "We are needed elsewhere." He asked for their pay, and Gotsro's face reddened.

"You have some nerve," he spewed, "and I have no intention of rewarding such impetuousness."

Morok said nothing but looked at him evenly. The elder stared back at him, smug and unbreakable.

"I am not your slave," stated Morok authoritatively, "and it is in your best interest to honor your obligations to your employees."

Gotsro's eyes narrowed. He was weighing his options.

"I will give you half," he bellowed finally. "The other half will compensate me for your inconvenience."

Morok nodded at him calmly. The air in the room was oppressive, but he was determined to hold his ground and not engage in the elder's angry ways. He tried to access the feeling of peace that came to him when he prayed.

They were set to leave the next morning. When Morok had put on his shoes and Loobal had finished washing, the couple said good-bye to the other servants and began to climb the stairs to the main hallway, which led out of the house. On their way up, their ears were attuned to some curses from below—the servants admonishing them for leaving the bulk of the chores to them—and a commotion upstairs. They ignored the disgruntled servants but paused to listen to what was going on upstairs before proceeding. It sounded like two men were having an argument. They slowly crept closer, and this is what they heard:

"I won't hear anymore of this! The soldiers were in position two weeks ago and nothing happened. You have failed in your duty as Captain. If you fail again I will have you deported."

"When do you want me to give the order then?"

"Prepare them tonight. Tomorrow they will march."

"And what if there is civil unrest?"

"That is unlikely to pose a threat to our cause."

"I will await your command then. The soldiers are prepared to do what is required of them."

"Good. Have a horse waiting for me."

"I won't disappoint you this time."

Footsteps were heard retreating down the corridor, and then a door was shut.

Morok and Loobal waited a moment longer, then quietly left the house through a side door. They walked briskly through the grounds, hand in hand, saying nothing. Both were tense, sensing a danger in the words they had overheard on their way out.

When they reached the main avenue of the city, a few blocks away, they sat down on a low stone wall to catch their breath.

"What do you think Gotsro is up to?" Loobal asked Morok, in a whisper.

"I don't know," he replied, "but we had better figure this out. Lives may depend on it."

Loobal stared down at her hands, her delicate brow furrowed in deep thought. "There is a celebration taking place tomorrow in the main square. Frantair, the Governor of Tanlar, is hosting a delegation from a city to the east called

Chapter 16

Menzoneal. It is a larger city, and we have always had good relations with them, until recently. Last year, so I heard, there was a skirmish, and some Tanlarians were taken prisoner there. They are trying to make amends."

Morok replied solemnly, "Do you think Gotsro's soldiers will be targeting the visitors, then?"

"That is the only thing that makes sense to me. But I don't know what his motive is," she added. "Why would he want to upset relations between our two cities? What could he have to gain?" She looked perplexed. But Morok brightened and changed the subject.

"Why don't we seek out that tailor whom the angel told us to find? Perhaps he has some insight. Remember, you've been away for quite a while and you are bound to have missed some news in that time."

Morok was right. Loobal nodded and stood up. "I know the way," she said.

They wound their way through the city streets, stopping only once to buy some food at the market. The tailor's house was easy to find, as there was a large sign outside, denoting his profession. He came to greet them at the door, and they were surprised to see that he was quite young; by the look of him, he was not much older than Morok.

He smiled and invited them inside. "What brings you here?" he asked courteously.

Morok and Loobal looked at each other, suddenly unsure how to answer.

"I guess you could say we were guided," Morok offered sheepishly.

The tailor was not busy, so he offered them each a chair and looked expectantly at them, awaiting a more lengthy explanation. After an awkward pause, in which no one spoke, Morok cleared his throat and began to tell their tale. He omitted a few details, such as angels and what had been overheard at Gotsro's—for these seemed like things one would tell a person only after one had gotten to know his political and spiritual views—but he did explain that Loobal had been raised here and had only recently emigrated to Palador.

"You were a seamstress!" the tailor exclaimed. "That's wonderful. Then you appreciate the work I do. It is not easy, and there are some people who are very difficult to please."

Loobal laughed. She well remembered the demands placed upon her and her sisters by some very particular customers who were rarely happy, no matter how fine the work.

"That I do not miss," she said.

Morok asked the tailor if he could give them shelter. He seemed taken aback by this blunt request and did not know how to respond, but he softened when he saw Loobal's innocent gaze. Morok explained that they had money to pay and at the very least could help him at his shop until they found other work.

"It is difficult to find lodging in this city. I have a small room at the back that I use for guests and sometimes to store cloth. The two of you may stay there until you can make a more suitable arrangement. I do need help, as the demand for my work usually increases in the summer. It is funny, but I wasn't going to hire anyone because I could not afford to. And now here you are—" he looked at Loobal— "a seamstress."

He showed them the room then invited them to sit with him and eat. They shared what little they had left from the market, and he brought out some bread and honey.

And now Morok took it upon himself to tell the man what they had overheard at Gotsro's mansion.

"Why, that could be the celebration tomorrow!" the tailor blurted out. He looked concerned. "I knew there was something evil brewing. I feel these things," he added.

Chapter 16

"The question is," Loobal joined in, "what are we able to do about it?"

The three of them pondered this while they ate. Finally Morok stood up. "We've got to warn them," he said sternly.

Loobal looked at him. "But how, Morok?" she asked. "They will be staying at the governor's mansion on the hill. And there's no way in there, for us. It's heavily guarded." She paused. "We don't even know if our guess is correct. It would be folly to spread such gossip about Gotsro. He is a dangerous man."

The tailor went to the window and peered out. He had a view of the hill and could see just the top of the governor's abode, peeking out from above the stacks of buildings in front of it.

"I don't like this," he said. "If what we suspect is true, and he intends to kill the Menzonealan visitors, then war will be upon us."

"Why would he want that?" Loobal asked.

"I'm not certain," the tailor replied, "but I suspect that there is something he can gain by creating instability in the city." He turned to Morok. "Let us see what tomorrow brings. We will attend the celebration and be prepared to act if the opportunity presents itself."

Morok smiled at him. "Thank you, Astnor. I am glad of your wisdom in this matter."

Morok tidied up the table where they had been sitting and then left with Loobal so they could put their belongings away in the room they had been given.

It was dusk when they spoke with the tailor again. He was sitting in his living room reading, his work finished for the day.

"Astnor," Morok called, alerting him to their presence, "may we sit with you?"

"Certainly. I have some new ideas for you to

The Darkness

consider." He walked over to the window again and looked out. "There was a skirmish here last year. The local guards were called to intervene. But the fight intensified and one of them was killed. After that it seemed as though they were reluctant to work. And I have noticed a general lack of respect for the governor of this city. He was jeered on one occasion. He came to make a speech in the town hall regarding relations with neighboring communities. I remember it well. I believe he offended many of the citizens who were not in support of his ideas about the trading of resources. He was a fine man, whom people could trust, but in recent times he has demonstrated weakness."

"So what are you saying, Astnor?" asked Loobal.

"That there is instability in the governing house of this city, and the guards of Tanlar cannot be relied upon."

Morok sighed. He did not like the fact that they had no chance to help in this grave situation. "Let us rest," he said. He bid Astnor good night and went to the back room, his wife following behind him.

They did not sleep well that night. Although the bed Astnor had provided was fairly comfortable, their dreams were restless.

Loobal dreamt that she was behind a great wall. No matter what she tried, she could not surmount it to see what lay beyond. On the other side she could hear cries from those who had fallen into darkness. Loobal was engulfed by a great light that spread over the land on which she stood. She was carried upwards, above the wall, into the source of this light. From up there she could clearly see the scene below. There was no help for those on the other side of the wall.

Morok's dream began with a song. Loobal was singing to the baby in a cozy room in a house. He could not see whose house it was. The song cheered him, for he was weary of his travels. She tucked the baby into its bed then turned to Morok. "I love you," she said. The scene faded quickly and he

Chapter 16

was in the boat. The storm was raging and Loobal said to him, "This is not over. A bigger storm is coming." Again the scene shifted, and he was back in Palador, at the home of Zev-ran. Zev-ran was playing with his sisters but turned to him and said, "Morok, all hope lies with you. I'll see you on the other side." Morok woke up at this point and cried miserably. His heart ached for his young friend.

Morok decided to get up, for he could not sleep now. He felt distraught. Not only was he haunted by his dream, but he felt the heaviness of the coming events. He got dressed and went over to the window to look outside. The sky was yet dark. Frustrated, he sat down upon the bed. Loobal was still asleep, her breathing soft and her eyelids aflutter as she dreamt. He felt so much love for her that he could hardly contain it. He planted a kiss on her forehead then closed his eyes, leaning back against the wall. He said a silent prayer, thanking God for his wife and asking God to guide him today.

Breakfast was a silent affair. Loobal and Morok joined Astnor for the meal. All three of them were particularly nervous at the thought of what was to come. They gathered up their things and left the tailor's house, following the road to the town square.

There were crowds of people present there, awaiting the procession down from the governor's mansion. Tables were set up in the center of the square, presumably for the honored guests to sit at, and there were a few guards present on horseback. The buildings surrounding the square were adorned with floral arrangements, and a troupe of jugglers was stationed near the center stage, preparing to perform.

The three wound their way through the crowd, attempting to get a better view. Morok was vigilant, keeping watch on every entrance to the square, lest he see signs of Gotsro or his men. For a while nothing happened. The crowd cheered as the governor, with the Menzonealan delegation, descended the hill on horseback. He got up on the stage,

The Darkness

addressed the crowd warmly, and made a presentation to the guests. At this point they were all standing upon the stage, receiving applause from the enthusiastic crowd.

Astnor turned white. "Oh no," he said. "I feel it..."

Morok quickly looked around, scanning the crowd and his surroundings.

"There!" he said, indicating a horse and rider approaching quietly from behind the crowd. Soon another and another appeared. Their riders were fitted with leather armor and helmets, and each one carried a sword.

Loobal gasped. "What do we do?"

Astnor grabbed her arm. "We run."

They pushed their way out of the crowd and to an open doorway at the edge of the square, just as the soldiers charged forward, circling the crowd and advancing to the stage. The two guards beside the stage were quickly overwhelmed, and they surrendered, begging for their lives. The governor was not so lucky. He was speared immediately by a soldier who had ridden right up onto the stage. The Menzonealans were left unharmed.

All was chaos as the soldiers quickly retreated to where they had come from. The quivering guards did not follow them but ran to Frantair's side. He succumbed to his wounds and died on the stage. The delegates were in shock. They sat and screamed, calling for help. Morok watched from outside the doorway where Loobal and Astnor were hiding.

"We must go to them!" he yelled, trying to raise his voice above the din of the quickly dispersing crowd.

In the square it was a tumult of fearful people looking out for themselves. No one was answering the Menzonealans' cries.

Morok approached them calmly, Loobal and Astnor trailing behind him. "Please," he called to them, "do not be afraid. If they had wanted to harm you they would have done so." He reached out his hand to the man nearest to him.

Chapter 16

The Menzonealans gathered close to Morok. His presence seemed to comfort them.

"You should return to your home," he told them. "There is nothing you can do for him." He looked sadly over to where the governor had fallen. Frantair's death was, to him, a shocking reminder that one's life was at the mercy of the will of other men in a place such as this. He gulped, feeling unsafe. Would this be his fate also? He was about to ask the Menzonealans about the whereabouts of their horses when a guard of Tanlar rode up, followed by two others.

"Stay where you are!" he commanded the guests. "I have some questions for you." He looked gruff and nervous.

Morok stepped back, maintaining eye contact with the Menzonealans to reassure them. The guard approached closer, focussing his attention on one particular man, who was the highest official of the delegation.

"Was this attack sanctioned by the Menzonealan people?" he demanded.

The official seemed shocked at the accusation.

"We came to Tanlar with the hope of restoring peaceful relations between our troubled peoples."

"Then who would *you* implicate for this unthinkable crime?" the guard asked.

He looked the guard straight in the eye and said pointedly, "Someone who seeks to usurp your governor's office."

"Get your horses. You will be escorted to the gate."

The guard gestured to his comrades, and they set to work, assisting the Menzonealans to capture their mounts, which roamed the square uneasily. Once the delegation was reassembled, it was ushered solemnly through the streets and finally out the front gate.

When they were out of sight a soldier followed after them, unseen. They rode to the top of a hill that overlooked the city. There, as they paused to let their horses eat, they were surrounded by a group of men on horseback—the same ones who had been in the square, the same ones who had murdered Tanlar's governor. The Menzonealans trembled in fear. They foresaw no way out for themselves. The soldiers said nothing, but decimated these innocent people with no hesitation. Their screams were not heard. The soldiers left their bodies on the hilltop and set their horses free to run home. Then they galloped to a concealed stronghold in the forest, awaiting Gotsro's arrival.

Morok had watched the Mezonealans leave, with some trepidation. They seemed so vulnerable in the aftermath of the bloodshed, and they had no guards of their own to accompany them home. He sighed and turned to his wife and his new friend and suggested they return to the tailor's house.

When they got home they sat, shaking, and discussed the events.

"We were wrong," Loobal stated. "The target was not the visitors after all, but our own governor."

"I was not expecting that," said Morok.

"Nor I," Astnor chimed in. "But I do feel a strange feeling, like the bloodshed is not over. I wonder what Gotsro has planned. Do you think he will try to blame the murder on the Menzonealans?" he mused.

"We shall see," said Morok. "But we know the truth, and we must find a way to prevent the spread of lies, lest they lead to more peoples' deaths."

"Oh, Morok," lamented Loobal, "what a horrible place this city has become."

He patted her arm comfortingly. "We are here for a reason, my dear. We must do as God wills us, and perhaps we may yet shed some light on this dark place. "

"I do hope so," she said.

Astnor was lost in thought. He was a thinker, by nature, always observing and analyzing, analyzing and

Chapter 16

observing. He would come to a conclusion and then re-analyze it from a different angle and change his answer.

"I have an idea," he said finally. "What if the reason Gotsro killed the governor was so that he could take his place?"

"Gotsro already has power, as an elder," said Loobal. "And he certainly has everything he needs in that mansion of his. What could he gain by that official title?"

"It's not what he has to gain, but what he has to lose," said Astnor.

"And what is that?" asked Morok.

"Opposition."

Astnor looked at the two of them and offered to explain. "Loobal, you have been absent from here for a while and have missed out on some political conflicts. Gotsro wanted to expand the shipping business from this port and charge a tax to all foreign ships entering our harbor. Frantair disagreed because he was focussed on improving relations with other cities, and felt that this financial imposition would cause more tension—perhaps have an effect on imports. There was also the issue of Tanlar's military. Frantair decreased the city's security, as an act of faith. This celebration today was supposed to be somewhat of a peace treaty."

"And Gotsro?" inquired Loobal.

"Gotsro wanted to get revenge on Menzoneal for the kidnapping of several of our citizens. He thought the guard should be increased. He maintained that Tanlar should have an army. But armies are expensive, and the city could not afford such an expenditure. It seems that he has funded his own army of rogues. I fear what their next target might be." Astnor was silent for a while. His thinking led him in circles, yet he could not come up with an answer.

"I think he will attack the city," Morok offered. "Menzoneal, that is."

The Darkness

"If so, how do we stop him?" wondered Loobal.

None of them had any good suggestions. They decided that their only option, at this point, was to pray. Astnor was happy to join them. He, too, was a spiritual man, but did not often share this with others. "Tanlar is a funny place," he explained. "Those who are truly spiritual say their prayers in the shadows, while the superficially devout shout their prayers from the rooftops. In the meantime, their houses are filled with sin."

They bowed their heads together and took turns praying aloud for guidance, for justice, and for protection from the evil that was spreading in the land. It was a beautiful prayer. They left their woes behind and ascended to a place of beauty and grace, a light-filled world where love reigned and peace was ever-present. Each received a healing and a blessing. They were shown, individually, the gifts they had to share with the world and the future that awaited them if they used these gifts in the flow of God's will.

Afterwards they talked for a long time, sharing their experiences and visions. The mood in the house was uplifted from what it had been earlier, and the three friends seemed hopeful that their obstacles could, in time, be overcome.

The next day they received word that Gotsro would be making a speech in the square that evening. They went about their business during the day, Loobal and Astnor working in the shop, and Morok fetching wood for the fire and buying food from the market. As evening approached they prepared for their walk to the square and hoped that no surprises awaited them there.

The scene in the square was sombre. Gotsro's men were lined up on either side of him, dressed in civilian clothes. Tanlarian guards were also present, positioned at the four corners of the stage and at various posts throughout the square.

Morok was puzzled. "That's pretty bold of him,

Chapter 16

bringing his army into plain view," he whispered to Astnor. But no one seemed to recognize that these were the men who had stormed the celebration and slaughtered the governor.

Gotsro began, "My fine Ladies and Men of Tanlar, I bring you solemn news: that our beloved governor, Frantair, was viciously murdered yesterday, by soldiers of our enemy, the city of Menzoneal. We have dealt with the traitors, who stood by while their men did carry out this vile deed, but justice must be served in full. I call upon you all to take up arms, to protect yourselves against a possible invasion, and to join me in ensuring that the people of Tanlar rule supreme in this land."

Loobal gasped. "He *is* starting a war!"

"As the elder of this community," Gotsro continued, "I have taken it upon myself to govern in Frantair's stead until a new governor can be elected. For now, we must focus on the task at hand."

"Loobal!" Morok exclaimed suddenly. "Do you remember the vision God gave us? The black cloud raining blood over Tanlar? This is it! This is what we must do—unite the people and stop this foolish war!"

"But Morok," she replied, "that would be almost impossible! These people will trust no one, let alone two newcomers like us."

"You're not a newcomer, Loobal," he reminded her.

"I feel like one," she said. "No one knows me here."

"I have an idea," Astnor interjected.

They turned toward him, curious.

"*If* it is Gotsro's plan to take over Frantair's office, then he will have a few 'in-house' issues to contend with. You see, it wasn't Frantair alone running the city; he had many advisors. And although they would defer to Gotsro, given his status as an elder, they wouldn't have to agree with him. I know one of these advisors, and I believe he can be trusted.

Perhaps we should make a plan to visit him—soon."

"We must make sure Gotsro does not see us associating with anyone involved in local politics. He knows us. And although he would not suspect that we knew his plans, it is plain that he does not like us. I stood up to him."

"Yes, Morok is right," Loobal affirmed. "The farther we can stay out of Gotsro's way, the better."

"Then I will go alone," said Astnor. "I have no ties to Gotsro and would not be suspect."

Loobal was relieved to be left out of any more involvement in this intrigue. She held on to Morok's arm and began to pull him away from the square. "Let's go back now," she pleaded with him and Astnor. "I am tired."

The crowd had already dispersed after Gotsro's very concise speech, and the three were left standing in the shadows, far from the stage. Gotsro's men had filed off the stage behind him and were now nowhere to be seen.

When they reached Astnor's home they all sighed, feeling they had returned to a safe haven.

The next morning Astnor gave Loobal instructions for the day's work and headed out to find the governor's advisor. Morok tidied up the shop, and since there was nothing much else to occupy his time, he sat and prayed.

God spoke to him in his prayers, beseeching him to pray more often, to focus his attention on that lofty connection rather than the troublesome state of affairs in the city. Morok understood, and made a commitment to do so. He received a blessing and felt his heart expand beyond the walls of the tailor's house and across the city. He felt alive and vibrant, fueled by God's love for him. He then called to Loobal to sit with him; he felt the need to have her join him in prayer. Together they sought to know God's will, to know how they should handle this delicate ordeal, which could shape the future of the city.

This time, Loobal was given a vision of what Tanlar

Chapter 16

had been in its glory days. It was open to all, bright and welcoming. Trade flourished, and the people knew each others' names. No one was suspicious or hoarded their belongings. It was ruled by a king in those days, long ago, and he was a just man. She saw that although he had many people who served him, the king also served his people. He would ask for their opinions on all matters that affected them and would base his laws thereupon.

The downfall of Tanlar came about when a chief of another people saw what the city had, coveted it, and eventually overthrew the monarch by force. Many people died in the attack, and many fled, in fear of what was to come. Those who had stayed remained loyal to their king. In his memory, they retained as many customs as they could. The new ruler was not particularly cruel, but he was greedy and did not care about the needs of the people. So by neglect, and by the infiltration of his own people, who were not kind or friendly, the people of Tanlar suffered. In time the walls went up, around the city and around the hearts of the people. That was long ago. In the changes of the years, both the king and the chief had been completely forgotten, although both had left their mark on the place.

In Morok's vision, he saw a place far beyond the world which he inhabited: it was a place of light and truth. The truth was simple; he could feel it as well as understand it, for it pervaded *everything.* The truth was love. When he became aware of his surroundings once again, he thanked God for this revelation and embraced Loobal.

Loobal took some time to relate to him the entire story she had learned, and then she returned to her work.

Astnor was gone a long time. They began to worry when he did not appear by suppertime. But it had taken him a long time to locate the advisor, and by the time he was finally sitting down to talk with the man, it was already late afternoon. And there was much to say.

The advisor, whose name was Josephus, did not take kindly to accusations of any sort, especially when made against an elder. Yet he had his own suspicions about Gotsro, and this encouraged him to listen to what Astnor had to say. Astnor himself seemed an honest sort, which added to the weight of his story. When Astnor was finished his tale, Josephus sat straight up in his chair and exclaimed, "This shall not come to pass!" He was referring to the war with the Menzonealans. "The damage that could do to both of our cities—the lives lost and the morale dampened—it's not worth whatever he thinks could possibly be gained from it. I will not consent. And I will do everything in my power to ensure he has no support from the Governor's Advisory Council."

Astnor was greatly relieved and thanked him profusely. They said farewell and Astnor returned home, wary of who could be observing him along the route.

Morok and Loobal were happy to see him and shared in his joy about the outcome of his meeting. They were, however, a bit concerned about the advisor's optimism.

"Do you really think he could sway the entire council?" Loobal asked Astnor. "And even if he did, would they have any chance of stopping Gotsro? He's the one with the army."

"That I can't say," replied Astnor. "But it's a start. We will have to see what Gotsro's next move is and then figure out how to counteract it."

They went to sleep that night feeling comforted that they now had an ally. Morok fell asleep thinking of one thing: love.

Chapter 17
The Great Truth

When Halfene left Dentino she was terrified. Not only had she separated herself from the one thing that brought her comfort, she was heading toward the forbidding landscape of her ruined life in Palador. What sort of nightmare awaited her return? One sister was already dead, she knew that. But was her mother as well? And how was Marfal? Stricken with grief? In shock? Alone? Her love for her sister and her desire to save Dentino kept her going. She ran when she could, rested when she fell from exhaustion. She ate little and slept less. Horrible imaginings kept her awake. The journey took her four days.

    Palador was unrecognizable. The aftermath of the destruction had left the town in worse shape than when she had departed with Dentino. And Dentino's house—the first place in which she sought refuge upon her return—had collapsed. She was frantic. She needed supplies—a horse—food. Starving, herself, she was having difficulty processing thoughts and was becoming delirious. She passed her sister in the street and did not recognize her.

    Marfal did a double-take. "Halfene!" she screamed.

    Halfene turned around, disoriented. When it registered that this was Marfal before her, some clarity returned. The arms of her older sister had always brought her comfort and made everything all right. She began to cry

Chapter 17

uncontrollably.

"Where is Dentino?" Marfal asked.

Halfene could not speak for her tears. Marfal sat her down and comforted her, allowing her time to calm down before she attempted, once again, to talk.

Halfene took a deep breath and wiped her tear-soaked face. "H-he is hurt b-bad. I had to leave him to get help. I miss him already. He is my world, Marfal. I can't lose him! We need a horse to carry him home. And bandages and food. Can you help me, please?!" she begged.

"Of course, Halfene," Marfal assured her. "But you *must* rest. You are exhausted and have no strength to make that journey. How far down-river is he? And did you not find Loobal?"

"I saw no sign of them," Halfene pouted. "I have no idea where they went, if they are even alive." She began to cry again. "Dentino is days away from here." Marfal hugged her tightly and let her cry. She did not want to add to Halfene's grief by speaking of their mother. Marfal was very concerned for her sister. She did not look well and was certainly not thinking rationally, but it was obvious that they would need to leave shortly if Dentino was to be helped, and they would need Halfene to show them the way.

Peter was able to borrow two horses in addition to the one he had ridden in on from Portshead. He saddled them up and fetched the supplies they would need for the trip. Although food was scarce, due to the destruction, he found enough to get them by. He said good-bye to his mother and then set off with Halfene and Marfal. Halfene had rested a mere hour but was adamant that they should not tarry. She was relieved to have Marfal and Peter accompany her.

It surprised Marfal that Halfene had not asked why Peter was there with her; but considering her sister's confused state of mind, it was forgivable that she could be oblivious to Marfal's good fortune.

The Great Truth

The three rode quickly and managed to cover much ground the first day. They camped overnight by a sheltered bend in the river and ate sparingly. The night was warm and they did not need to light a fire. It finally dawned on Halfene that there was something going on between her sister and the violinist. The long stares, the furtive hand-holding, gave her cause to wonder what had transpired during her time on the road with Dentino. Finally, she could bear it no longer and asked them to relate what had happened since she left Palador. It was a long story and both were too tired to tell it, but Peter assured Halfene that they would have time the next day while they rode. Halfene was disappointed but resigned herself to going to sleep. She certainly needed some.

The weather took a turn for the worse the next day, and they were pelted with rain. It was uncomfortable, but they pushed on, concerned for Dentino's welfare. That night they did build a fire in the forest, and it was there Marfal finally had a chance to tell her story. She gave Halfene a fair warning that it was not a pleasant one and that she had some sad news to share. Halfene nodded, having expected as much. She cried, of course; a new wave of grief washed over her as Marfal described their mother's death and Serbrena's lonely funeral. She was horrified at how close Marfal had come to death herself and was deeply grateful to Peter for rescuing her.

Peter told his tale as well, relaying the events in Portshead that led to his decision to return to Palador and seek Marfal's company. Halfene was happy that her sister had finally found true love, and it made her heart ache for Dentino.

The next day the clouds parted, and they set off once again, in better spirits. Halfene traced the route back to where she had left Dentino. He was not where she had left him, and this set her off into a fresh panic, questioning her own memory. Marfal sat her down and reassured her that he

Chapter 17

had probably just gone off in search of food.

Peter was the one to finally locate Halfene's man. He had followed a trail into the trees, and there he saw Dentino, limping toward him.

"I thought I heard horses!" Dentino yelled to him excitedly. He was surprised to see Peter, who he thought had left Palador weeks ago. "Is Halfene with you?"

"Yes," Peter answered, "she is with Marfal by the—" But his words were interrupted. Halfene came springing up the trail and embraced Dentino so hard that he almost fell over. There were no words to express her joy that he was alive and well, and he had no words for her either.

Peter turned away to allow them their privacy, and he followed the path back to the river to spend some quiet time with Marfal. They sat and watched the water rush by and appreciated the greenery, which was a welcome change from dusty, broken Palador. Marfal placed her head on Peter's shoulder and sighed. It was quite a journey to take so soon after her recovery. She was glad to have her sister back and to know that Dentino, as well, was safe. But where were Morok and Loobal? Their sudden disappearance had flustered her, and she had no point of reference to concede which direction they had gone. She spoke of this to Peter. He did not know them well—he had only met Morok once; but he understood Marfal's desire to find her sister and was intrigued about the couple's awakening, which Marfal had described.

"I've wondered about God often," he said.

Halfene and Dentino were reluctant to come out of the woods and join Marfal and Peter. Their world was a world for two, and they were lost in it, happily. Halfene could not believe the change in Dentino. She stood back to look at him. "Why, you're a new man!" she exclaimed. "You haven't looked this well since before the storm!"

Dentino's grin spread from ear to ear. "I needed rest,

The Great Truth

Halfene, and now I've had six days of it. I feel great! I didn't starve. I didn't get dragged off by wild animals. And I have you here again, all to myself. What more could I need?"

Halfene reflected his bright smile and gave him yet another hug. She held on for a long time.

"I suppose we should head back," she said finally, when they had stepped apart. They walked slowly, hand in hand, back to the river, where Marfal and Peter waited patiently for them.

"Hello, Dentino!" Marfal called warmly. She hugged him and made space on the blanket for him to sit down. Halfene joined them. They began to tell him of their journey. Dentino was keen to hear all the details. He marveled at Halfene's endurance—having not had a break between running home and riding back; but she assured him that her love for him had given her amazing strength.

The group decided to camp there for the night and start back to Palador in the morning. They lit a fire and spent the evening sharing stories of their time apart and singing songs they had practised with the choir. Peter felt self-conscious without his violin, but he made an attempt to sing anyway. His happiness made up for his lack of vocal skills. All four of them slept soundly that night under a starry sky.

At daybreak they were awake and searching out food to eat before the journey. Peter prepared the horses. The largest horse, the one Peter and his mother had found, was chosen to carry Halfene and Dentino.

The pace was slower for the return journey, but as their mission to save Dentino had been accomplished, there was no reason to hurry along. They were enjoying this little interlude in the tale of strife and struggle that had been their lives of late.

Chapter 17

Back in Tanlar, tension was building. The city guard had been increased to include street patrols, and the gates were now closed day and night. One could only leave—with permission—at a certain time of day when there was a brief opening of the front gate. Traders from other places had to wait for hours to enter the city, and they were subject to questioning and inspection. Gotsro was getting his way.

Astnor, on his daily jaunts to meet clients and purchase supplies, was privy to many rumors. He would relay them every evening to Loobal and Morok, who spent most of their time at home.

The latest news was that Gotsro had put a stop on all ships coming into port, lest they be harboring soldiers. Ships leaving the harbor were inspected, to ensure that no civilians were trying to escape. Gotsro would need every able-bodied man for his new army.

Morok was distressed. He did *not* wish to be conscripted. He retired to his room, alone, to pray.

"Beloved Heavenly Father, I seek your comfort tonight. In this time of darkness and chaos, I ask to be kept in the light and to see the truth, which will bring clarity to my confusion. I pray for peace, dear Father, peace for all people. May the peace of the Heavens descend upon us here, in this world, and change our way of living. Show us how to love one another, and please forgive us our sins, that we may have a fresh start. I humbly ask for Your blessing, dear Father."

God replied to Morok, deep within his soul. He said, "My son, your love for this world is great, and My love for it is great too, for it is My creation. Be at peace, knowing I have a plan for it. But you fight for the unjust, the wicked, even. My love and blessings cannot change or save those who don't *want* to be changed. Should I force My love upon them when they have no desire for it? Should I bring them peace if they seek war? Those who ask shall be given to. Those who seek shall find.

"My son, it is not right to try to change the will of another; instead you must love him, and in doing so you allow him to change in response to your love. I would not have any of my children subjugated to the will of another, for it is My will that they be free.

"And now you, My dear son, who comes to Me with such concern for the affairs of this world, I ask you to listen. Listen deeply, with your soul, for I speak in this simple way: My truth is love. *Love* will heal this world."

Morok blinked as he integrated those words into his consciousness.

"But God, what shall I *do*?" he asked.

"Love," God answered.

Morok felt a great number of angels surrounding him. He felt light and uplifted. There was peace in his soul. He had received an answer, although it was not the one he sought. *God knows best*, he thought.

Chapter 18
Two Paths Diverge

Astnor sat alone that night, thinking. Morok and Loobal had gone to sleep and he was left alone. He was used to being alone; twenty-two years old and unmarried, he had spent many years in this house, by himself. His parents were dead and his one sibling, a brother, had left Tanlar years ago. He envied Morok. Loobal was a beautiful girl. He wished that he, too, had a wife with whom to share his life. His thoughts dwelled on his misfortune, for a time, but then shifted to the current threat: war. He had never seen battle; he knew only how to make clothing. He thought of running—of trying to escape the city before the situation worsened—but that frightened him also. Where could he go? The thoughts circled through his head incessantly. He wished he were brave. What could *he* do to stop this war? He already did the one thing he thought might help, yet he felt somewhat uneasy about his talk with the advisor.

As he was thinking about their meeting there was a loud knock at the door. He froze, not knowing what to do. The caller persisted. Astnor stood up and went over to the door cautiously. He opened it a crack and said, "Who calls at this late hour?"

The door was flung open and in stormed Gotsro, followed by two of his men.

Astnor was taken aback. He could not speak, for fear.

Chapter 18

Gotsro stared him straight in the eye. "I have a question for you, young man," he said, sneering.

"What is it?" Astnor asked, clearly ill at ease.

"Where are you hiding those two servants of mine?"

"W-what servants?" he stammered.

The noise had woken Morok. He entered the room, then stopped short when he saw Gotsro.

"Ah—there he is!" Gotsro shouted.

Morok's first instinct was to run. But then he remembered Loobal, sweet Loobal, asleep in the back room. He summoned his courage. "Gotsro!" he exclaimed. "What brings you here?"

"I have heard that you are now working for this man—" he looked over at Astnor, who was backing up to the wall. "You see, your departure from my mansion has caused me distress. Many things are now left untended. I'm a busy man, Morok; I have a city to run. I must insist that you return at once and resume your duties."

Morok looked at the guards and then back at the elder. The situation was plain. He would have to submit, or risk being killed fighting them.

He turned to Astnor. "I'm sorry, Astnor, it appears I must leave your service." Astnor's face was white. He said nothing.

"Gotsro," Morok addressed the elder, turning back to him, "might I have a few moments to pack my belongings?"

Gotsro's eyes narrowed. "That won't be necessary."

The guards took Morok by the arms and led him briskly out of the house, pausing only to let him put on his shoes.

Loobal, by this time, had woken up and now stood, unnoticed, at the back of the room. When Gotsro left, she ran to Astnor and began to cry. "Where are they taking him?" she wailed.

"To Gotsro's house, I presume. He said he needed

Morok to work."

"I don't trust him! What if he knows that you told his advisor what Morok and I overheard? I can't bear the thought of Morok going back there!"

Astnor did his best to comfort Loobal, but she seemed inconsolable. She would not sit down; she paced back and forth across the room, crying bitterly.

"After all we've been through—now this! Oh, my poor Morok!" She held her protruding belly with both hands, as if to comfort the baby inside.

Astnor felt guilty. It was his idea to visit the advisor. Did Gotsro know the whole story? If so, Morok really was in danger.

Astnor hung his head. He wished he knew what to do. Then he heard a voice. It was a quiet voice, and calm. It said, "Do not fear what has happened. There is more to this than you can perceive. Your friend is not in danger."

"Who are you?" Astnor whispered.

"An angel, sent to comfort you in your distress. I am glad you are able to hear me."

Astnor felt a deep wave of warmth come over him. He smiled, in wonder, and looked up at Loobal, who was still pacing anxiously.

"Loobal," he called softly, "there is an *angel* with us."

She stopped her pacing and came over to sit with him.

"Why don't we pray," he suggested.

They sat together in silence. Astnor continued to perceive the angel's words, while Loobal directed her own prayer at God. She asked her Heavenly Father what she should do in this crisis. She felt His loving presence enveloping her and lifting her out of her grief. She listened to what God had to say. He said, "My beloved daughter, you must release your fears and your doubts. I have chosen you—and your husband—to do my work here, in this troubled city, in these troubled times. Your path will not always be

Chapter 18

easy, but it will lead you to where I need you—both of you—to be. Trust in me, my daughter. You must be strong. You must be wise. You must be brave. Do not fear what will happen to your husband. My hand is upon him. He will not be harmed. I have much work for him to do yet."

Loobal relaxed into her chair and sighed, finally letting go of her terror. She allowed God's embrace to heal her, to reach to the very core of her being: her soul. She was at peace.

Astnor came out of the silence slowly and readjusted to the conditions in the room where they were sitting. He looked at Loobal, who still had her eyes shut. He sat and waited quietly for her presence to gradually return, and then he began to tell her of his revelation.

"The angel told me I was to lead a group of devout worshippers of God in prayer for a peaceful resolution to this conflict. I am to gather them in a public place so that more people will witness the effort and may join in if they so choose. I am excited about this, Loobal; I feel passionate and inspired to act. My fear—which overcame me when Gotsro appeared—is now gone."

He was smiling broadly and leapt to his feet. "I know just who to ask!"

"May I go with you?" asked Loobal. "I'm afraid to be alone."

"I will take you in the morning."

Loobal did not sleep well, despite the reassurance she had received from God that Morok was safe. She took her time getting ready in the morning, as her fatigue was great.

Astnor, on the other hand, was unusually full of energy. It was a stark contrast from his quiet, unassuming nature. He could not wait to begin his quest.

They walked through the streets, stopping only to eat some fruit at the market. The house Astnor was looking for was at the far end of town, near the mill. An old widow lived

Two Paths Diverge

there, one who had known Astnor since he was a boy. She met them at the door. Loobal was struck immediately by her resemblance to Geminus, the wise man of Palador. She gave Astnor a warm hug and then turned to Loobal.

"And who are you, my dear? Is this your wife, Astnor? I did not know you had gotten married."

Astnor laughed. "This is Loobal, Farentina. She is not my wife, but that of another man, who has been taken into Gotsro's custody."

"Oh!" She seemed alarmed. "What may I do to help you?"

"May we come in?" Astnor asked. "There is much to tell."

She guided them indoors to a comfortable sitting area and offered them some water. Loobal was on edge, still thinking of Morok and their predicament. The old woman took her hand. "Tell me your troubles, my dear, I see that you are ill at ease."

"I am well enough," she replied, "but I worry for my husband."

Astnor took it upon himself to explain the entire situation, as far back as the day he met the couple, and what they had revealed to him about Gotsro's secret army. He explained the guidance he had received from the angel that led him to seek her, for she was the most God-loving person he knew.

She was a wise woman, and she knew they would need to gather a large group of people for this to work. She fetched some food and a few blankets, which she gave to Astnor to carry.

"Come!" she bade them.

Astnor and Loobal followed her out into the street. She walked past a number of houses and then rapped at someone's door. The elderly man who answered stood there and listened while she quickly explained her need for him to

Chapter 18

follow, and after a few moments he, too, joined them.

By the time they reached the town square, there were about twenty people with them. They gathered on the main stage, which was not in use at that time, and formed a circle, seated on blankets. And then they started to pray.

By this time, Morok had been up for hours, working—not at Gotsro's mansion, as he had thought, but in Frantair's house on the hill. This place was much larger than Gotsro's and more lavish. The grounds were immense and in need of tending—all had fallen into disarray at the house after the governor's sudden death.

Morok was mystified. Was this all Gotsro had in store for him—endless hours of toil? Or was there a more sinister plan? It made him nervous, not knowing. Yet he felt a strange distance from true fear. He could *feel* the presence of God in his life. He knew he was safe.

The servants in this house were a mixture of Gotsro's own servants and ones who had remained with Frantair's house. Gotsro's servants—the ones who had previously shared a room with Morok and Loobal—were strangely civil toward Morok. This amused him, but he treated them kindly.

The work was not difficult, but it was tedious. Morok missed Loobal terribly, and he worried about what she thought had happened to him. Would Astnor be of any help to her? He had looked very frightened when Morok last saw him. Morok's thoughts were convoluted and unclear. He felt like he had no control over anything that was going on in his life, and he was oblivious to Gotsro's plan for him.

The group on the stage attracted a lot of attention from passers-by that day.

"What are they doing?" whispered one to another. A few approached close enough to listen. What they heard were beautiful prayers for the healing of Tanlar and its people, and for peace between Tanlar and Menzoneal. It was uncommon in this city to see an altruistic gathering. It shocked people out of their self-serving reveries and into the realization that they were all in this together. If war broke out, all of them would be suffering.

The mood in Tanlar was grim. Soldiers walked the streets and were questioning anyone who was deemed to be suspicious. This included the group on the stage. It was Loobal who spoke for the group. She was unafraid and radiated a peacefulness that was mildly disarming to the small group of soldiers who had been called to the scene.

"We are here to pray," she told them simply.

"Why are you doing this here?" one of them asked, indicating the public stage.

"Not long ago our dear governor was slain here, on this stage. Since then there has been naught but distrust and fear in these streets. We seek to bring about a peaceful resolution to this tension by asking our all-powerful Heavenly Father for his grace, his blessing upon this city. We pray for the people of Menzoneal also. Our governor was trying to bring about peace between our cities, and he was killed for it. But war will not bring him back, nor will it restore peace. War begets war. Not one of us here wishes to see this city destroyed and its people slaughtered. And whether the battle is fought here or in Menzoneal, our people will be among the dead. You soldiers, who die because someone else orders you to fight, throw your lives away. Is this how you planned to live your life? To die in a fight you did not start?" She paused, allowing the words to fully sink in. The soldiers said nothing. "I ask you to let go of your hate and your anger. See this for what it is—an excuse to murder and pillage. You are better men than that, and your lives do not need to be shed so

Chapter 18

lovelessly."

By this time a curious crowd of listeners had gathered in the square. They were absorbing Loobal's words, given with authority and love, as were the soldiers to whom she addressed her speech. The soldiers felt the pressure of the crowd, and were hesitant to act. The group on the stage continued to pray. Loobal faced the growing crowd. "You are all children of God," she told them, "and your Father wishes you no harm, but only to live peacefully, coexisting with your fellow humans in this world. It is His desire that you are happy. War—and the destruction it brings—will not bring you happiness, but only lead to chaos and ruin. Be aware of your choice, for it is in your power—each one of you—to choose war or peace. If enough of us choose peace, there can be no war."

The soldiers were flustered. They had already chosen war, and were being paid for it. To turn away now meant more than losing their jobs, it meant being disrobed of the only thing that kept their fears at bay: their weapons.

One of the soldiers made a move toward the stage, an act of defiance toward this woman who was preaching at him, but he was suddenly repelled backward. He was flabbergasted. Had someone pushed him? But no one was in reach. The other soldiers stood still, unsure of what to do and afraid to make a similar move.

Loobal looked kindly toward them and said, in a gentle voice, "Leave us in peace, brothers."

She had won this show of power, for her power over them came from a place deep within her where she and God were connected. It was His will, His words that were coming forth through her. She sat back down with the group and continued her prayers, while the soldiers slowly turned and left the square. They did not venture far; they were still considering action. But Loobal's words had struck a chord within them, and now, to them, a violent demonstration against the group seemed unpalatable—wrong, even. They continued to observe from a distance, confident that they were doing their duty as long as they maintained a presence.

The crowd had started to disperse. A few onlookers lingered, feeling a pull to stay and observe. Astnor took notice of this and called over to them. "Please, come and join us." They looked at him awkwardly, suddenly aware of their own doubts and insecurities. One shook his head and turned away. Another excused herself, saying she was running late and had to be somewhere else. One, however, paused momentarily and then marched right up to the stage and sat down.

They prayed until sundown, taking breaks, as needed, to stretch their legs. When their time on the stage was finished, they packed the things they had brought with them and broke up into smaller groups to go to their respective homes. The consensus was that they should return the next day and continue their vigil as long as it took to create change in the city.

Loobal was exhausted but elated. She felt as though she was serving a purpose for which she had been previously ordained.

The walk home to Astnor's was tiring indeed. Loobal's pregnancy weighed heavily upon her, and the day's heat had caused her feet to swell. Now, as she walked, she held on to Astnor's arm for support. When they reached the house they retired to their separate rooms and were both soon asleep.

Morok lay awake in his bed. The sound of other servants snoring was distracting, and he could not sleep. The day had been a busy one, and he had thought of Loobal often while going about his work. Where was she now? What was she thinking? How was the baby? He wondered when he would see his wife again.

Chapter 18

His thoughts drifted to God—God, who had led him on this unexpected and eventful journey, from Gate-Town to Palador and now here. The journey had changed him greatly. He thought about the man he used to be, the man who hated work and routine and sought only to escape, to be on his own. He thought of that beautiful town of Palador and the many gifts he had received there—friendship, family, a wife. He felt that it was in Palador that he finally grew up and became able and willing to take on responsibility. There he saw himself as part of a whole, a community, where the efforts of one could benefit many others. In Palador he gained wisdom and clarity—and finally met God. The gratitude he felt for all of these blessings suddenly overcame him, and he wept. But oh, the pain—all he had then lost—his home, his friends, the family that became his when he married Loobal. Where were they? Were any of them yet alive? Had anyone survived the destruction of Palador?

He decided to pray. He asked God to show him what he could not see; he asked for those he loved to be brought into his presence, somehow. He drifted deeply into a state of stillness, where the questions ended and the answers were waiting. He felt a presence, a familiar presence, of one his heart ached for. And, in a dream-like way, he saw Zev-ran.

"I love you, Morok," said the child, reaching out to him. His voice was as Morok remembered it, and the boy appeared in a halo of light.

Morok struggled to stop his tears. There was so much he wanted to say to the boy, and he did not know where to start. He asked Zev-ran what had happened to him and his family. He was able to perceive most of what Zev-ran then described, although it was terrible to hear of their suffering. All were dead—his whole family.

"But we are happy here," Zev-ran reassured him. "We are together and we are happy."

"Where is 'here'?" Morok asked.

"The Realm of Light, of course! It is so beautiful here. Like Palador, but different, too. We don't need to go to work here, Morok. We play, and learn, and go places...and when we want to be with someone we just think their name and POOF! there we are. I like the trees here. They're shiny. And the birds are always singing really lovely songs. The water is like music and the games we play are so much fun and I've seen an angel a few times." He paused for a moment and Morok laughed. This was Zev-ran; that he was sure of. Zev-ran could talk for hours.

"You would like it if you were here."

"I'm sure I would, Zev-ran. But it might be a long time before I can join you. There is work for me to do here and I must carry it through. I miss you, though. I wish we had had more time together." Morok began to cry once more.

"Don't cry for me, Morok. I am happy. We will see each other again someday." He faded into a bright light and Ansera appeared, looking calm and radiant.

"My dear son," she greeted Morok, "I have come to reassure you of our whereabouts, and to tell you that Marfal is yet alive, as is Halfene. They are in Palador, trying to rebuild their lives. They believe you are lost. Halfene searched for you along the river for many, many days, but finally gave up to save her injured man." She paused, sensing his question. "Dentino is well, yes. I have come to you to tell you of your wife, my dear daughter, for I can see her now as you cannot. She is well also. She is safe and she is well. She is finding her way in this world. You would be quite surprised to know how she stood her ground today and conveyed God's truths to many."

Morok was surprised and intrigued. "Do tell me," he encouraged her.

"She led a group in prayer at the main stage of this city. When the soldiers approached them she was able to fend them off with her wise words."

Chapter 18

"What else can you see, Ansera?" Morok was desperate for information, being trapped, as he was, in Gotsro's custody.

"I see that you are in danger, but it is not yet close. Your keeper intends to kill you after you have served your purpose. He feels threatened by you."

Morok gulped. This news was not welcome.

"Keep your head low and your ears open," Ansera advised. "Morok, you have many powerful angels keeping watch over you—I have seen them. I think you are well cared for."

Morok was relieved. Although he could feel the presence of angels at times, this confirmed that he was not alone.

"Thank you, Ansera. If you see Loobal, please give her my love. She is the most precious thing in the world to me."

Ansera smiled and faded away as Zev-ran had done.

As Morok fell asleep that night he was truly at peace. He had let go of the fear that Loobal was in danger and allowed in the confident feeling that comes with being in the care of a loving, ever-watchful God.

Chapter 19
Borne into the Light

It was a dark evening in Palador when the couples returned on their tired, but eager, horses. They dismounted outside of Mortin and Saminelle's house, where Peter's mother had remained, and sent Halfene in to get some immediate attention and rest. She had overexerted herself for many days and was now worthy of the ministrations of others.

Dentino was aware that his house had collapsed—Halfene had told him as much—but he wanted to see it himself, so he rode off alone.

Peter and Marfal took their time tending to the other two horses. They wanted to be alone together after so much conversation with Dentino and Halfene on the ride back home. Marfal was exhausted but tried to hide this so that she could keep up with her man.

The mood in Palador had shifted since they had left. People were beginning to show themselves, to come out of the shock that had kept them hiding in what remained of their homes. Some had begun the arduous process of gathering the dead for burial, and some were tasked with rebuilding the structures that needed to be saved.

Marfal saw many people she recognized that evening and heard some of their stories. It was overwhelming, and she desired only to curl up in a bed and forget the world for a while. Peter led the horses to a field where grass had finally

Chapter 19

begun to push through the mess of dust upon the ground. Many horses were there, running loose, as the fencing was too damaged to contain them. Peter was not concerned. He had let go of many concerns lately in the need for survival. Marfal waited for him outside of the house where Halfene lay resting. He sat next to her and placed his arm around her aching shoulders. There were no stars to be seen above them that night, only dark clouds. But in spite of this, they remained hopeful that tomorrow would be a clear day and that the sun would shine upon them.

Halfene sat upright in the bed she had been sleeping on. She had awoken from a frightening dream. *Where is Dentino?* she wondered. She glanced around the room, seeking the comfort his presence always brought her, endeavoring to find that calm within the storm of her thoughts. Dentino was not in the room, however. It had been weeks since she had had a good sleep, and this was affecting her mind. She let herself cry, releasing some of the unrest within.

When morning came, the situation had improved for her. Dentino lay asleep on a mat beside her, on the floor. Marfal and Peter were also asleep on the floor. She reached down and grabbed Dentino's hand and held on like he was her lifeline.

The mood in the house that day was sombre. Rain pelted the town, making it difficult for work outside to continue. Dentino was in mourning, not only for his home, but for his parents and brother. He had learned of their deaths but was unable to see the bodies so he could say good-bye. Halfene comforted him but was barely able to rise above her own grief. Being back in Palador brought up the worst memories.

Many in the town gathered that day, in what was once

Borne Into the Light

a barn, to discuss the town's future. There was little hope to be seen in the once-bright faces. The task of rebuilding seemed a huge burden for those left alive, but there was no help from outside to be brought in. Peter had relayed the tale of Portshead's similar fate. A plan was made to construct a group of temporary shelters in the least-damaged area of town, and to care for the people who were injured. Food was also a concern, but since it was midsummer there were berries to be found and fish to be caught. A group was tasked to do this also.

Marfal did not know what to do about the farm. There was little to salvage there, and the thought of going back, when her mother's body still lay there, was unbearable. Peter knew what had to be done, and unpleasant as it was, he took Ansera's body and put it with the rest of the bodies. Marfal was ever so grateful but ashamed that she had not helped him.

"It is not so easy when it is your own mother," he said, consoling her.

The days went by in a blur of hard work with little joy except for the companionship the sisters had with their mates. Although the sun had returned and the grass continued to grow, there was a sense of foreboding that no one could quite explain. It was as if a storm were on the horizon.

***

Above Tanlar a storm was brewing. It had come off the sea and now hovered above the city, dark and ominous. Daylight had turned gray-green.

There were patches of heavy clouds blanketing the land, as far away as Portshead to the west, and over above the hills to the south.

The land was unstable. What began as just a tremble deep beneath the soil quickly manifested as a great shaking

Chapter 19

of the land. It was felt throughout the city, although the damage was minor. Something of this nature had never occurred before in Tanlar, and people were frightened.

Loobal's group, now twenty-five strong, paused in their prayers to look about with wide eyes. Loobal knew, somehow, that this was a sign from God and that the destruction she had foreseen was forthcoming. As the rumbling died down she went deeper into prayer, reaching out to God for answers and for guidance.

"We must leave the city," she told the group, after an angel had given her abrupt guidance. "A storm is coming, and we will not survive if we stay. We have little time. Gather what you must, and meet at the far gate."

"But only the front gate opens now," Astnor said worriedly. "We'll be trapped!"

Loobal looked at him calmly.

"All right, I will follow you," he decided. He helped her off the stage, and they hurried to his house, which, fortunately, was on the way to the gate. When they arrived at the house they changed into clothes for travel and gathered food and supplies into two packs. Astnor gave Loobal the lighter one to carry and locked the house.

"Am I saying good-bye to this place, Loobal?" he asked, already knowing the answer. She nodded grimly.

The rain held off until they had just about reached the gate. It began slowly; the large drops were interspersed with momentary pauses. And then it poured: a deluge. With it came thunder and lightning. At the gate the guards lingered uneasily; they desired to abandon their post and take shelter.

"Let us through!" Loobal called, when a number of her group had arrived.

"We have orders to keep this gate closed," a guard responded.

"Destruction is upon us, and the gates of this city will not stop it, closed or open."

The guard looked at his partner. The other shrugged.

"Very well," he said finally. "You may seek your death outside of these walls. But don't expect me to let you back in!"

The group nervously exited the city, taking a last solemn look over their shoulders. The gate closed.

Morok paced about the mansion anxiously. He was supposed to be cleaning, but his inner voice was warning him of a danger from without. He could hear the storm raging and thought of Loobal. *Was she safe?* Gotsro had left for a meeting that morning and had not returned. Morok knew that there was a window of opportunity for his escape, but he feared what would occur if he should fail. He closed his eyes and prayed fervently for deliverance from this place of evil.

After a few minutes one of Gotsro's guards appeared and said, "Morok! Go clean the stable!"

Morok smiled inwardly. One step closer to his escape. He rushed out the door and sprinted to the stable.

Marfal looked out the window of Mortin and Saminelle's house, squinting her eyes at a disturbance on the horizon.

"Something's coming, Peter, and I don't like it." They had stopped in that day to have some lunch before returning to their duties with the townspeople. Peter joined her to look.

"Nor do I," he said. "It reminds me of the day this *mess* got started."

Marfal took his hand. "Whatever happens," she said to him tenderly, "I'm happy to have found you."

Chapter 19

"I cannot fathom this world without you in it. Say you'll marry me, Marfal. Let's have some happiness in this hopeless town." He looked at her with so much love in his eyes that she almost swooned.

"I would love that, Peter," she replied, reflecting the same love-filled look. The couple's tender kisses lasted well past the lunch hour, and they had to rush back to their duties as caregivers of the wounded.

Halfene and Dentino were working at a building to house homeless citizens when the earth-tremors began. A ladder that Dentino had been standing on earlier fell to the ground. There were shouts in the streets as sink holes began to appear in random places.

Halfene was not afraid, at first, but rather stood confused next to the house she had been helping rebuild. And then fear gripped her—the type of fear that overcomes one when one's life is threatened. She held on to the wall to steady herself as the ground shook again. She wept, afraid of what could only be seen as another injury to the town's already-broken state.

Dentino left the building and held her tightly, not saying anything. The two braced themselves, as yet another tremor shook the building, this time throwing logs loose from their temporary bindings.

Dentino jumped back, dragging Halfene with him. They fell to the ground but luckily were not hit. One of the other men working there was not so fortunate—his leg was trapped beneath a fallen beam.

Marfal and Peter were running back toward the shelter for the wounded when the first tremor occurred. They were thrown off their feet and remained on the ground long enough to withstand the next two from a safer position.

"What is happening to this world?" cried Marfal. "When will it cease?" The sky was blackening, and she could see the distant streaks of lightning. "Where can we hide?"

she whimpered.

Peter was shaken. He felt suddenly very small and powerless against the forces of nature. He looked at Marfal, wishing he had the answers she sought and the ability to bring her happiness and peace. *But only God can do that,* he thought. Where was God in this?

"Marfal," he said, "will you pray with me? There is not much else we can do now."

"Okay," she whispered. "What do we say?"

Peter laughed. "I don't know."

Marfal closed her eyes, trying to shut out the frightening scene around her and tune in to a force she had never really tried to connect with before.

"Dear Father," Peter began, "I don't know what to say to you, or whether you can actually hear me..." He paused, formulating the words in his mind. "I want You to know that I'm sorry. I'm sorry that it has taken me this long to finally reach to You in this way. Please come to our aid, Father. Reach down to us and bring us closer to You, to the goodness and love that You are. We are lost, Father. Lost and hopeless."

He hung his head low in silence. Marfal was still praying. He could hear her gentle whispers, as she beseeched God not only to help them, but also to save the town. She prayed for her sister and Dentino, and then for Peter's kind mother, who had cared for her when she was in shock. Peter listened closely to her words. He was comforted by them, by the love that his beautiful Marfal had for everyone she prayed for. She prayed for him too, that he would have the strength to help others who were frightened by these strange and devastating events.

When she was finished, Marfal got to her feet. "I feel better, having done that," she told Peter. She meant it. It truly brought her peace to know that she had done her best for those she loved—by asking God to help them in a way she

Chapter 19

could not.

Peter took her hand and led her to the shelter. As shaken up as they were, they knew they were needed by those who were in worse condition.

Halfene and Dentino decided to stop working and seek shelter instead. Rain was now pouring relentlessly upon the town and the thunder boomed above. They went inside a nearby house that stood empty due to its leaky roof. There they found a place to sit where the floor was relatively dry, and they leaned upon each other for support. Halfene rested her head upon Dentino's shoulder. She wondered aloud, "Why is this happening? It seems strange, doesn't it, Dentino-my-love?"

"I don't know," he replied solemnly. "Halfene, I'm worried—for you, for us, for this town...for human life. I'm scared to just die and rot away."

"You are going to be with me. When we die, sooner or later, you are going to be in the Realm of Light, with me, having a wonderfully happy life."

"Do you really believe that?" he asked her.

Halfene sighed and looked away. "I don't know, Dentino. It's what I was told would happen, by my parents. I believed it when I was young."

"And now?"

"I don't know."

Dentino said nothing. He, too, had been told of the Realm of Light, and had participated in many of the rituals the townspeople engaged in when someone died or got married—the prayers, the blessings. But he doubted. And that left him feeling empty somehow. He wanted hope—something to hold on to in times like these when all seemed so grim, so out of everyone's control. But Halfene—who was generally quite bright and optimistic—could not even give him that. He wanted to cry. They held each other silently. The rain continued to pelt the roof, making puddles on the floor.

~~~

Morok was an honest man. The thought of taking one of Gotsro's horses to make his escape was painful to him and almost stopped him from moving forward with his plan. *But what good am I dead?* he reasoned with himself. *He's going to kill me.*

He grabbed a saddle and buckled it onto one of the smaller horses, one who seemed friendly. He led it out of the stable, cautiously checking this way and that for guards. They were all inside the mansion, though, avoiding the rainfall that now blasted the hill. Morok mounted the horse and rode quietly but swiftly down the hill to the edge of the grounds. There was no gate here, only a narrow entrance that a small wagon could pass through. He left Gotsro's world, not looking back.

It was difficult to see where he was going. The blackened sky and heavy rain were an impenetrable veil. No one was about; he was thankful for that. But he did not know the layout of the city very well, nor did he know where he was going. He wanted, very much, to see Loobal. Would she be home? He headed in the direction of Astnor's house, careful to avoid being seen. He had a cloak over his head and walked beside the horse at times. When he got to the market—which was now deserted—a strange feeling came over him. *She's gone,* he thought. He was terrified. Somehow he knew Loobal had left the city, that she was on the run. He panicked, not able to imagine how he would ever find her. And in this weather—he hoped she was not alone.

He looked up at the sky. The rained poured upon him, and he blinked to clear it from his eyes. *Where was she?* Instinct told him to turn right. He got back up on the horse, caring less now who saw him and more that he could reach one of the gates.

Chapter 19

The first gate he came to was the south gate. It was heavily guarded. He passed quickly out of sight and headed for the front gate. This, too, was guarded, and had a lineup of drenched traders who had fled the market in their wagons and were seeking refuge outside, where they could get under the trees. *I'll never get through there,* Morok decided.

His last hope was the west gate, a smaller one that was used mainly by hunters to get up into the hills. Backtracking nervously through the edge of town, he finally came upon it. At first glance there was no one there. He approached cautiously. He saw someone in a cloak and startled, fearing the worst. But it was an old woman, standing alone in a shelter not far from the gate. She approached him.

"I need to get through the gate, sir. Can you help me?" To Morok's surprise, she smiled and held out her hand. "I am Sinwela. I was expecting a rather large group of people here, to travel with; but, alas, they must have left before me."

Morok did not know what to say. He was afraid to tell her anything, lest he give himself away. But he did not want to cause her to miss her companions, and so he did his best to lift the heavy beams that barred the gate. He followed her through, checking to make sure no one saw them, and closed the gate. *It won't take them long to figure this out,* he thought, and braced himself for a quick gallop into the hills.

The woman stopped him. "Wait!" she called. He rode over, tentatively, dreading what she would say.

"Thank you," she said.

"For what?" he asked, looking about anxiously.

"You let me through the gate. Thank you," Sinwela repeated. "Now where is Loobal?" she wondered, out loud.

"What did you say?" Morok asked, not believing he had heard her name.

"I said, 'Where is Loobal.' That's the name of the young woman I was to meet—Loobal and the rest of our group. We have to hurry and leave this city," she explained.

Morok looked at her, incredulous. "Loobal is my wife!"

"Oh my! Well, perhaps you should join us then. Is that why you are here?"

Morok smiled, not wanting to divulge the truth. "I am looking for her, yes."

They began to walk slowly up the steep hill that led away from the city. The heavy rain made the going difficult, especially for Sinwela. Morok followed the muddy tracks as best as he could. Although he wished to race ahead, to find Loobal as quickly as possible, he knew it was wrong to leave this old woman on her own in the storm. They walked together, leading the horse over the slippery ground.

Morok was soaked. He had brought nothing else with him. There had been no time to gather what was his. He was on the run. This frustrated him greatly, the instability of his life, moving from one place to the next—out of desperation—with no food. He felt sorry for himself and almost angry at God for putting him in this predicament again and again. *What have I done to deserve such a fate?* Morok lamented. He closed his eyes for a moment, willing himself to stop those dark thoughts. He could not even pray. Of all the dark times he had endured since leaving Palador, this was the worst.

Sinwela sensed his distress and placed a calming hand upon his shoulder. Her compassion, a kindness offered to him despite her own suffering, brought him to tears. "I'm sure your wife is all right," she reassured him, "and I will ask God for help in finding her."

She walked in silence for a while, keeping her eyes on the path but her mind on God.

"Ah," she said finally. "I see." She pointed to a cluster of trees up ahead. "They went there."

Morok almost broke into a run and had to check himself so that she could catch up to him. The rain had abated, somewhat, but a mist now covered the land, and he

Chapter 19

could not perceive whether there were actually any people up ahead.

The ascent to those trees was quick; however, the horse balked when they reached the spot and could not be encouraged to go further.

"Let him go," Sinwela advised. Morok did, and the horse galloped back down the hill, toward his home in the city. Morok shook his head, regretting his action.

"What is done is done," said Sinwela firmly.

They moved on to the trees. Someone was in there—he could feel it. But it was not a comforting feeling.

A man stepped into view. He was dressed as Frantair's attackers had been. "Who are you?" the soldier demanded.

Morok opened his mouth to speak, but Sinwela spoke first. "I am Sinwela of Tanlar. My son and I are seeking our group of fellow travelers who are making a pilgrimage to the land beyond these hills."

"Strange weather for traveling," he commented suspiciously.

"That could not be avoided," she said. "Have you seen anyone pass by?"

The soldier paused, wary. But the old woman and her companion did not look to be a threat. He waved them past, indicating the direction in which their group had gone.

Morok gripped Sinwela's hand tightly and led her onto a path that wound to the right. Their presence was soon obscured by fog and the soldier did not follow them.

When they had walked for another hour and were approaching a rocky cliff face, they heard voices—not the gruff voices of soldiers, but more soft-spoken ones.

"Loobal!" he called, desperate to find her. There was silence. He called again, louder.

This time a figure emerged from a small shelter in the rock. It was Loobal.

Sinwela greeted her, but she had eyes only for Morok.

Borne Into the Light

She ran to him, shaking with overwhelming emotion. They embraced and clung to each other, crying in each other's arms. Sinwela stepped aside and headed toward the shelter, seeking the remainder of the group.

There were fourteen in all, with the new arrivals. Morok stepped into the shelter, relieved to have a safe place, at last, to rest. He did not recognize anyone there but Astnor, whom he was very happy to see. He hugged his friend and said, "We have much to talk about!"

"We were just about to say a prayer, Morok, when Loobal heard you call her name. Would you like to join us now?"

Morok beamed. "Yes!" he exclaimed. "I have much to be thankful for!"

Astnor began the prayer as Morok and Loobal cuddled side by side on the dry floor of the cave. "Heavenly Father, for our blessings this day we are deeply humbled and grateful. You have brought us together in safety and in love, to where we can now praise You and offer You ourselves to do Your will, in joy, upon this earth. Please guide us this day and each day forth, and keep us safe from the dangers of this changing world. Help us to love one another in greater depth; to share this love with all the people we meet. Thank you, beloved Father."

The group prayed quietly for a long while, offering each their own silent petitions, apologies, and gratitude. Many angels were present; Morok could feel them. He was amazed at the synergy of this group of strangers, at the conditions of love and stillness that were brought about in their presence, in response to their soulful desires. And Morok, himself, spoke to God of many things. He prayed for the group to be guided and safely escorted wherever it was that God needed them to be. He thanked God—profusely—for bringing him out of the darkness of Tanlar and into his wife's loving arms. And he humbly begged forgiveness for having

Chapter 19

doubts about God's loving touch upon him. He was cared for and well-protected, he knew that now. Sinwela's sage advice to let the horse loose may well have saved his life.

As Morok opened his eyes and looked around the dimly-lit cave, a great feeling of love welled up inside of him. Whoever these people were, who had followed his wife and Astnor here, he loved them. They were his sisters now.

Eventually, everyone ended their prayers and rejoined the group, chatting happily about the adventures that brought them together. Morok was mystified that they were all so willing to follow Loobal, but God had guided their exodus and they could feel her righteousness.

Loobal told Morok of the urgency she had felt when the tremor occurred: "Something terrible is going to happen to that city," she proclaimed, "I know it!"

Astnor agreed. "As much as I was frightened to leave my home, I felt it too. It would not be safe to stay there." The others nodded in agreement.

They shared some food they had brought and began discussing their next step. There was some concern about the soldiers who lurked on the hill and a desire to be far from them.

"I don't trust them," stated Loobal. "They are at Gotsro's command." She held her belly. The baby was an active one and had been poking her. "I must go somewhere safe to have my baby," she added quietly.

"How much time have you got?" one woman asked.

Sinwela smiled. "A few weeks yet, by the look of her."

"How do you know?" asked Loobal, who was not sure of it herself, being a first-time mother.

"I had thirteen children of my own, and helped many of them give birth to their own children. One of them is here with us!"

A young woman smiled. "My name is Ana," she said to Morok, to whom she had not yet been introduced.

"Well, Ana, I am happy to meet you. I am much indebted to your grandmother." He looked at Sinwela affectionately. "She delivered me from a tense situation today, and I am very grateful." Sinwela smiled.

No one seemed to have any ideas about where they could go to find proper shelter and care for Loobal. She looked worried. But Morok was optimistic. "After today, my dear, I shall no longer doubt our Heavenly Father and His plans. He will find a place for us."

That night they all huddled together for warmth in the coolness of the cave. They had not built a fire, mainly because there was no dry wood to be found in the storm. Wet and cold, they suffered through the night, praying for a better day ahead.

Morning brought with it some hope. The storm had blown past, and though the air was now cooler, it looked as if the sun would shine. The group ate a small breakfast, tended to their bodily needs, and then sat down to pray before making a decision as to their course.

Loobal was the first to receive an insight to share with the others. "We are advised to stay here," she told them, "to rest and to gather food, for the journey ahead will be a long one. We are not to stray far from our camp, lest we attract more attention from the soldiers. I feel we will be okay, though. Let us make a fire today."

Loobal was right. The rest and warmth did them much good. They foraged for food, cooked it over the fire, and had plenty of time to pray and to discuss with Morok all the things that had happened since he and Loobal had been separated.

Morok told Loobal, in private, of his experience connecting with the dead. "Your mother looked radiant, Loobal. She is watching over you. I did not see your father or Serbrena. But Zev-ran had much to say. He always did..." Morok trailed off, briefly mourning the boy's absence. Loobal

Chapter 19

put her arm around him.

"He was a good boy, Morok. A wonderful boy. He could have been our son."

"We would be very lucky to have a son like Zev-ran," he said, rubbing Loobal's large belly.

Loobal decided to take a nap, and Morok took that opportunity to speak with Astnor. He wanted to enlighten his friend about the politics that were playing out at the governor's mansion, where Gotsro was now lord. He told him of the continual comings and goings of various dignitaries from other lands who were especially aggressive in their collective approach to intercity relations. These men—they were always men—would stay for days and plot takeovers and embargoes. Morok had secretly overheard many things. He told Astnor about Gotsro's use of deceit in dealing with almost everyone: what he told one man was not what he told the next. The story was always changing, and Morok doubted that anyone had heard every part of it. Gotsro was clever; however, his great flaw was his inflated sense of self. It matched that of his adversaries—the ones he invited over as allies—and this ensured a never-ending competition with no winner. He deluded himself into thinking he was indispensable, and the truth was that at least two others were plotting his assassination.

Astnor was intrigued by the complexity of it all. He wondered what would become of Tanlar. Would their prayers for peace be answered?

Morok looked at him solemnly. "Astnor," he said, "we have been guided to leave Tanlar. Although we all wish for peace, there is a choice being made by those who live there. How many times did a citizen walk by your prayer group and choose to ignore the effort that was being made on his behalf? How many of them chose to follow Gotsro's orders and take up arms, steeling themselves for an invasion? How many believed his self-serving lies?"

Borne Into the Light

Astnor had no answer, but reflected upon Morok's wise words. "I see what you are saying," he said, after a pause. "We all have a choice. Our group has chosen to leave Tanlar and to find peace elsewhere. We tried, Morok, we really tried."

"I know," Morok said. "And if you and Loobal had not followed your hearts, how many of these people—" he indicated their new family— "would still be there? So indeed, your efforts did bear fruit."

Astnor smiled half-heartedly. "I wish we could have helped more people."

Loobal emerged from the cave entrance. "Morok!" she called to him. Morok excused himself and walked over to her.

She looked perplexed. "I had a dream," she said.

Morok nodded and sat down on the grass with her, so that she could tell it.

"It was night time. The sky was so black we couldn't see anything. You were with me, Morok, and the baby was too. There was nothing anywhere. It had all just fallen away somehow." She paused, straining to remember the details.

"What happened next was quite strange. All that had been dark fell away—like a curtain was pulled back. We were bathed in light; it was almost blinding. I said to you, 'We go now.' But you said you weren't ready and pulled back. The baby was in between us. I asked you again to come along. Still, you hesitated. I left you there, Morok, at the edge of...something. I could not resist the pull of that light. And you cried out to me, and I could hear you, but I did not turn back. You faded away and I was met with the most beautiful scenery: trees unlike anything seen here, shimmering with colored lights; animals and birds, all around, welcoming; and the most glorious people, so kind and loving. I felt so light, so free. Our son was full of joy. The dream ended there."

Morok was puzzled but did not take the dream seriously. He told Loobal not to worry, that they would

Chapter 19

always be together, in this world and the next.

They returned to the group, for it was nearing dark now. It was time to gather in prayer once again, each one of them seeking her own guidance within her personal connection to God.

Loobal prayed about her dream. It was still troubling her, and she sought an explanation. The quiet voice inside her had but a few words to share: "There will come a time when each person has a choice to make, and it must be made by that person alone."

Morok went deep into a state of communion with his Heavenly Father. He prayed to know the truth of what was going on in the world. His yearning was strong, and the response was clear: "My son, what you are beginning to see is a cleansing of the earth, a renewal, a rebirth. It is a beautiful thing and will bring healing to all. What is being cleared away is that which is dark and sinful. It must be destroyed."

Morok heard no more but felt a sense of complete stillness. He received much healing that evening, and his strength was restored.

Astnor, too, had been given some insights. Although he was not as attuned to his Creator as were Morok and Loobal, he was able to hear the spirits who guided him. He addressed the group. They had all finished praying and were eager to share their experiences. "I was told that there is something we must wait for before we leave on our journey. It is a sign that will tell us something has been fulfilled in this land." Astnor laughed. "Unfortunately, I was not given any specific details!"

"I heard something," offered a woman who had not said much to anyone since they had met. "I was told that I would be losing all I had worked for my whole life, and that I could not ever return to Tanlar." She paused, absorbing their shocked silence. "However, what I was shown was that which awaited me—us, I mean—and it was a place more magnificent and full of joy than anything I could have imagined. I felt so much love from our Father and His angels. We really are lucky to be here." She smiled, sharing the upliftment she was feeling.

Sinwela commented next. "Well," she said, "I did not hear, and I did not see. I can now move my leg without pain. It has been aching for years." Her satisfaction with this apparent healing was obvious. She beamed at them.

Morok did not tell anyone what he had learned. He wanted to reflect on it for a little while first.

The moon was full that night. A clear sky sparkled with bright stars, and Morok slept soundly.

Chapter 20

A Summons

The morning arrived with a glow that invited the enthusiastic group out to readily receive the sign of which Astnor had informed them. When nothing had occurred by mid-morning, some of the followers began to question the veracity of his guidance and were restless to start their journey.

"It's such a beautiful day," one murmured, "a perfect day for travel." It was difficult for them to sit around, not knowing what to do. They were rested and eager to get on with the journey, to distance themselves from Tanlar and its corruption.

Even Morok was indecisive. He questioned Astnor about the details of the guidance that kept them lingering at the cave. But Astnor had nothing to add to his original report.

Morok was on edge. With every day that passed he felt more certain that a patrol would be out searching for him. Surely, by now, Gotsro had learned of his escape. Loobal was no comfort to him in this regard. She trusted Astnor's guidance and would not leave the area until she was certain his prophecy had been fulfilled. Morok decided to wander off, alone, to pray.

He climbed to the top of the ridge above where they were camped. The view up there was spectacular, and he now wished that Loobal was with him—although she would have had a difficult time making the climb. From where he

Chapter 20

stood, looking east, Morok could see Tanlar, far below, at the edge of that vast sea. He saw nothing unusual in its environs. Perhaps he was expecting an army on the march. There was none to be seen. He sat on a rock and closed his eyes, enjoying the peaceful sounds of insects buzzing and birds sweetly chirruping. A prayer was needed. He gave thanks to almighty God for the beauty of the earth and for this time of rest after the trials of his sojourn in Tanlar. As he was reflecting on his many blessings, he felt the ground quiver, ever so subtly, beneath him. *Oh no*, he thought. He moved closer to the edge of the cliff and called down to those he could see outside the cave, below. "Get out of there!" he shouted.

They looked up, startled. Shielding their eyes to focus clearly on Morok's face, they waited for an explanation.

"Get everything out of the cave—quickly! I felt a tremor!" The ones who had heard him complied. They called to the others to gather upon a flat grassy area away from the cliff.

"Is this our sign?" one asked.

"I didn't feel anything," asserted another. And many had not.

Morok climbed carefully down the rock face and joined them. "I feel wary about staying here," he said to the group.

Loobal closed her eyes. "There is more coming," she said firmly. "I have the sense that it will bring death to many."

The others were confused. How could one pair the glory of such a beautiful summer day with the death of God's children?

"It is those who are on the other side of the walls who are in danger," Loobal continued as her guidance flowed. "We shall be spared." She lowered her head, thinking back to the destruction of Palador and to those she had left behind.

A Summons

She did not linger long in that state, however, as a great tremor of the earth then shook her to her very core.

There were screams from the others as the ground shifted beneath them. Rocks cascaded down the cliff and bounced in all directions, narrowly missing the place where they had gathered.

"Sit tight!" yelled Morok. The rumbling continued for a moment, then everything stood still.

Far off in the distance it was utter chaos. Buildings had collapsed in a matter of moments. Streets cracked open, exposing great chasms and holes. The walls—those great, tall, forbidding walls—stood unchallenged. They held Tanlar prisoner, encased within its own error, crying for mercy. On the top of the hill in the governor's domicile lay Gotsro. He was dead.

"I'm going to climb back up and take a look," said Morok, once he was confident the tremor was finished. Astnor went with him. The terrain was more challenging now, due to the displacement of many rocks, but they managed the ascent, and stood heaving, breathless, at the top of the ridge. Below was a scene quite unlike the one Morok had laid eyes upon not an hour before: Tanlar was a mess. Even at this great distance they could see that. A horn sounded, echoing through the hills. Astnor recognized it at once.

"Why, that is the call that summons the people of the city when someone of importance has died."

"I don't remember hearing it when Frantair was killed," said Morok, confused.

"Nothing followed proper protocol *that* day," Astnor explained. "But in the past it was used in such a case. The

Chapter 20

horn is kept in the governor's mansion."

Now that he thought about it, Morok *had* noticed a large, hollow instrument of sorts; it was held aloft in the gathering room.

"Gotsro!" he exclaimed finally, when the answer came to him. "It must be Gotsro."

Astnor went white with the realization. "This is our sign, Morok!"

They rushed through the trees, taking the safe course to the bottom, and rejoined the others. They quickly described what they had seen of Tanlar. Everyone had heard the horn and surmised its meaning and implication. It was time to go.

They packed up what little they had and soon began their journey westward to leave Tanlar and its memories far behind them.

That night they camped by a stream in a grouping of tall, delicate trees. A gentle breeze rustled the leaves, bringing with it a soothing scent.

Morok led them in prayer. There was a solidarity to the group now, a common drive and purpose; before, the ties that bound them had fit loosely. But now, Loobal's prophecy had manifested, and this increased everyone's faith in her, as their leader, and in God. Together she and Morok were a strong team, one that could be trusted. And the couple felt a strengthening of their commitment to each other, to their followers, and to God.

"Dear Heavenly Father," Morok began, "we gather together here in joy and in sorrow, and come to You with these great emotions, asking for Your healing touch upon us and upon those who suffered so terribly in this most recent disaster. We thank You, with great sincerity, for delivering us from this event and for leading us ever onward. We ask Your forgiveness for the doubts we once harbored. Please take us into Your care—always—and make us Your servants, as we

A Summons

endeavor to do Your will and to bring about change in our troubled world. Thank You, most gracious Father."

By the end of the prayer, Loobal had the distinct impression that the group was to change direction and head north toward a hilly region of the land. None of them had ever been that way before. Her guidance was to complete the journey as quickly as possible, so that she would have time to rest there before the baby was born. This was a daunting task. Loobal's endurance was flagging. She tired easily and preferred to take long naps and short hikes.

She spoke to Morok in private. He was concerned for her welfare and for that of the baby, but he decided they should trust in the guidance given. He found her a walking stick for support and helped her along, himself, when the trail was wide enough.

The first evening of their lengthy excursion, Loobal excused herself from food preparation and went straight to sleep. The womenfolk—who comprised the entire group, save for Morok and Astnor—were compassionate and caring and took turns carrying Loobal's pack. They washed her clothes and fed her and rubbed her tired feet. Loobal was deeply touched by the loving support she received, and she vowed to do her best to keep up.

On the third day of travel rain came. It slowed their progress. They took shelter in some trees and used the time to go within, to seek the guidance that would confirm or redirect their course.

Morok was able to connect deeply with God that day. He shared his worries with and gave his burdens to his Heavenly Father, who then provided him with much comfort. They all prayed for Loobal. Morok was told that the help she needed was coming.

On the fourth day the trail they were following widened. Although there were no clear indications that this area was inhabited, they took this as a favorable sign. Not

Chapter 20

fifteen minutes into their walk along this road they met another traveler. He was coming up the hill on a cart laden with goods. He was about to pass them by with a mere nod, but then he spotted Loobal. She was exhausted and walked slowly, supported on both sides by her women-friends. The driver pulled up his horse.

"Where are you going?" he called to them.

Morok approached him. "We are headed to these hills, but know not what awaits. Is there a town here?" He was tired, and there was a hint of desperation in his voice.

The man, who was middle-aged, looked at him kindly. "There certainly is," he said. "It is not far, about two hours on foot." He looked at Loobal once more. She returned his stare.

"I could take the young lady," he offered. "And some of your packs. There is a bit of room in my cart."

"I would be most grateful," said Loobal, "but were you not traveling in the other direction?"

"Well, yes, I was," he responded. "But it's not every day one comes across a traveler so in need, and I would be happy to help."

He was showered with gratitude from the group as they helped Loobal onto a layer of blankets that he had placed on the cart for her. Astnor and Morok helped him turn the cart around, for the road was narrow and the horse had to be unhitched to do it; then they were on their way, with Loobal bouncing along in the cart while the others followed.

Chapter 21
The Effort to Save Halfene

The rains in Palador were horrendous and unrelenting. For days it poured, and the work on the shelters slowed to a stop. The townspeople began to despair. Their lives were not improving, despite each person's will to make the effort, and this hopelessness set the tone for what was to come. There were arguments about the division of labor and concerns about the food that would have to be gathered to keep them all alive. Most of the livestock had been killed or had run away. The crops were spoiled, trade had ceased, and the future looked bleak.

Peter and Marfal kept the news of their engagement to themselves, having decided that others might find a wedding frivolous in these dark times.

Halfene became despondent. In the search for Loobal and the ride to save Dentino she had been so well occupied that she had no time to think about or mourn the loss of their mother and Serbrena. Now it was all she could think of. She cried for days on end, and not even Dentino's loving care elevated her mood.

Marfal was deeply concerned. Although she herself was still in mourning, she had gotten some closure by witnessing her mother's last breath and by having seen Serbrena burned to ashes. She thought of them now with love and peace in her heart, remembering them for the

Chapter 21

beautiful women they had been.

It was Peter who finally suggested that they leave Palador. "There is nothing more for us here, Marfal," he concluded.

"And where shall we go?" she asked. She was relieved that he had made the suggestion. Many people had begun to talk about abandoning their town.

"I think we should follow the river," he replied. "It will take us somewhere."

"But which way?" she wondered. "We've already been part way down. There was nothing to find. Shall we ask Halfene and Dentino?"

"We must," he said determinedly. "We should keep our family together. I will speak to my mother as well. I think she is well enough to travel."

They spent a few days in discussion until the rains abated. Halfene was indecisive. On the one hand, she desired to continue searching for the missing couple; however, it was apparent that what the group needed was a secure and stable home and not another futile mission.

Marfal suggested they try the other direction. "Mama always wanted to continue up-river," she told them. "She believed her sister was there."

"That just sounds like another pointless quest," Halfene blurted out.

"We could go that way anyway," said Marfal. "I'm not suggesting we have to look for someone."

Peter tried to calm them. "All right, ladies, you have said your piece. What do you think we should do, Dentino?"

"I've lived here, in Palador, my whole life, Peter. I wouldn't know what to do. But I'm willing to come with you. Anything is better than this...misery," he concluded.

Peter's mother spoke next. "Perhaps we can find a map—or someone who knows the land—to give us direction."

Peter smiled. Why had this solution not come to him?

The next day was spent gathering information and supplies. Although the skies were now clear, the ground was a mess of mud and debris. Work on the shelters did not continue. No one wanted to stay. Many of the townspeople—the ones well enough to walk—were looting the abandoned houses, searching for preserved food or anything useful that could be carried easily on a long journey. There were arguments over the horses—who would claim ownership of the ones whose owners had perished. Some bitter feuds developed in the once-peaceful town. It was a fight for survival now, and the sacrifice of goodwill seemed worthwhile.

Marfal returned to the farm. She had avoided the scene for too long, and now it was time to collect what she could and to say her good-byes. It had been difficult to convince Halfene to join her; the memories were far too painful. But together they went. And in the end it was not as bad as Halfene had anticipated, and it brought some peace into her heart.

Peter was easily able to claim one of the horses roaming the town—the one he had rescued from Portshead. But one horse was not enough for a group of five.

"We will have to take turns," he told them. "And our horse can carry some of the packs."

Peter's mother was able to locate an old book with a roughly sketched map of the region. It named Gate-Town and Portshead and another smaller place called Yulert.

"Why don't we head to Gate-Town!" Halfene exclaimed, when she saw the map. "That's where Morok's family lives!"

"We would have to deviate far from the river," Peter said, concerned. "But it is not a long journey, if this drawing is accurate."

The group agreed that this was their best option and made a plan to set out at dawn.

Chapter 21

Marfal's dreams were disturbing that night. It was so unsettling, leaving her home with no experience of the place she was going to.

She dreamt that she was lying on the side of a steep slope. Trees lined the side and she could not see past them. The wind was howling, and it blew them from side to side, thrashing the branches and leaves. No one was with her. A darkness crept up from the bottom of the hill, engulfing everything in its path. *Who will save me?* she thought. The encroaching darkness did not touch her, however; it merely passed by. The wind died down. She got up and walked to the other side of the hill. There the sky was brightly lit with angels, shimmering in the light of the sun. A song was heard on the horizon. It was hopeful and uplifting.

Then the scene shifted to a confusing montage of images from her past. She saw Tanlar, but it was broken in half. She saw her sisters—all three—washing clothes in the river. She saw Peter at choir practice and Bekren on the farm and thousands of garments she had sewn. The images swirled together, blending disharmoniously, and she turned in her sleep, trying to get away. She then saw a man she knew not. He was dark and menacing. He began to chase her, yelling, "Where did you hide my keys?" She ran through a forest, and where she ended up was at Serbrena's funeral. She saw no one there. Serbrena was lying on a bed of leaves and grass, with flowers in her hair. The scene shifted again, and Marfal was enclosed in a dark box. It was smoky in there. She began to scream, desperately trying to break free of her confinement. No help was coming. The door then opened and light burst forth into her prison. She was free. She flew to a hilltop with a company of angels, and there she rested. Alone.

When Marfal awoke she was crying. She remembered her dream but could not make sense of it. Peter consoled her and urged her to let it go.

"A new day is upon us, Marfal. Let us step forward and leave our darkness behind."

They gathered their packs, which they had prepared the night before, and went out to meet the others and get the horse.

Marfal was the first to ride. Peter walked beside her, holding the reins. He wanted to be close to her, as she seemed disturbed. The group said a quick farewell to Palador. It was the last time they would ever see the town.

The day grew bright as they passed through the fields where cows had once grazed, and they quickened their pace. Dentino was now astride the mare, leading them confidently to the far boundary of the only home he had known. When he reached that far hill, he gave the horse to Alemara and stood for a moment, looking back at his life. Halfene took his hand and squeezed it gently. Then they turned and followed the horse onward, toward a hopeful future.

Peter saw many things that day that filled him with awe. There were kinds of trees in this more rugged terrain that were not commonly seen in Portshead or Palador. He caught a glimpse of the distant mountains and marveled at their height and grandeur. It would be his first time climbing a mountain, and it excited him. The weather was warm and flowers proliferated, dotting the land with bursts of color. Marfal, too, was uplifted by the change in scenery. It was fresh and bright, unlike grim Palador. But oh, how she missed the Palador she had known. It had been paradise to her. She shed a tear at the memory.

Halfene was starting to feel better. Leaving Palador was like throwing off a great weight. She laughed as Dentino presented her with a flower, on bended knee.

Alemara consulted the map frequently. Although it was loosely drawn, there were some obvious landmarks designated, and she was able to match them with what she observed along the trail.

Chapter 21

The first night they camped in a hollow and enjoyed the display of the stars above. By this time Marfal had forgotten about the past night's dream and was beginning to relax.

"I love you," whispered Peter as she fell asleep beside him. It was music to her ears.

On the second day, Halfene took the lead, map in hand. She was so enthusiastic about reaching their destination that Dentino had to run to catch up to the horse.

As they neared the mountains at the end of the day, a strange feeling came upon them. It was as if a light had been snuffed out. The mountains suddenly seemed foreboding.

Marfal, astride the horse, pulled up. "Let's not go any further today," she said to the others. "It doesn't feel right." The others, tired from walking, consented.

They felt cold that night despite the fire they had kept blazing. Marfal's sleep was restless, plagued by bad dreams.

In the morning, they reached a trail that supposedly led through the mountains.

"Are you sure this is the right one?" Peter asked his mother, looking at the map.

"Yes, Peter," she confirmed. He hesitated for a moment, then began the slow, winding ascent, carefully maneuvering the horse around fallen rocks. The others followed slowly behind.

At noon, as the sun was beating down upon them, the earth shook. The tremor was massive. Peter's horse reared up and threw him. Then it bolted, narrowly missing the others as it sought escape down the trail they had come from. Marfal was in shock. She lay where she had fallen, close to Halfene and Alemara. Dentino, who had gone up ahead of them, was nowhere in sight. A large rock had fallen upon the trail, below, and they could not now see where the horse had gone.

Halfene had only one thing on her mind—to find

Dentino. She scrambled to her feet and ran up the trail. The sight that met her eyes when she rounded the corner was horrific: Dentino lay motionless, half piled under rock. The scream that escaped her lips was unearthly. Marfal, now alert, grabbed Alemara's hand and pulled her to her feet. Both were unhurt. They followed the trail to where Dentino lay. Halfene was at his head, sobbing miserably.

"This can't be happening!" she cried, through a wall of tears. Marfal went to comfort her, but there was a growing sense of unease in her own heart.

"Where is Peter?" asked Alemara, voicing Marfal's primary concern.

"The horse..." Marfal remembered. "He was riding the horse—he must have fallen!" She left Halfene and ran ahead, climbing over more fallen rock.

"Peter!" she called, hoarse with fear. Alemara followed slowly behind. Peter was moaning on the ground, hurt, but fortunately, alive. His head was cut and his arm looked broken. Their packs were scattered around him.

Marfal approached him gently. "Peter," she whispered, stroking his hair. He winced as he turned to look at her.

"This is not good, Marfal. I am a broken man."

"Dentino is dead!" she blurted out. It was the wrong thing to say.

"Then we are doomed," he whispered. "Is my mother alive? And Halfene?" he asked her.

"Yes," she said quickly. "They are unhurt."

Alemara approached, covering her mouth. "Oh, my Peter!" she cried. "What has befallen you?"

"I fell, and I hit the ground hard, Mama."

Alemara examined his wounds. "Your arm is broken. How shall we splint it?" She looked around for something straight—a stick, perhaps. There was little to work with among these rocks.

Chapter 21

"Halfene had a walking stick," Marfal suggested. "I will go see her." She looked longingly at Peter. "I love you," she said.

Alemara busied herself looking through the packs for something that could be fashioned into a bandage and for a flask of water to wash out the wound. Peter, meanwhile, writhed in agony.

Marfal hurried back down the trail. Halfene had not moved. She explained what had happened to Peter and that they needed help. Halfene gave her the stick but would not leave her man. She continued to stare at his body, her tears welling and abating in an endless cycle.

"Thank you, Halfene," Marfal said, patting her shoulder. "I will be back. He is in a lot of pain..." Marfal knew that her sister needed her, needed someone to validate her grief. But her calling to help Peter was stronger, and she left Halfene, alone, to face the manifestation of her life's biggest fear.

When Marfal got back to Peter, he was sitting up. His mother had stopped the bleeding from his arm—at least temporarily—and was washing out the cut on his face.

"I wish I could give him something for the pain," she said to Marfal.

Marfal looked at him sympathetically. She had nothing to offer. Peter looked back at her. In his eyes she saw fear.

Alemara looked up at Marfal. "I will leave you two," she said. "I'm sure Halfene could use some company right now." She kissed her son on the forehead and walked away, stepping carefully over the debris.

"Marfal—" Peter began, "we must find our horse! I cannot make it out of here without it."

"It ran away, Peter. It was so frightened."

"So was I," he admitted. "That tremor was much worse than the one in Palador. Will there be more?" he wondered.

The Effort to Save Halfene

"God only knows," whispered Marfal. She began to cry. "Oh, poor Dentino! He was so young!"

"And so in love," added Peter. "I worry for your sister. This may be too much pain for her to bear."

"I don't know what to say to her, Peter. What words could I give her to make her life bearable?"

"I wish we had never come here. And now, we have no choice but to continue on to Gate-Town. There is no turning back."

"Perhaps a brighter future lies on the other side of these mountains, Peter," she offered.

"I have little hope for that," he said solemnly. He started to get up. Marfal put out her hand to stop him.

"No. You must rest. We can sleep here tonight." Peter did not like the idea but was in too much pain to argue.

Alemara did not have any luck consoling Halfene. She was broken—irreparably broken. So the older woman left Halfene alone, once again, and returned to her son.

Marfal had done what she could to make Peter more comfortable and then set about following his orders as to how they should arrange themselves for the night. There was little food and almost no water—that had been used on Peter—but the sky remained clear and that was one less worry to contend with. What now weighed upon them was what they should do with Dentino's body. It did not look like the rocks on top of him could be easily moved; Peter was certainly not able to help. The thought of leaving him there for all time saddened them greatly. Marfal was especially sensitive to this matter—it reminded her of her mother.

"Let us say a prayer for him," suggested Peter. "It is the least we can do."

"The Funeral Prayer," said his mother.

"Should we get Halfene?" asked Marfal.

"I think not," said Peter gloomily. "Leave her to mourn."

Chapter 21

Alemara began:

"Oh, Heavenly Father, so gracious and bright,
Please take our Dentino to everlasting light.
Make him a home in Your Heavens above,
And bless his dear soul with Your inflowing love.
May all then be healed of his earthly wounds,
And, by Your grace, may his life be resumed
Up there, in peace, with the Angels of Light.
We love him, dear God, and we bid him good night."

All three of them wept for a long time after the prayer. They did not notice Halfene's presence, standing above them.

"He's gone," she said quietly, grabbing their attention. "He left. I can't feel him here any longer."

They stared at her for a moment, speechless. Then Marfal spoke up. "We were just praying for him, Halfene."

Halfene dropped to her knees. She looked so small, so vulnerable. She burst into great sobs. Marfal approached her, and this time Halfene accepted her comfort. They embraced each other tightly, the last of their family. Peter found this heart-breaking to watch.

The night was cold. There was no wood for a fire; they had only each other to keep themselves warm. Halfene could not sleep at all. Exhausted as she was, she was too disturbed to fall asleep. She suffered greatly.

Peter was in pain. Every time he moved the ache in his arm was amplified and irritated. He, too, found sleep elusive. Only Alemara and Marfal managed to get any rest, and little at that.

The sunrise was stunning, but not even beauty could eclipse the ugliness of Dentino's death. The mourning continued. No one wanted to leave the body yet, nor did they wish to linger in that place. They packed up, changed Peter's bandages, and made one last trip back down the trail to say good-bye.

Peter had not seen the body yet. It shocked him. His compassion for Halfene's loss grew ten-fold, and he held her close, offering what little warmth he could to comfort her.

Halfene could not bear to leave. Suddenly, she became childishly stubborn. Pouting, she crossed her arms and demanded that they all wait another day—until all of them were ready to go on.

"Halfene," Marfal said cautiously, afraid to ignite a tantrum, "I don't think another day is going to help you—or any of us. It is not going to bring Dentino back."

Halfene was furious. "I'M NOT GOING!"

Peter looked at Marfal.

"We can't leave you here alone. You will die," she said to her sister. And then it suddenly occurred to Marfal that this is what Halfene wanted—to die at his side rather than face life without him.

Marfal went white.

"Oh, no—Halfene," she called to her sister, gently reaching out her hand.

"I'm not coming," Halfene repeated bitterly.

Marfal's mind whirled. What could she say? "Halfene, I'm the only family you've got left. Please, let us go from this place of sadness."

"Everywhere is a place of sadness now, Marfal! Do you think I'm just going to forget about him? About this nightmarish life that just gets worse and worse?" Halfene's eyes were blazing. "IT'S NOT FAIR!" she yelled.

Marfal hung her head. Halfene was right.

Peter spoke softly: "Halfene, we love you dearly. And we wish you would come with us and let us take care of you. But you are a grown woman, and you must choose your own fate. We will proceed slowly. If you wish to join us, you should be able to find us." He gave her a quick hug. Halfene

Chapter 21

just stood there, emotionless. Alemara, too, gave her a hug good-bye and wished her peace and good health. Halfene gave no response. When it was Marfal's turn, it was as if a small door cracked open in Halfene's heart. She blinked, and a tear fell. And then another. And then the dam burst. Marfal just held her. Peter quietly urged his mother to step away with him. He was hoping that Marfal would be able to get Halfene to leave.

At this point, Marfal was crying too. Halfene's grief—and anger—was also hers. Why—after everything else they had been through—did this have to happen too? Dentino did not deserve to die. And neither had Serbrena. Would Halfene be next? Marfal was afraid for all of them. What if it had been Peter instead of Dentino? How would she have felt? Would she leave him?

"Halfene—" Marfal said suddenly, as the idea came to her— "why don't you climb to the next viewpoint with us, some place where we can get a glimpse of the land below. Then, if you do not like what awaits us, you can return here."

Halfene looked at Dentino and then back at her sister. "All right," she said. She knelt down beside the body one last time and kissed his still, pale face. "I love you forever," she whispered. And then, without a backward glance, she took Marfal's hand—as she had done as a child—and proceeded up the trail.

They caught up with Peter and Alemara at the site of Peter's fall. Peter said nothing, but he smiled at Marfal after Halfene had gone past.

The climb was difficult. Much had changed due to the tremor, and the map was not helpful. They used the sun for guidance, hoping that, if they went in the general direction of Gate-Town, they would eventually arrive there.

They curved eastward that evening. Here the way was easier. There was not much of a view yet—except for the mountains. Gate-Town was still some distance beyond.

The Effort to Save Halfene

Peter's injury was causing him a lot of discomfort. He tried to be stoic and ignore the pain, but it was constant. He awoke that night with a fever. Marfal was woken by his murmuring.

"What, Peter?" She sat up and looked at him; his face was aglow in the light of their dying fire. His eyes were glassy and his hair was soaked with sweat.

"Let me see your arm!" she demanded. She undid the bandage, carefully, and exposed the site of his injury. It was red and swollen. "Peter, I fear you are infected." He did not respond, but closed his eyes in response to the pain. Marfal shook Alemara, rousing her from her dreams.

"What is the matter, my dear?" she asked.

Marfal motioned her over to where Peter lay and showed her the wound.

"I was afraid this would happen," said Alemara.

"But is there nothing to treat it?" whispered Marfal. She was frightened but did not want to alarm Halfene, who had finally fallen asleep.

"The plants we need I have not seen at this elevation," she said sadly.

Marfal began to panic. She could *not* lose Peter. His presence was the only thing that kept her sane. She began to cry.

"Oh, God, no," she whimpered. She held Peter's face in her hands. "Look at me, Peter!"

His eyes rolled around, trying to focus on her face. He was shaking. "I—I'm c—c—cold, Marf—fal!" he stuttered. Alemara gave him her blanket and mopped his brow with her kerchief. The two women held him and cried upon him as he writhed. Halfene awoke from the commotion. She said nothing but simply stared at the two women who were clinging to a life that could barely hold on.

At daybreak Peter was mildly better. He was able to focus on their faces. But he was in no state to travel.

201

Chapter 21

"I...need...water," he said, desperately.

Halfene finally spoke up. "There is a tiny stream up ahead. I saw it yesterday, when we were looking over the edge. I will go. Give me all the flasks you have."

They complied, and she bundled the flasks into a small pack. She left immediately.

Peter was exhausted and soon fell back to sleep. Alemara hung his sweat-soaked blanket on a rock to dry and wrapped him in another. His clothes were wet too, but he did not have any other that he could wear.

Halfene did not return until after noon.

"What took you so long?!" scolded Marfal. Halfene shrugged. She handed them the flasks, half-full, and sat down, facing the other direction.

Marfal quickly gave the water to Alemara, for Peter, and walked over to Halfene. She was parched, herself, but did not want to take what Peter so badly needed.

"Halfene," she said, trying to keep the anger out of her voice. "We *need* you. *Please.* Do you want to see him die too? So I can suffer as you do?"

Halfene turned around, her face red with shame. "I'm sorry, Marfal. I don't know what is wrong with me. I'll go back—"

"I will go," Marfal asserted. We all need water." She kissed Peter good-bye. He looked at her like *she* was water—*she* would bring him back to life.

Marfal ran quickly down the trail. She had not seen the stream the day before and was not sure where it was, but that did not concern her. She was on a mission. She found it easily about ten minutes later. Now she saw why Halfene had lingered there: it was a beautiful spot, calm and peaceful. The water was mesmerizing. It sparkled in the sunlight, reflecting many hues. Marfal leaned over and washed her face, her hands, in the running water. She soaked her kerchief, to take back to Peter, and she drank until her thirst was quenched.

She even dipped her feet in; the cool water was soothing after the long days on the trail. When all of the flasks were filled, she left. This small pleasure, this simple gift, lifted her spirits, and she returned to the group with new hope.

Peter was sitting up when she returned. She gave him a fresh flask of water and the wet kerchief. He used it to wipe his dusty face.

"Are you feeling better?" Marfal asked him sweetly.

"Some," he admitted. "The swelling has gone down."

"I am amazed," said Marfal. "I felt sure you were going to die!"

"I have much to live for." They locked eyes. She knew then that he had fought hard to stay.

Halfene, who had overheard them, turned away. She could not tolerate scenes of love, where she had none. She took it upon herself to forage for food. "I know there are some berries here somewhere," she mumbled as she left.

Alemara was elated that her son had survived the night, but she was tired from the drama of it. She lay down to rest. Peter and Marfal discussed the next step of their journey. He felt he would be able to go a little ways the next day, if the night was peaceful.

At dusk, after a meal of berries, they built a fire and lay down for the night.

It was a long, dream-filled night. Halfene was able to rest, on and off. When she did sleep, she dreamt of Dentino. They were back in Palador, in the innocent days before disaster struck. This dream was happy. But she also dreamt of his death—the ultimate parting of ways for them. She dreamt that he was trapped on the other side of an invisible wall. She could see him and hear him, but they could not touch. Dentino looked despondent. When Halfene awoke, she felt completely alone in this world.

Marfal's dreams were intense. She was trying to escape from the man from her previous dream. As fast as she

Chapter 21

could run, he would always catch her; he then demanded, "My keys! I need my keys!"

Peter did not dream. He slept in fits, and when he was awake, he was ruminating about his future. He felt cautious, as if he should not get his expectations too high. Worse things might yet befall them, although he could not imagine what. He wondered how they would live, if they ever did reach Gate-Town. Would there be any place for them to call home? Would he be able to work? He doubted he could play the violin with such an injury. In any case, his own instrument had been left in Palador. There was no room for it. The thought saddened him; music was his great joy in life.

Of all of them, Alemara fared best that night. In her long life she had experienced many trials—although never this serious—and she had learned to count her blessings rather than to hold on to what was gone. She had her son. For now, that was enough.

The sun rose above them well before they were set to make their way over the mountain and into the valley beyond. Peter knew this was his only chance to prove to himself that he could survive these dark times. He pushed himself to his feet and drank some water, then he took the lead; the women, laden with the packs, followed behind.

They stopped briefly at Halfene's stream to wash and to refill the flasks, and then they veered south, following a windy trail that was now covered with fallen rock.

It was not easy going, especially for Peter. Several times he stumbled and had to catch himself with his good arm. Marfal offered to help him, but he kindly refused, saying that she would need her strength. The descent was awkward and slow, but they reached the lush green of the valley shortly after midday.

"Let us rest for a while," said Marfal. After snacking on berries, they stretched out in the tall grass and allowed the sun to warm them. It was peaceful there, and only the deer

The Effort to Save Halfene

took notice of them, pausing in their perpetual grazing to take a look.

They stayed there for a full day, for Peter needed the time to recover from his first hike since the accident, and the women wanted to forage as much as they could before crossing to the other side. The mountains beyond were great, and they looked intimidating to the weary group.

Peter and Marfal were not at ease. Although it was certainly a beautiful place, and it provided abundant food, water, and comfortable places to lie, there was something wrong. They could sense it. It was like a shadow creeping up behind them—whenever they looked, it disappeared. They held hands as they sat—at least that small comfort was theirs.

Halfene stayed away. Not wanting to intrude on their togetherness, nor remind herself of what she had lost, she wandered off into the trees to be alone and think. Although her tears had stopped, for the moment, she felt quite hopeless.

Alemara spent the evening reading the book that contained the map, for the vivid descriptions of the surrounding area piqued her interest and contained some practical information. She ignored everything else that was going on around her and was not aware that her son was feeling a looming danger.

"It felt like this before we went up the mountain," said Marfal. The sun had set and the foreboding feeling was getting stronger.

Peter wrapped his good arm around her shoulders. "I know," he whispered, glancing nervously around their camp. He stiffened suddenly. "Where is Halfene?"

Marfal sat up straight and looked around. "I don't know, Peter!"

"Mama!" he called to Alemara. She was bundled in her blanket by the fire. "Did Halfene come back?"

"I think so, Peter."

Chapter 21

"I'm here," a voice called quietly from the shadows.

"Thank God," said Marfal. Her heart was pounding. "Get some sleep, okay?"

"You too," said Halfene half-heartedly. She lay down and stared blankly at the sky.

Clouds rolled in overnight and they awoke to fog and drizzle. Halfene, who had not slept, was already sitting under a large tree. The others grabbed their blankets and packs and went to join her.

"This is not ideal," said Alemara. "I was hoping we could make some progress today. I can't even *see* the other side of the valley now."

"No worries, Mama," Peter said, patting her arm. "We will get there eventually."

Marfal was restless. The dark feelings of the night before had not left her, although their source, like the valley, was shrouded in mist. Halfene seemed distant to her, as if she were fading away. This was entirely out of character. *What is she thinking?* Marfal wondered. She missed the closeness that she and her sister once shared. Halfene looked at her only once that day. Marfal tried to engage her with a smile, but Halfene quickly turned away.

The day was spent listening to Alemara read from the book and describe some of the other passages she had read the day before. They built a fire—ineffective as it was—and started to gather material for a small shelter, in case the rain should stay.

Peter's arm ached and he felt a chill again. It was hard to stay warm in the dampness of that place. But he kept himself busy, thinking thoughts of the past and of the future and humming little tunes that he used to play on his violin.

After another night in the valley, Marfal was very much on edge. She was eager to leave, believing that the place, itself, was the source of her fears. She could not convince the others, however, and they continued to linger there, awaiting fair weather.

After two more days, during which time they completed a shelter, they spotted another human in the valley. It was a man, traveling alone. He came over to them immediately, happy to see someone on the path. He was from Gate-Town, and his name was Mar-hook. He was an older man—probably older than Alemara—and he was curious to know their tale. Peter was happy to narrate it, although there was so much background information to be added that it took a long while to explain why they were headed to Gate-Town.

Marfal was not interested in hearing their tale of horror yet again, but wanted to ask Mar-hook about Gate-Town, and if he had known Morok.

"Why, yes!" he said brightly, after she had had a chance to speak. "Morok was my nephew. An impulsive young man. He left years ago."

Marfal explained their relationship to him and that he—and her sister—had gone missing during the initial event that destroyed Palador.

"Oh, my," said Mar-hook. "I do hope they survived. His parents and sister would want to know about this. Please do tell them." He described how to find their home. "I'm sure they would offer you shelter," he added. "They are kind people and have an extra room or two."

The group was happy to hear this good news, and they welcomed Mar-hook to stay with them in their shelter that night; however, he declined. "I mustn't linger," he said. "I have come to check my trap-line and then must return home."

They did manage to convince him to share a meal and to tell them more about Gate-Town.

"You will like it, I'm sure," he told them. "It is a solid community—we work hard and are proud of what we have achieved. Visitors are always welcome."

Chapter 21

After giving them clear directions to the trail that led to the easiest pass through the remaining mountains, he left them. They were sad to see him go. His presence had been a welcome distraction from their worry and sorrow.

That night the ground shook again. This time it was colossal. Peter did not survive. He had left Marfal to gather more firewood, and then the tremor hit. What had been a trail through the meadow quickly became a deep chasm. Peter was thrown forcefully off balance by the shifting ground beneath him and was cast into the chasm. The impact of his fall was fatal. His last thought—in that brief, terrifying moment—was of Marfal.

She knew he was gone. The moment the tremor hit, she knew it. She screamed his name as she, herself, was thrown to the ground. Halfene grabbed her and quickly pulled her out of the way of their shelter, which was in the process of collapsing. Alemara lay trapped inside. There was nothing heavy upon her—the branches that had fashioned the walls and roof were not exceptionally large—but it smothered her nonetheless, and when Halfene tried to get in there to pull her out, she, too, became trapped.

It was not long before Marfal, working in the dark, had managed to pull off the largest branches and drag her sister and Alemara out. Halfene was breathing steadily, but Alemara was gone. Marfal helped Halfene to sit up and checked her for injuries. She was bruised but not seriously hurt.

"I have to find Peter," said Marfal, her voice shaky, "though I fear he is gone." The last word came out as a squeak. Halfene jumped to her feet.

"I'll go with you." She grabbed a branch and poked it in the embers of their fire, trying to make a light to help them navigate the trail. It failed. After another attempt, she left it. "Stay close to me," she told Marfal.

They hurried forward to where Peter had disappeared

The Effort to Save Halfene

to at dusk. It was difficult to see, but they could feel a path through the grass.

And then Halfene slipped. She screamed in fright as the ground gave way beneath her, tumbling her down a steep slope where the trail had been. She hit the ground some ways down with a thump. It was dark as pitch; she did not know where she was at.

Marfal could not see what had happened, but she stopped walking and got down on her hands and knees, feeling the ground before her where Halfene had been.

"Are you okay?" she called to her sister.

Halfene managed a "yes." Marfal could feel the edge of the chasm, where the grass was uprooted and the soil torn loose.

"I can't see anything, Halfene! What are we going to do?"

Halfene was terrified. The ground she was sitting on seemed unstable. She could hear soil and rock falling whenever she shifted her body.

"Please don't leave me!" she called to Marfal.

"Of course I won't!" she replied. "I will lie here until first light, and then we will find a way to get you out. But where is Peter?" She had, in her panic, forgotten about Peter. She called his name. There was no answer.

"Ahhh!" she screamed. The pain in her heart was unbearable. She lay awake, in utter torment, until the birds began to sing. She was afraid to move at all, lest she join Halfene in that hole. But the pale light of dawn eventually crept into the valley, and she could finally see the layout of the area and understand what had happened. She peered over the edge at Halfene. Her sister looked pale and cold. She wasn't that far down—the height of a tall man, perhaps. Marfal carefully crawled backward to a place where the ground was undisturbed and stood up. She quickly found a large, solid branch, and crawled back to the edge to offer it

Chapter 21

to Halfene. Halfene was able to grip the stick but could not get any traction with her feet. The soil was loose and the slope too steep.

Marfal started to sob. "Not you, too!" she cried. "I can't lose you—I won't!"

Halfene felt helpless. She looked around but could not see another way up. The drop off below her was sheer. It was then, looking down, that she saw Peter's body, wedged between the rocks. He had fallen far.

"Oh, Marfal!" she cried. "He's down *there*..." She pointed, but Marfal, from her vantage point, could not see him.

"Why did we stay here?!" Marfal shouted. "I KNEW something bad was going to happen!"

Halfene said nothing. There was nothing to say.

As the sky brightened, Marfal and Halfene made an attempt to set aside their grief and focus on the task of raising Halfene from the chasm. First, Halfene wanted Marfal to go back to their camp to fetch water and anything else that might appear useful. Although Halfene was nervous about being left alone, even for a few minutes, she was very thirsty.

Marfal did as requested and returned not long after with a flask for Halfene and a small rope—one they had used to tie up the horse. Marfal lowered the flask down to her sister and then pulled the rope back up. If only there were something solid to anchor it to...Unfortunately, nothing of that nature was close enough to secure a proper line that would reach Halfene. As Marfal pondered the situation, they became aware of the sound of hoofbeats across the valley. Marfal looked up. In the distance, far from their camp, she spotted a horse. It was cantering haphazardly across the meadow, shaking its head as if to rid itself of an irritating insect. As it came closer, she could see that a saddle dangled under its belly.

The Effort to Save Halfene

"It's our horse!" she exclaimed, amazed that it had made its way to the valley and had survived the tremor.

"Go get it!" yelled Halfene. "It can pull me up!"

"It is far, Halfene, but I will try."

Marfal summoned her strength and ran off in its direction, careful to avoid the edge of the chasm. She called its name and waved her arms. At first it did not respond. She yelled again. This time it saw her and whinnied. It slowed to a walk and meandered closer to where she was headed. As she neared it, she could see that the reins were dangling from its neck and that it had been trying to shake off the bridle. She approached it calmly, speaking in a low voice. It settled immediately and allowed her to right the saddle and pick up the reins. She rubbed its head gently, happy to see a familiar face. Then she led it carefully back to where Halfene was trapped. This time her plan worked. With the rope tied firmly to the saddle, she was able to pull Halfene up the slippery slope.

Halfene was ecstatic. "Oh, thank you, Marfal! I realized down there that I don't wish to die, as bad as things have gotten. I do still have some life in me. Let's get back to camp and figure out how to get out of this valley!"

"Wait!" exclaimed Marfal. In her enthusiasm, Halfene had forgotten about Peter. "I need some time with him. Alone. You take the horse. It probably needs a break from the harness. Set it free. We can catch it again when we're ready to leave."

Halfene nodded solemnly. She gave Marfal a meaningful hug then led the horse back up the trail. Marfal watched them go. She sighed deeply. Then she made her way around the gaping crevice in the ground, looking for a clear view of her fallen man.

There was nothing that could have prepared her for the excruciating feelings that arose when she eventually caught sight of him. He lay face down. She would never see

Chapter 21

his kind, beautiful face again. She wished she could climb down there—to touch him one last time—but there was no way.

"Peter," she said, her voice choked with sorrow, "wherever you are, if you can hear me...please forgive me. I didn't listen well enough to the warnings within. We should never have stayed here. I miss you so much! And you haven't been gone a day. I love you with all of my heart. You were—and are—my only love. Be well, my Peter. May God carry you ever higher up in the Realms of Light. Oh, Peter..." her voice trailed off. She sat and wept. And then something remarkable happened: she felt a hand touch her shoulder—his hand. Love poured into her. She felt calm...and whole. The feeling enveloped her. In her head she heard his words: *I'm here, Marfal. Think of me only with love, not sorrow.*

Her tears stopped. "Thank you, Peter," she whispered. She closed her eyes and allowed herself to be with him, with that great feeling of peace. She was nourished by it. Her worries melted in its warmth.

When she returned to the camp, she greeted her sister with a humble smile.

"What happened?" Halfene asked, trying to understand the look.

"Peter came to me," she said peacefully.

Halfene gave her a sad smile and nodded. She looked over at the ruins of the shelter. Alemara's body lay just beyond it. "What do we do with her?" Halfene asked.

Marfal walked slowly over to the body. "We say the Funeral Prayer. She would have wanted that."

"I don't remember it, Marfal."

"I will say it then." They sat next to Alemara, gently placing their hands upon her.

"Oh, Heavenly Father, so gracious and bright,
Please take our Alemara to everlasting light.

Make her a home in Your Heavens above,
And bless her dear soul with Your inflowing love.
May all then be healed of her earthly wounds,
And, by Your grace, may her life be resumed
Up there, in peace, with the Angels of Light.
We love her, dear God, and we bid her good night."

All was still. They could hear their own hearts beating, that gentle rhythm of life that mysteriously continued in them but not in her.

"I will miss her," said Halfene.

"So will I," added Marfal. "She was to be my mother. I loved her very much."

They sat in silence, reflecting on their time with this kind woman whom they had been so fortunate to meet.

After a while, Halfene stood up. "I would like to say good-bye to Peter." She gave Marfal a tearful look and disappeared up the trail.

Marfal set to work, tidying Alemara's clothing and hair and gathering a small bouquet of flowers, which she set atop the old mother's chest. She then sorted through the packs, combining as much as she could into two of them. The rest of the items, including some of Dentino's belongings, she set by the remains of the shelter. *Perhaps someone will find these useful,* she thought.

The horse was grazing peacefully by a narrow stream. Marfal approached it slowly, offering her hand. It snorted and pushed at her hand with its muzzle. She stroked its neck and then gently slid the rope over its head, fashioning it into a makeshift halter. The horse was somewhat reluctant to leave its idyllic grazing. Marfal coaxed it gently, and eventually, it walked at her side willingly.

Halfene was waiting at the camp. She, too, had gone through the packs. "Let us not forget the book." It had been under the rubble of the shelter, where Alemara had been.

Chapter 21

Halfene added it to her pack, along with Dentino's spare shirt, and then went over to the horse.

"Well, old girl," she said to it, "are you ready for another adventure?" There were still a few hours of sunlight left. Halfene buckled up the saddle while Marfal fetched the bridle and replaced the rope halter with it.

"You first," said Halfene.

An eagle called. They looked up, trying to spot it. High in a tree, it watched over them. Marfal mounted the horse and off they went, zigzagging through the long grass of the meadow, with the mountains ahead in their sight.

Chapter 22
Truth and Prophecy

The air was chilly that night. "We're losing summer," Halfene said, as they gathered firewood at the foot of the mountains. They had made it this far and were now very much in need of rest. Both women had recovered surprisingly well from the emotional trauma of the previous night's loss, but physically, they were exhausted. They got a good fire going and lay as near to it as they could, bundled in everyone's blankets. The horse stood guard nearby, its eyelids heavy with sleep.

In the morning they refilled the flasks, saddled the horse, and began their ascent. Marfal did not have any particularly bad feelings about this mountain. She felt rather detached from the experience of trudging up its rocky trails. Halfene, however, was wary. She was especially cautious on the back of this horse—the one who had thrown Peter—and she stroked it gently as she rode, calmly suggesting to it that all was well and that there could not possibly be another upsetting tremor.

Marfal followed slowly. She was reluctant to leave Peter's body, although she knew his spirit was with her. She felt him with her now—as a presence in her dreams as well as in her waking life. She would think of him and, shortly thereafter, she would feel a touch or hear a familiar whisper. It gave her hope that she would see him once again some day.

Chapter 22

They reached the highest point of the trail later that day. It wound around the mountain well below the peak and offered a clear view of the land beyond. Gate-Town was a mere speck in the distance. Marfal estimated that it would take them one more day to get there.

The lookout was a perfect place for a rest. They unpacked their blankets and stretched out on the rough ground beside the trail, shading their eyes from the bright sun. The horse, who was keen to forage, had few choices in that place.

Halfene was looking at Marfal as she lay, wondering what she was thinking. She felt like starting a conversation. "I said the prayer for him."

"What?" asked Marfal, turning toward her.

"The Funeral Prayer. For Peter. Of course, I couldn't remember it exactly. But I tried, Marfal."

Marfal just looked at her. Halfene surprised her sometimes. "Thank you, Halfene. That means a lot to me. How are you?"

Halfene looked off into the distance. "Not well at all—I miss him too much. I miss his smile and how he would hold me and sing to me. I miss everything about him. Now what do I have to look forward to? Growing old? Old and childless?" She kicked at the dirt under her feet.

"He's not the only man in the world, Halfene."

Halfene glared at her. "He was the only man for me. And what about you? Will you just move on and find another one?"

Marfal shook her head. "No...I just meant that you are still young, Halfene."

"When I was young I had plans to get married and have five children. I've missed my chance. I feel old, Marfal. We've been through so much."

"I know." She gave Halfene a hug. "Let us go."

They stood up, took one last long look at the view to

get their bearings, and began their descent. Marfal rode, and Halfene wandered behind, focussing her attention on just putting one foot ahead of the other.

By nightfall they had made it down the mountain and had found shelter in a grove of trees. There was a light rain—not the kind that gets one wet—but they sought shelter anyway. Their bellies were grumbling, and they hoped that the morning would bring a profitable opportunity to forage.

Marfal's nightmare recurred. He—the one chasing after the keys—was there yet again. This time Halfene was in the dream; she was telling Marfal where to hide. The dream was exhausting, and Marfal awoke feeling grumpy.

Halfene slept in peace through the night. Perhaps it was the presence of the horse that gave her comfort. It was nice to have someone watching over them. It never strayed far.

Their worries about finding food were soon over. They recognized a type of bush that had edible leaves, and there were a few varieties of berries in the vicinity as well.

When they were well sated, they packed up and continued on their way, map book in hand. The landscape was not exactly as described therein. Marfal concluded that the effects of the three tremors—plus the growth of trees over the years since the map had been drawn—accounted for the discrepancies. Nevertheless, they found their way.

Gate-Town was not as far away as it had appeared. Remembering what Mar-hook had told them, they circled around to the left, following the trail past a row of houses and through a small gate that served as an entry-point to the town. The town had been hit by the tremor—that was obvious—but the damage was negligible, and they were witness to many people hard at work, achieving all of the necessary repairs, together. It was like a hive of bees, the way they buzzed about. Halfene and Marfal stood there—Marfal astride the horse—just watching.

Chapter 22

Eventually, a tall man approached them. Marfal dismounted and walked toward him, smiling. He seemed disconcerted by their presence and looked at them with one eyebrow raised. Marfal was slightly taken aback and stopped.

"Where are you coming from?" the man asked.

"Palador," said Marfal. "It is in ruins."

"Ah, yes, Palador. Some people from that place have arrived here of late, seeking refuge. I dare say we are running short on space here." His look was stony.

"We have relatives here—sort of," faltered Halfene. "Mar-hook met us in the valley and told us where to find them. He said they might have room for us."

"He did, did he?"

Another man approached, and this one turned to him. "From Palador," he explained. "Who are these relatives?" he asked Halfene.

"I don't know their names. Morok was their son. He married our sister last year."

"What do you mean, 'was'?" he demanded.

"They are missing," said Marfal. "We do not know if they survived the great storm."

The man nodded to his friend, who then left abruptly. His voice softened. "We will let them know you are here."

"Oh, thank you!" exclaimed Marfal. She began to cry. The stress of their journey had pressed upon her, and now, the emotion was difficult to contain.

"Shall I take your horse?" the man asked, hoping a change of subject would allow this woman to compose herself. "We have room for it in the town stable."

"Yes, thank you, sir." She handed him the reins and removed her pack from behind the saddle.

The horse nickered as it was led away. Halfene sighed and turned to Marfal. "It seems as if our luck has improved."

The other man approached again with an older couple. From the concerned looks on their faces the sisters could tell

Truth and Prophecy

he had told them about their son.

The woman, who resembled Morok, spoke to the sisters. "My dear daughters, you have traveled far. Please join us at our home. There you may rest and tell us your tale."

The couple led them down a lane to a small wooden house with a garden of flowers in front. There they were joined by another woman who looked to be Marfal's age. She wore colorful paint on her lips and eyelids. She bade them enter and offered them each a comfortable chair to sit on. The mother then fetched for them a drink of water and some fruit. The girls were ravenous and ate quickly. Seeing their hunger, the woman then brought them nuts. When they were finished eating, the husband sat facing them.

"Please—we are anxious to hear of our son," he said.

Marfal began, her last mouthful still in the process of being chewed. "We met him a couple of years ago by the river's edge in Palador. We were four of us then, my sisters and I. He was kind, and he showed us our way back to town, for we were newly arrived from Tanlar, a great city by the sea. He visited us often at our parents' farm, and he fell in love with our youngest sister, Loobal. They got married in the winter. She was expecting a child—" Marfal broke off. In all the chaos she had actually forgotten that Loobal was pregnant. A tear rolled down her cheek.

Halfene took over. "A storm hit Palador earlier this summer. Our mother and our next youngest sister were killed. We looked for Loobal and Morok but could not find them. The cabin they had been renting had collapsed."

Morok's family members looked at each other in shock.

Halfene continued: "But I had the strongest feeling that they escaped—by boat—down-river. In fact, I journeyed far along the bank—for many days—looking for signs of them. I found nothing and was forced to return to Palador. Our town

Chapter 22

was damaged beyond repair, and many people did not survive. We decided to leave—there were five of us—" she looked at Marfal, who looked at the floor, sadly. "Now, we are two."

"How awful!" Morok's mother gasped.

Marfal tried to hold back the flood of tears that was growing within her. "So, we cannot tell you of your son's fate. He may be yet alive. Our sister would have had the baby by now, I am sure. Your son was a fine man. You should be very proud of him."

"What about the boy? He brought a young boy to visit us once," said Morok's sister.

Halfene looked down. "Zev-ran. A sweet child he was. Unfortunately, his whole family died. They took good care of your son, that family."

"That saddens us greatly," the father said, wiping a tear from his eye. "Yes, we enjoyed Zev-ran's visit. He brought out a side of Morok that we had not seen before."

"And what a talker he was!" added the sister.

Marfal grinned.

The parents excused themselves to talk in the kitchen, leaving Morok's sister with the visitors. She asked them many questions about Morok's life in Palador and the nature of their journey to Gate-Town. Halfene, distracted from her sorrow by this new person, had many questions for her as well. Their conversation was quite congenial, and although the sisters could sense some differences between them, they did feel that they had found a new friend.

Morok's mother returned and offered the sisters the room that had been his, if they wished to stay. There was only one bed, but they could provide a mat to serve as another.

The sister, whose name was Perchant, led them outside to view the garden so that her mother could prepare the room. The flowers were beautiful. Some of them the sisters had never seen before. While they were outside, a couple from across the street beckoned to them. Perchant introduced Halfene and Marfal to her neighbors and briefly described the girls' connection to her brother. They seemed friendly and offered to help in any way they could.

By the time Perchant had finished touring the sisters around the house, Marfal and Halfene were ready to sleep. They thanked the gracious family many times and retired to their new room to unpack what was left of their life's belongings.

Halfene slept well that night. The feeling of being under a roof—a real roof of a real house—was wonderful. She still missed Dentino terribly, though, and clung to his shirt as she slept, the way a young child would cling to its favorite doll.

Marfal was feeling fragile. As relieved as she was to be welcomed into someone's home, it was not *her* home—not her home, not her town, not her people. She felt isolated. If it weren't for Halfene...but why think about that? Halfene was here, beside her. They had made it through this great trial together; whatever life brought upon them next, they would still have each other's assistance and friendship. It was this comforting thought that finally allowed Marfal to fall asleep. She dreamt of Peter, beautiful Peter. She was dancing to the music of his violin.

When Loobal and her group of followers arrived in the town, they were greeted by a throng of curious inhabitants. It was a fairly isolated place and few travelers ever made their way there. Loobal was relieved that the cart had finally stopped; the bumpy ride had been uncomfortable, though she was thankful she did not have to walk.

Morok gave her a big hug. "We made it!"

They followed the man, on foot, into town; he had

Chapter 22

wanted to leave his horse in a shady area.

Loobal was amazed at what she saw. There were pools and fountains, rockwork and gardens, surrounding the most beautiful little stone houses. Grass grew in abundance between these structures. It was peaceful there. Many of the women traveling with Loobal had spent their entire lives in Tanlar. Astnor, as well, had never traveled from the city, except to take a short excursion once, by boat, to a nearby island. All of them were overcome by the beauty of this place. It awoke in them a deep sense of awe at humanity's potential to create beauty and to live in perfect harmony. The people who met them that day were pure. One could see it just looking at them. The love in their hearts shone through their welcoming smiles; the peace within showed in their gentle movements. Their laughter rang with the song that is sung when one's needs are easily met. Loobal was captivated by their openness and keen interest to be of service to the newcomers.

A woman approached her and gazed deeply into her eyes. "Welcome to Akenrah. Come with me!" The woman took her by the hand. Loobal looked at Morok, who was following along behind. He gave her a huge grin and shrugged his shoulders. They were led to a lovely house not far into the village, and the woman told them it was there they could have the baby.

"It is kept for that purpose, you see," she said.

"We will help you, if you need it," said another woman, who had just appeared at the front door.

"Is there a place we can wash?" asked Morok. "We have traveled far."

With a gracious smile, the second woman bustled them in the front door and showed them all of the conveniences the birthing home had to offer. There was a fireplace, a kitchen, and two sleeping rooms—one for the expectant couple and the other for midwives and helpers. In the back of the house, adjacent to the midwives' quarters, was a room for bathing one's body as well as for washing clothes. The latrine was also a part of this area. Morok suggested that Loobal take her time washing and then lie down. Meanwhile, he could look for some food.

"That will not be necessary," the woman said happily. "Fathers need rest too—especially tired ones. I will prepare a meal for both of you."

They thanked the kind stranger and asked her name.

"I am Senelka. This house, and anyone who stays here, is in my care. Please, feel you are at home." She left them and disappeared into the kitchen.

"Why, Morok," exclaimed Loobal, "it is the place we were promised!" She looked at him, wide-eyed. "This place of love and beauty!" But Morok was silent.

"I think," he said finally, "that we are in a place of transition, a doorway to that place we were shown."

"How do you know?" she asked.

"It's just a feeling—but a strong one."

"All right, my dear. I wonder where Astnor and the others have gone?"

"I'm sure they have been well taken care of, Loobal. But hurry now, bathe yourself, that you may rest. That baby may well be eager to meet his family."

He gave her a quick kiss and closed the door behind her. His mind was running in two directions: although he very much wanted to get out and explore this new place, he thought that it would be wiser to lie down and rest, to save his strength. Wisdom won, and he lay down in their new room, on the most comfortable bed he had ever had. He fell asleep quickly and soon began to dream.

In his dream he was approached by an angel. This angel was one Morok had met many times before in dreams and visions. He recognized him by the colors he wore and by a rod that he was holding. "Come," the angel said. Morok

Chapter 22

followed him into a dense woods, where he was suddenly overcome with intense longing, a deep soul-felt desire to be with his Creator. They came to a small clearing among these trees, and here Morok saw what he could later only describe as the brightest light that he had ever seen. It hurt his eyes, that light, and made him alert to every bit of his own self that was, in contrast, dark. He fell to his knees, sobbing, wishing only that he, too, could shine that brightly. He felt sick. In the presence of that light everything else seemed tainted, imperfect, ugly. He cringed, wanting it to stop yet also wishing to be a part of it. It was a push and a pull, repulsion and attraction: a drawing of his own inner light toward it, while the darkness he held, as one suffering within the earth's lowly realms, was sifted out. "Agh!" he cried. He spoke to the Holy Light, calling to his beloved Father to heal him, to forgive him his earthly sins. And then he heard a voice. It was no earthly voice, to be heard with human ears, but the sound of life itself, a vibration of the highest love, sent forth from oneness to feed and nourish a tiny seed that had been planted in the field of its self. Morok received that nourishment; he soaked it in to the depths of his being. He began to grow, reaching out hungrily to the source of this goodness, the plant from which he had fallen, the ground he was germinating in, the air and the light—which were all as one. He continued to absorb, and feel nourished, and feel the vast potential within him awakening, answering a call that came from the place where he and his Creator were connected. His soul was burning.

The dream ended there, and he awoke, soaked in sweat. He sat up and blinked his eyes. What had happened to him? The dream was clear in his mind—he could recall every detail. His body was throbbing with pulses of energy. He felt vibrant and strong and dizzy. When Loobal entered the room she stopped, staring curiously at him.

"Why, Morok—" she gasped— "you're so colorful!" She

giggled, delighted by what she was perceiving with her inner eye. She sat down on the bed to listen to his explanation.

He repeated the dream, describing what he had seen and how he had felt. "Loobal, I was so close to Him—the power of His presence is awesome. I felt so fragile. And now, I feel strong; my faith in His power is deeply ingrained. Our future has its beginnings at God's doorstep. Let us proceed over the threshold and not look back."

"How, Morok?" Loobal asked, innocently.

"Rather than seeking God's love the way a child seeks love from a distant parent—by trying to please in exchange for the security of the parent's approval—we must seek it knowing that it is the true food of life everlasting and that it will be given to us—unconditionally—when we ask Him for it."

Loobal looked confused. He continued, searching for the words to explain something that he only understood as a deep knowing.

"Loobal, He loves us. Each one of us. His love is not the kind of love that is given one day and taken away the next, dependent upon whether we have been saintly or sinful. His love stays within us. It flows into our soul and lodges itself there, and it will remain there *forever*. His love is a part of Him, Loobal, and He gives it to us—to any one of His children who seeks it. It doesn't matter who we've been or what we've done; He is always waiting for us—each child—to ask for it."

"But why would we need to ask for it, Morok, if He is such a loving God?"

"Love is not something you can force on another. Some people, as strange as it may seem, do not wish to be loved. To desire God's love is to allow its inflowing. It is like saying, 'Yes, my Creator, bring me closer to You. I choose life, and peace, and goodwill to all!' Loobal, it is time for us to open up to God on a much deeper level—to walk through that door, knowing that what awaits us is a new life, lived in

Chapter 22

Him—in perfect harmony with His will. Loobal, I desire—passionately—to serve God. Not because I fear I will lose His love if I don't do His will, or that I will gain some reward if I do, but because I love our Heavenly Father so deeply! Am I making myself clear to you?"

"I understand, Morok, I really do." She looked at him with great love in her eyes. "I am happy, Morok. This has been such a trial. But I feel that it is over now—for us. I am ready to meet our son."

"So am I!" Morok beamed.

They heard a light knock at the door. Morok got up and let Senelka in with the meal she had prepared for them: fresh fruit and vegetables, cheese and bread.

Loobal's eyes widened. "Delicious!" she exclaimed. She thanked Senelka and immediately began to eat.

Senelka laughed. "You really were starving!"

"We were not prepared for the long journey that led us here. Yes, we are very hungry!"

Senelka turned to leave.

"Thank you, Senelka. I'm very grateful—for everything you have done for us."

"It brings me joy to serve." She closed the door behind her, and Morok and Loobal shared the most delightful meal they had eaten since their wedding.

～～

Astnor was brought, along with the others in the group, to a large building that served as a gathering place for the community. There they were greeted by the elders, who served together as leaders for the village.

After everyone was seated, a female elder got up and spoke: "Welcome! We are pleased that you have come. Not long ago, we received a vision of a child being born in our little village. There was no one pregnant here, so when we saw you arrive with such a person in your midst, we knew

Truth and Prophecy

this was the fulfilling of the prophecy. We are prepared to house all of you, for this was also shown to us: that our numbers would be increasing. We extend our warmest welcome to you, fellow children of our gracious Creator-God, and hope that you will be at peace here, as we are. Please, get to know us. Speak with us, and tell us of yourselves, of your journey."

They were seated in a circle, the inhabitants and newcomers together. Astnor looked at his companions and, seeing their encouragement, stood up and addressed the group. "We are from Tanlar, by the sea," he began. Seeing the blank look on the strangers' faces, he added, "It is a large city—a troubled city, experiencing dark times. There was treachery and the threat of war. We, here, were praying for peace but were guided to leave. It is well we did, for, soon after, there was a great tremor of the earth. We fear it destroyed much of the city. We mourn the loss of our homes and friends and family. But we have chosen to follow God. He led us here. Thank you for your warm welcome. It is a gift beyond imagination to be here, to be embraced in such a manner. And we shall be happy to contribute to your village in any way that we can. My name is Astnor. I am a tailor, by trade." He then indicated his fellow travelers, one at a time, saying each one's name to the villagers. The villagers did likewise.

After they mingled and chatted for a while, Astnor asked to be taken to see Morok and Loobal. A kind man offered to lead him to the birthing house. The man's name was Fazpen. He was born in Akenrah and had known no other life but this one of peace and harmony. He did not understand what Astnor had suggested about Tanlar and asked him to explain.

"My friend," Astnor said, "if you do not know of the sins of man, it is all the better. Live as God wishes us to live. Do not burden your heart with the fall of some of your

Chapter 22

brothers. Some day they will redeem themselves and know the grace that is your experience."

Fazpen smiled, shyly, and continued down the lane.

Senelka let them in; Fazpen, however, chose to wait outside the door and take Astnor to his lodging once he had spoken with his friends.

Loobal was asleep, but Morok was delighted to have Astnor's company. He longed to know more about the village and what had transpired with their remaining travel companions. They talked in the sitting area by the unlit fireplace to give Loobal peace. Astnor told Morok of the gathering he had just attended.

"They knew we were coming?" Morok asked.

"So they say. But I am no longer shocked by such prophecies. God has shown us the way here just as He has shown them of our coming. It makes life much easier, doesn't it?" he said with a laugh. "So what now, Morok? We are here. What do we do?"

Morok reflected on his question. "We rest, I think! And pray. And learn. I am sure these good people will have much to teach us. And I am going to learn how to be a father!"

Astnor clapped him on the back. "I can't wait to meet 'Little Morok'. I must be going now, my friend. I will come and visit again soon."

"Thank you, Astnor," said Morok.

Fazpen led Astnor on a tour of the village, since he did not feel the need to rush home.

Astnor was captivated by the intricate details of the stonework. "Were you not hit by the tremors?" he asked. "We felt more than one. I would have expected much of this—" he indicated the garden walls— "to have collapsed from that second one. It was exceptionally strong."

"A few days past, I recall feeling unsteady on my feet for a few moments. Perhaps that is what I was experiencing.

But no, there has been no damage here."

They met some children along the way, two older girls and a little boy. The children eyed Astnor curiously.

"Have you come to stay with us?" the boy asked.

"I have," replied Astnor. "Is this a nice village? Will I like it here?" he asked.

The girls giggled. The boy circled around them, singing a joyful tune, unaware of the need to answer Astnor's question. Astnor laughed, and they continued on their way.

"Here it is," Fazpen announced finally, "your new home." They stood at the entrance to a tiny bridge that spanned a quaint oval-shaped pool at the front of a tall house. "Upstairs in this house is a room for guests. I will introduce you to the family that lives here and then leave you to get acquainted with them."

Astnor nodded with a grateful smile, then they crossed the bridge to the front door. They were welcomed immediately by a man and his wife and their small daughter. Although it was hard for Astnor to have left Tanlar after all of his years there, he had the strongest feeling that his new life here would be the balm he needed to heal those wounds.

Morok had left Loobal briefly after conversing with Astnor, to do his own bathing and wash his only clothes, and when he returned to her she was awake and moaning softly. Morok joined her on the bed and held her hand.

"I think our baby is preparing his journey," said Loobal anxiously.

"Would you like me to call Senelka? I'm sure she will know what to do."

"Thank you, Morok—but don't be long, I don't wish to be alone."

Morok hopped off the bed and left the room, leaving the door open. He found Senelka in the kitchen.

"Could you help us, Senelka?" he asked. "I know nothing of babies. My wife thinks something is happening

Chapter 22

now."

Senelka gave him a reassuring smile. "I will fetch one of the midwives, and we will tend to your wife. Go, be with her. I will return soon."

Morok gave Loobal the news and rubbed her back for a while to help her relax. She breathed slowly, trying to calm herself and allow a relaxation of her belly, which had become very tense.

It was not long before Senelka returned with a midwife. This woman seemed very motherly, although surprisingly young, and Loobal was calmed by her presence. Senelka excused herself with the promise that she would return if needed.

Loobal allowed the young woman to check her over to see if the baby seemed in line for the descent. She was then encouraged to go for a short walk. Morok helped her up, and they walked carefully out of the house and along the path beside it, trying to distract themselves with the lovely sounds and scents of the warm evening.

Loobal was distressed. Something pressed upon her pelvis in an uncomfortable manner. She alerted the midwife, who was standing not far off, and the woman and Morok helped her to maneuver safely to the birthing room.

When she arrived there, there was an immediate outpouring of fluid from inside of her. She had not expected this and did not understand what had occurred. The midwife explained that the sack of water surrounding the baby had burst and that this would help her to birth the baby. She cleaned where the fluid had splashed onto the floor then fetched a dry skirt for Loobal to wear.

Loobal was experiencing intense pain. It upset Morok to see her so, yet he was aware that this signaled the impending birth. He held her and whispered encouraging words as she moaned and swayed, often changing her position from sitting to standing then sitting again. And then

Morok became aware of a presence in the room. The midwife paused in her work; she sensed it too.

"An angel!" exclaimed Morok.

"Angels," corrected the midwife. "These ones watch over birthing mothers and bless the babies."

Morok knelt down with his hands pressed against Loobal's bulging belly. "Oh, Father," he prayed, "I thank You with all of my heart for this precious baby. Please bless him mightily—and my dear wife—keep her in Your care as she releases this baby from her body. Help her to move through this passage with grace. We love you, dear Father."

Loobal was moaning loudly now and drew the attention of Senelka, who rushed into the room.

"Fetch me water," said the midwife, "and another blanket, please." Senelka left.

There was a pause as the moans stopped—for just a moment—and Loobal was able to focus herself once again. And then it began in full force. She felt urges that were deep and primal. She was compelled to scream. She pushed with all of her strength against the tissues inside of her that held the baby. Morok was lost in a swirl of emotion—his and hers and perhaps the baby's too. He wanted to cry and sing all at once. He felt Loobal's pain: she had reached her limit. Wordlessly, he gave her the strength to go beyond that limit, to exert the full force needed to bring their son into the world. Loobal pushed again, bearing down with furious passion. She gripped Morok tightly, clinging to him as if he were a lifeline. The midwife positioned herself where she could see the baby's head beginning to emerge. She said nothing, but allowed the drama to unfold, the beauty of the couple's music to play on, uninterrupted.

"My God!" yelled Loobal, "I need You!" Her cry was felt in the Heavens. It rang from her soul to His and was answered, in full, with a thunderous rush of energy that took over her body, her mind, her will. She succumbed to its

Chapter 22

forceful flow and felt at once outside of herself. In that moment she viewed herself—from outside of her body—giving birth to her son.

Morok felt the wave of love and power that had been invoked by his wife, and he held her trembling body as the midwife received the baby—the slippery, shiny, perfect tiny body with its trail of twisted cord following it. The baby's cry split the air; it was not a cry of fear or anger, but an announcement of his *being*. "I am!" it sang.

Loobal collapsed in Morok's arms and turned to face the one she had been waiting for. The midwife gently passed him into her arms, and as Morok steadied her trembling body, she brought that little soul close to her pounding heart, and every beat of her heart was an expression of love for her son. Morok began to cry the moment he laid eyes on that face: that sweet creature who gazed, blurry-eyed, at Loobal, seeing, for the first time, a human being. Loobal gently touched his head and spoke to him in a quiet, soothing voice. She smiled at him and planted a kiss upon his brow. Morok reached out to him, touching his tiny hand. "My son," he said, bursting with joy. The midwife then placed a blanket over the baby's back. She gently dried him, wiping away the traces of his mother's blood, and positioned the cord of life so that it would continue to feed him as his body adjusted to his new world.

Senelka tiptoed into the room with a clean blanket for the baby and a bucket of warm water to wash Loobal.

Loobal tried to nurse the baby, but he was not responsive to her prompts. He chose, instead, to nestle in against her breast and sleep. She rubbed his back, ever so softly, and sang to him as she had been sung to as a child. Her sweet lull-a-bye stilled the room, bringing an overlay of peace to what had been, so recently, chaos. When she was finished, the baby squirmed, searching for the gift she had presented him with before he slept. She guided his mouth to

Truth and Prophecy

her nipple and held him close while he drank the first offerings of her breast.

As the night wore on, Senelka and the midwife tended to Loobal. The proud father was given his son to hold, and as the cord of life was severed, he felt the responsibility of the baby's care shifting from Loobal's alone to a shared one. It felt right that it should be so. The baby had, as of yet, no name, but as Morok finally drifted off to sleep that night, a whisper of "Sol" graced his ear. He smiled and thought, *Yes.*

Loobal was up most of the night. She encouraged the baby to feed often. He slept frequently, and as he did so, she gazed upon him in the dim light, marveling at the perfection of his being and feeling a deep love of a kind she had never known. The midwife assured her that he was healthy and left to get some sleep herself, although she would be close by if needed. Senelka, too, had left the room, leaving the new family alone for their first night together.

It was near dawn when Senelka came in with a message from the elders. "They say we are to leave the village. One of them received a sign last night, and it is time for an old prophecy to be fulfilled."

"But we just got here!" exclaimed Loobal, alarmed. "And I am in no state to travel..."

Senelka looked deep into her eyes and said, calmly, "You may stay, Loobal. But this means you must travel on your own. There is a wave of change coming. In part, it is a change of thought. However, it brings with it a change of the land. You have experienced this, to some degree, already. I know you are afraid. The Lord has carried you this far, and He shall bear you yet further. Your child will be safe."

"What of the others?" asked Morok. "Our fellow travelers—will they be staying with us?"

"That is for them to decide. They have all been informed of the situation. It is comfortable here, I know. And you are all weary from your long journey. But time is short.

Chapter 22

The wave is approaching."

"Where are you going?" asked Loobal meekly.

"To a place our elders were shown, in a dream, long ago." She did not elaborate.

"Should we go there too?" asked Morok.

Senelka paused, searching for a way to tell them. "You must follow your own guidance," she said simply. "Your path may lead elsewhere."

Morok sighed. He looked at his son, who was peacefully asleep upon Loobal's chest. "Thank you, Senelka," he said, rather sadly. "I suppose it is time to pray."

"Your needs will be met," she said. "We will leave you with food and supplies. You may take whatever you like, once we have gone. We do not plan to return."

When she had left the room to begin packing, Morok held Loobal tightly. She was shaking with silent sobs. "We must have faith, Loobal. As she said, God has carried us this far."

Loobal laid her tired head on his shoulder. "Morok, I am not ready for this. And I'm frightened."

Morok looked down at his son, so tiny and new. He did not know what to say to her. How could he console her when he, himself, did not know how they would be able to travel, nor where they should go. He closed his eyes and said a silent prayer, thanking God for the baby and for getting them safely to this beautiful place. And then he beseeched God, to know His will for them, to guide them forward on this journey. His answer came in the form of a vision. He saw himself tending to Loobal and their son and preparing to travel. Then he was shown a building decorated with stars. In it was a collection of medicines. One was for the baby. He saw himself carrying the infant on his chest while Loobal walked beside him. He could not tell where they were going.

He gave Loobal the details of the vision and asked Senelka about the meaning of the stars. Senelka confirmed

Truth and Prophecy

that there was such a building in the village and that there he could find herbs of different sorts for healing. He would have to hurry, though, if he sought advice from an elder.

Loobal assured Morok that she would be fine while he was out, and he took his leave quickly, following Senelka's explicit directions to the elder's home.

Loobal decided to say a prayer of her own while the baby was still asleep. She asked for God's grace in all that she did. And then she remembered what Morok had told her of God's wonderful love, and she asked for this also—whatever God had to offer her, she would gladly receive it.

She was surprised by the feeling that followed her request. It was as if something she longed for had been returned to her. It gave her a feeling of satisfaction and wholeness; although, afterward she became aware that there was so much more of this yet to receive that she would never be truly full. The love felt, to her, like a flood of warmth and goodness—not unlike experiences she had had before in prayer, yet somehow more profound in its effects.

"May I have some of this love for my son as well?" she asked humbly. She knew immediately that her request was granted, and the baby opened his eyes. Holding him close, she prayed for his wellbeing and safety on their journey and asked God to guide every step. She felt at peace afterwards, with the faith of one who has tried God many times over.

When Morok returned, Astnor was with him. "Look who I found, Loobal!" he said happily.

Loobal shared her experience with Astnor, but he was more interested in meeting the baby.

"Would you like to hold him?" she asked. He looked at Morok, seeking his permission.

"Please," said Morok, smiling. "You are family."

Astnor tenderly reached over and lifted him from his mother's arms. The baby looked up at him and did not cry. "God speaks to us in many ways," said Astnor. "When I see a

Chapter 22

baby, such as this, I see the miracle of our kind. He is pure. We could only aspire to be as pure as this baby."

Morok smiled. "We were, once, were we not?" But Astnor did not reply. He only had eyes for the baby. Loobal excused herself to care for her wounds, and Morok and Astnor sat down on the floor to talk. Morok held the baby, tucking him into his shirt to keep him warm.

"We are leaving with the others," said Astnor. "I feel deeply that it is the right thing to do."

Morok was dismayed. "I was hoping you would stay. But in my vision you were not with us. I hope we will meet again, Astnor, you have been a good friend to us. I owe you much for keeping my wife safe while Gotsro had me in his keeping."

"Morok, I wish I were staying too. God knows I need a rest—and I prefer your company to those who are new to me—yet I feel it is God's will for me to accompany these people, and I trust in His plan."

"When do you leave, then?" asked Morok, his anxiety building.

"At sunset. They say we must travel by night, as it is cooler. I plan to spend the day resting. I have little to pack."

"Is this farewell, then?"

"I'm afraid it is, my friend. I will pray for you."

"And you also. But please don't leave before Loobal returns. She will wish to speak with you."

Loobal returned shortly thereafter, and with many tears she bid her friend good-bye. She knew she would not see him again.

Chapter 23

The Wave

Morning, the next day, brought an eerie silence to the village. The entire populace had left during the night—although it was well after sunset. The women of Tanlar had been by to see Loobal and to bless the baby, but now they were gone, and Loobal felt utterly abandoned. She cried in Morok's arms, lamenting the fact that she knew so little about the needs of babies. The midwife had given her instructions for his care—but only basic information, and nothing about how to handle an injury or infection. She was frightened. The baby sensed her unease and became fidgety. He cried and would not take her milk.

"This will not do!" cried Morok. "We must pull ourselves together, Loobal—for his sake. Let us pray—" He paused, to regain his composure— "Dear Father, we cry out to you in our fear and confusion. Please light our way! Fill our hearts with hope and our minds with peace. Show us what to do, that we may follow Your will. Help us to overcome the temptation to hide here, where we feel safe, when our future is unknown to us. Be with us, dear Father."

They held each other, with the baby snuggled in between, and hoped fervently for this heavenly help that they so desperately needed. And their cries were heard, and the healing was sent and received. The baby nuzzled at his mother, for milk, and she gladly met his need. Morok felt the

Chapter 23

presence of an angel, and he was then told to begin packing for their journey—that they would need to leave in two days. Loobal received a deep healing that not only brought her mind into a state of peace, but also stemmed the flow of blood from her empty womb. She was startled as the contractions briefly intensified, and then her womb began to grow smaller, back to its original size!

"Morok, it's a miracle!" she gasped. But Morok was unaware of her words; he was in deep communion with his Heavenly Father, receiving a blessing of love that flooded his soul. And when his consciousness returned to the room, he was a changed man. Gone were the feelings of apprehension and doubt, replaced with the sure knowing that God would be with them every step of the way and that their safety and wellbeing were assured. He looked at Loobal confidently and said, "I know the way now, and I know that our needs will be met."

Loobal shared with him her miracle. Morok beamed and felt his faith grow even stronger. He left her, to scour the building for items they would need on their journey, and then he would search the entire village, using the angels' guidance as a compass.

Loobal was content to spend the day with her little one. She gave him his first bath and nursed him frequently. He seemed content. She felt drawn to sing to him, and it was healing for her to express herself in this way. She felt a deep longing to be with her family—her sisters—and to share with them her greatest joy. For a brief time she felt that dark pull of despair. The memories—good and terrible—flooded into her mind, dampening her heart and causing an ache there. However, her son drew her back to a place of wonder and beauty, innocence and purity. He was the medicine she needed. She thought of Morok, and how truly blessed she was to be with him after the threat of separation. When she had left Tanlar with her prayer group, she believed she was leaving him behind. Her will to follow God had been stronger than her will to stay; the hope that she could find and save her husband, in the weakened state of her pregnancy, had been a small one.

Morok returned late afternoon. He had found many things that would aid them on their quest, including packaged foods, large flasks for carrying water, a blanket that could be formed into a shelter, and a walking stick that fit him perfectly.

Loobal was impressed. She had an urge to go out herself, to explore the village and look for useful items, but she did not wish to leave her son, even for an hour. Morok told her that there was not much to see, now that the people were gone. "They were the soul of this place. It is empty without them. Even the flowers are drooping."

Loobal satisfied her curiosity with a quick tour of the birthing house and its most proximal neighbors. She peeked in rooms and walked through gardens, selecting a few pieces of clothing and some produce that she wished to eat for supper.

Morok was happy to have these tender moments alone with his son while she was exploring. He loved to simply hold the baby and look at him. It calmed him and brought within him a state of peace. He whispered the name he had heard the previous night, to see if there would be a response. The boy continued to sleep, however, oblivious to his father's voice.

When Loobal returned from her foraging, Morok was asleep in bed with the baby. She giggled and decided not to wake him but instead went into the kitchen and prepared their evening meal. She prayed over it as she cooked, thanking God for the abundance of this day and asking that their needs continue to be provided for. She hummed to herself as she worked, feeling lighter and more secure than she had in many days.

Chapter 23

Morok eventually woke up and joined her. They supped together at sunset, watching the ever-changing colors of the sky as they sat on chairs on the bridge with their newborn baby wrapped in blankets in a basket beside them.

It was the calm before the storm; the last days of the way things were in the world. The change that was coming gave no warning but for a whisper on the night breeze that called, "I am here."

They felt the beginnings of it as they were falling asleep that night: a sensation of aliveness that pulsated in the air. *What is this?* wondered Loobal. Morok held his breath for a moment, trying to become so still that he could detect the subtle change. He felt it though; it had an effect on him. It was as though something was lifted from him—something he would not have missed; perhaps something he had never been aware of before, for it was a part of him. If he were a rock that had formed over eons, with layer upon layer of experiences as his outer shell; then this layer—now removed—would have been the densest one, the one formed of the most difficult experiences of his life, the darkest thoughts, the deviation of his will from God's will. Its leaving was not detrimental to him; no, he would not miss this. Unbeknownst to Morok, it had weighed upon him, drawing in doubts when his natural response would have been faith. The love that he now felt—in the room—was more easily able to penetrate his being, to sink in and take hold. He breathed it in, gulping for it like it was his last breath. The sensation intensified, lifting now a further layer from his deep past. *The sins of my forefathers,* he thought. Morok looked at his hands. They were tingling intensely. He had felt this before, on occasion, but it had never been this strong.

Loobal did not know what was happening, but she let herself be carried by the wave of change that was manifesting itself within and about them. Her faith was strong, and she called to God, saying, "Your will be done,

Father." The baby slept.

It was at this time that the third tremor had hit the valley where Peter and the three women were camped. What Morok and Loobal experienced as an upliftment and a healing was to them an experience of horror and chaos. Marfal did not feel blessed. Halfene did not feel uplifted, although she was happy to have escaped death. Peter, the lucky one, saw then what they could not. He saw a light on the other side, a light that expressed only one thing: love. He was swallowed up in it, bathed in its luxurious intensity. He was carried to the place of rest he had been told about when he was young—a place within the Realm of Light where healing occurs for those who need it before beginning their journey onward. He was there momentarily, or so it seemed, and then he felt a strong pull to come back, to be with his mate, who had not joined him. Her tears were, to him, a sobering reminder of the deep sadness of the earth, of its pitiful lack of those qualities that would ensure and maintain the happiness of its people. He reached out to Marfal with love, just as love had reached out to him, and he held her there, in that place, as she wept over his broken remains, below. He felt her love for him and knew, in that moment, that however short or long her years there would be, her love for him would endure. And he knew, without a doubt, that he would be waiting for that glorious day when she would join him.

Morok and Loobal were far removed from the drama that unfolded in Gate-Town in the days that followed. They were too absorbed with their own affairs to be sensitive to the cries of Loobal's sisters and Morok's family when the wave finally crashed upon their lives. It was as if they were in

Chapter 23

a world of their own, untouched by the devastating destruction of the godless mentality they had left behind. With their son bundled into a blanket on Morok's chest, they journeyed on foot to a land beyond the peaceful dwellings of Akenrah. Here was their destiny: a road leading up to a high ridge which overlooked a cool blue lake, fed by a mountain stream. There was a cabin there, built long ago by a man who had lived alone in the wilderness and had spent his days in peace and prayer.

"This is our home, Loobal," said Morok, as they approached the cabin at sunset after three days' journey. "We will be safe here until the wave has washed over this world."

"And then?" asked Loobal, disconcerted, for in her focus on the care of her baby she had not had the means to receive detailed guidance about their future.

"I do not know, Loobal. God has told me this only."

"I am so confused, Morok."

"I see it this way, my dear," he said softy. "There is a time for seeing and a time for living. Let us live our days here; years, perhaps. And when it is time to see, to understand, we will be shown. Be at peace here. We will be fine. I know it."

She smiled and held his hand as he led her through the doorway into the cozy cabin that was to be their safe haven in the coming storm.

The days were passed getting to know their son, establishing sources of food in the vicinity of the cabin, and praying. Now, more than ever, they felt a strong urge to commune with their Creator, to ask for help and blessings for everyone.

Loobal thought of her sisters often. Now that she was settled and had much time in her day for quiet reflection, she did make the attempt to connect with Halfene and Marfal. She beseeched God to watch over them—if they were, in fact, still living; and she also prayed for Serbrena, that she would find healing in her new life in the Realm of Light.

Morok was despondent. He knew something had happened to his family, and it was unsettling to him that he should be so far away and unable to help them. He told Loobal of his worries, and she suggested that they both attempt a connection with them, although she had, unfortunately, never met his parents or sister. He had told her much about them over the months of their marriage, and about Gate-Town too. She regretted never having gone there.

The two of them sat inside. The baby slept in his bed. Loobal closed her eyes and said a prayer, asking for God's blessing on their attempt to reach out to *all* of their family members and to understand what had befallen them.

First they called out to Serbrena. They felt her presence immediately, peaceful and light. They could see her in their mind's eye. She noticed the baby and went over to him, reaching a transparent hand so tenderly toward him. She turned to Loobal and smiled. Loobal thanked her for responding to their call and told her how much she missed her.

"You can talk to me any time, Loobal," they heard her say. "I am not so far away!"

They felt another presence in the room, and another. "Mama and Papa are here too," said Serbrena.

Loobal smiled through her tears as she began to perceive them in the room. "Isn't he beautiful, Mama?" She longed so deeply for her parents to share in the joy of her motherhood. "Your first grandchild!"

Bekren and Ansera beamed. They were radiant, like Serbrena. Loobal felt them hug her. It was not the same as receiving the hugs they had given her when in the flesh, but she felt their love for her, and that was a valuable gift.

Morok, too, was able to perceive them and communicate with them. He had much to say and many questions to ask. He asked for *their* help in locating his

Chapter 23

family—if they were among the dead.

The spirits seemed hesitant to answer that request. "We must leave you, Morok," Bekren told him. "It is not our place to share with you their fate." The couple sadly bid them good-bye.

"Remember," called Serbrena, "we are not so far away..."

The room felt empty when they had left. It took Morok a while to regain his focus. He was hesitant to call out to his parents, fearing the worst for them.

At first there was no response. He could not feel a connection with either of them. He turned to God for help. "Oh, loving Father, please grant me my deep desire to know of my parents' fate."

He emptied his mind of the thoughts and fears it harbored and went into a state of calm receptivity. Waiting patiently, he simply thought of his family with love and with gratitude for the love and care they had given him in raising him. Finally, he felt something. It was Perchant, his sister. He could hear her voice in his head. *Morok?* She sounded perturbed. He called her name, mentally, and focussed all of his attention on making that connection with her.

Perchant was alone when the strange feeling came over her. "Morok"—she said his name, wondering why she had suddenly thought of him. The thought persisted. It occurred to her that, perhaps, he was thinking of her too. *Where are you?!* she thought. She closed her eyes. An image flashed in her mind. It was Morok and his wife. There was a baby too. *Where!* she repeated. This time she saw, quite clearly, a ridge with a cabin at the top, overlooking a lake. She felt him ask the same of her: *Where?*

Gate-Town, she replied. *Your wife's sisters are here.* She hoped he could hear her. Halfene rounded the corner and almost bumped into her.

"Halfene!" she exclaimed. "My brother is talking to me—in my head!"

"He's alive?" she asked.

"Yes! I mean, I think so. Could he talk to me in this manner if he were dead?"

Halfene didn't answer. She closed her eyes. Her longing to know if Loobal was alive was so strong. She focussed her thoughts on her baby sister, sending all the intensity she could muster.

Loobal! she called, to that part of her sister that was more than mere flesh and bone.

Loobal felt it instantly. And she knew it was Halfene who was reaching out to her in this way. She focussed on her connection with her sister—the place where their hearts had danced together, all through the years of growing up—and she hung on tenaciously, allowing no other thoughts to pierce her consciousness. *Halfene, I'm alive and I love you. Where are you?* It was a moment before she felt a response.

Halfene was not accustomed to being in silence and found herself easily distracted, but she closed her eyes firmly and received a vague impression of Loobal's words. Loobal was asking where she was. She formed the words carefully in her mind, that there be no mistaking them: *Gate-Town.*

Loobal received her thought clearly. *Is Marfal alive?* was her next question.

Halfene struggled again to grasp what was coming through. She perceived an image of Marfal. Happily, she informed Loobal, *Marfal is here. Baby?* Halfene inquired.

Loobal sent her sister a message of love: *Yes!*

Halfene felt her joy and knew, without words, that the baby was okay. But Loobal's next question disturbed her. It awoke in her a feeling she had been desperately trying to suppress. *Dentino?*

"Agh!" Halfene yelled, aloud, and ran. The connection

Chapter 23

was broken. Perchant snapped out of her trance and ran after her.

"Wait!" She caught up to Halfene and put a hand upon her. Halfene turned to her, her face streaked with tears.

"What happened?" Perchant's eyes were wide with compassion.

Halfene shook her head. She did not want to talk about it.

"Come," Perchant said. She took Halfene's hand and guided her along the pathway where it opened up into a cluster of trees. There they sat, further away from the eyes of nearby townsfolk.

"Please," said Morok's sister, "let me help you."

Halfene could hardly speak, she was so overcome with emotion, but she did try. "I could feel Loobal. We were connected, however that is possible. I think she is okay, and she has had the baby."

"Then why are you so upset?" she inquired innocently.

"She asked me about Dentino!" Halfene wailed.

Perchant had not been told the whole story of who he was and what had befallen him. Halfene could see that she did not understand, and so, with a deep breath, she began her story, starting with their falling in love at choir practice. By the end of her tale, Perchant was sharing her tears.

"Halfene," she whispered, "it is good news for us all that my brother and your sister are alive. Let us hold on to that for now. Shall we tell my parents?"

"You go ahead. I would like to be alone."

Perchant hugged her and dashed back down the path, anxious to spread the news of her brother's survival.

Morok looked up, adjusting his focus to the contents of the room. "Loobal!" he said, and she opened her eyes. "I spoke with my sister. Marfal and Halfene are with her in

Gate-Town!"

"I know," Loobal said quietly. "I was able to connect with Halfene, and she confirmed they were there. But something is wrong, Morok. I asked her about Dentino, and I got the most uncomfortable feeling—and then she was gone. I couldn't feel her anymore."

"I fear the worst," Morok said solemnly. "He must have died."

He did, said a voice in the room, one they could hear only in their minds.

Who are you? Morok asked silently.

Dentino.

Their hearts opened; they reached out to him with love and with deep compassion. Morok could see that he was unsettled and asked him what had happened.

I was killed on the mountain. It happened so fast. There was a tremor, the ground shook, and I was pelted by rocks. Immediately I could sense that something was not right. I could feel no pain. I walked around and around looking for Halfene, and then she was there screaming instead of embracing me.

Loobal looked at Morok. She could not see Dentino's spirit but had heard him all the same. "Oh, poor Halfene! How she must have felt, seeing you there. Why, you were her life!"

I know... he replied. *And she won't hear me or talk to me. I wish to console her...but she cannot bear to think of me. I have followed her—for much of her journey—but it is hopeless. She is lost to me, and I to her.*

"Can we help you, Dentino? In some way?" asked Morok.

Go to her—please! Comfort her, and tell her I am with her!

"We can't," said Loobal. "I am sorry, Dentino, but we must remain here—until God tells us otherwise."

Chapter 23

Then is there no hope for her? he asked.

"We will pray for Halfene," Morok offered kindly. "God will help her."

"And for you, Dentino. I will pray that you find peace."

There IS peace for me, Loobal. I have all I need. My home is beautiful...but it's empty without her. I wait for her.

"You must move on, my friend," said Morok.

Loobal disagreed. "He loves her, Morok. How can you ask that? Dentino, God has made for you a new home, and if it is His will that Halfene joins you there someday, so shall it be. Let her live her life—however much of it she has left—and send her love from afar. But do not send your longing and your grief. Sometimes we must leave those we love, and in our absence, they may grow. She will regain her strength."

Dentino then left; for where, they did not know.

"Morok, I'm exhausted," Loobal said.

"Yes," he agreed, "That was a more trying experience than I expected. Let us rest. Loobal—I do think we should keep contact with our loved ones. We may be able to help them yet."

"Could you sense anything about your parents, Morok?"

"No. But I did not perceive, through Perchant's manner, that there was anything amiss."

Morok looked at Loobal, trying to decipher how he should reveal that which he knew to be true.

"My dear, I was given a revelation—last night, in a dream—and I hesitate to share it with you but feel that I should." He paused, seeking her approval to continue.

"I saw myself floating high above the ground. Below was the remains of, well, the earth. It was dim and shadowy, like the life force had been extracted from it, leaving only an empty vessel. No one was there. No plant, no animal either. It was desolate. And then I saw someone plant a seed: it grew instantly. Somehow it initiated the growth of a whole landscape of plants, vibrant and colorful. From these plants sprang forth animals of all kinds. And finally, the people appeared. The light returned and all was clear and alive. I felt joy, Loobal. Pure joy. But I was not there, among them. I was watching. What I saw was the unfolding of the great rebirth of the world that will happen after the wave of change has done its work. It will not happen overnight, not like it did in my dream—I know this; however, it will not be like the stages of growth, long and arduous, that led us to this day and age. It will be hard, at first, to adjust to the new life, but help will be provided. Those who cannot see the agents of God will have their eyes opened, and truth will be revealed. God is not going to let us fail this time; we will be given the tools, the guidance, and the inspiration to build anew what was ripped from our world by this necessary cleansing. He knows it will bring peace. We must trust, Loobal. No matter how bleak things look, we must remember this promise—the new world awaits us. Now I have seen also a vision of our own lives, but I feel uncertain as to what will actually come to pass. My sense is that there is a choice to make. Do we wish to stay and usher in this new world, knowing that we must pass through darkness to do so? Or do we move on to the Realm of Light, our true and eternal home?"

Loobal just stared at him. "Why, Morok, that is a heavy weight to bear at this moment. I would not be ready to make such a decision, knowing so little of what is to come. My dreams and visions have not all come to pass yet, and the ones that did happen were not exactly as foreseen. How can you say that this will be so?" Her brow was furrowed with concern.

"You're right, Loobal. I can't confirm what I have seen. Perhaps it is impossible to know the future with such certainty. And perhaps every choice we make informs the unfolding of our future."

"I would like to ask God, Morok."

Chapter 23

"Very well. And let us not forget to ask for a blessing of His love."

"How could I forget that?" she laughed.

Morok began, "Oh Father above, who guides us with a wisdom much beyond our simple understanding, please hear our call for clarity and truth. Show us the way forward during this time of change, and help us to know Your will, that we may follow it as desired. Grant us the great blessing of Your love; that, as Your children, we may grow to be more alike to You. Keep us within Your heavenly embrace, and shine Your light upon us always. Thank You, dear Father, for Your grace in our lives."

They bowed their heads and allowed the angelic presence that was filling the room to uplift their thoughts toward the highest Heavens, that they might truly come to be in the presence of their Holy Creator.

Loobal opened her soul and immediately felt an inrushing of the divine substance. It permeated her being and touched the deep well of grief and loss that existed inside of her. She cried openly; her tears spilled upon her dress in great, dark splashes. Morok was sensitive to her pain, yet the angels had carried him to a place where he could not respond to or console her.

Eventually the tears stopped and were replaced with the feeling that the well had run dry. Her sorrow was gone, lifted, and she knew peace. God was then able to meet her in that place beyond tears. He showed her a place within herself where she could go, anytime, to be with Him. He told her that she had a great purpose and that, if she would listen and try, always, to follow His will, she would indeed fulfill her role.

Loobal was afraid to ask what this purpose was, lest it be something that was beyond her strength to follow through, but God knew this, and He said, "Be not afraid, daughter, for I ask only what is possible, and I will always help you find strength when you falter. You are a leader of the people, Loobal. And you must have hope—not only for them, but for yourself. You have much work ahead of you, but you will be guided. I have sent many angels to be with you, and you may call upon them when you are unsure of the way. Have faith, my child. I am with you. Always."

"But who am I to lead? I am here alone with my husband and son."

God did not answer. The light grew brighter, around and within her. She was bathed in it. It filled her and it changed her, bringing into alignment all those parts of her that seemed, at times, estranged. She felt strengthened and new and was aware of the great potential within her that awaited to be awakened. As she returned to the room, not yet fully present but with open eyes, her awareness drifted to her son. How long had he been sleeping? Did he need to nurse? Was he warm enough? Her motherly urges took over and she went to him, now fully focussed and aware, and woke him up. She cradled him in her arms and stroked his soft hair, gently calling him by name: "Sol."

Morok quietly approached them and gave his son a kiss. "Loobal," he said, "you were right."

"Right about what?" she asked.

"The future. Our prophecies may not come to pass. Only our Father can know—He told me that."

"He told me that my purpose is to be a leader of the people. I have heard this before, Morok, but how can it be? There are no people to lead! I feel that we are all alone in this world."

"For now we are," Morok agreed. He stood up and walked to the door. "I will get wood for the fire. There is a chill in the air."

Loobal held out her hand to him, beckoning him back to her side. "Morok," she said sweetly, pulling him close to her, "I would like to ask you something."

"Yes, my dear?" he asked.

Chapter 23

"When you first met me, did you ever think we would be living in this way?"

"Why, no! I had no idea, at that time, that we would be married, and I certainly wouldn't have entertained the thought of living so far from Palador, with no neighbors or friends."

"It is funny," she mused, "how unpredictable our lives are. Do you think we will be here another year?"

"I doubt it!" he laughed. "But wait and see."

"Morok, wherever you are is home to me."

He looked deep into Loobal's green eyes. "Wherever God is, is home."

That night, as they sat together, enjoying the fire, with their baby asleep on Morok's lap, the wave made its approach. It struck the earth in full force, bringing everlasting change to what had been there. Inside the cabin, safe within God's loving arms, the young family slept in peace. And when they awoke, God whispered to them, "Your time has come. Go. Be with your people. I will show you the way."

The darkened sky had not served as much of a warning to those still dwelling in Tanlar after the devastating tremor. The storm was fast upon them, and the torrents of rain that flooded the streets were like tiny droplets compared to the swelling sea that soon breached the walls of the city, spilling over and bursting through the rocks like they were of no consequence. Those who could swim, swam. The others were lost in a sea of chaos and terror. Farentina, who had been in prayer at the time the first droplets of rain fell, was given a stern warning to leave her house and climb onto the roof of one of the tall buildings near her home. She did not hesitate to heed the message, and wearing naught but a nightshirt and her cloak, she did her best to scale the wall of the building and scramble up onto its roof, her wizened hands shakily grasping at the tiles as she slowly turned herself over to sit down. The chimney was the only thing up there that looked solid enough to grab on to, so she inched toward it and hung on for her life. When the waters crashed over the city her humble home was engulfed. She was spared.

Marfal felt unsettled when she went to bed that night. Halfene had already fallen asleep, and the rest of the house was quiet. She lay in bed with her eyes open, watching shadows on the wall, which were created by the moonlight filtering through the trees and into her window.

Peter's voice whispered softly in her ear. "Marfal." She heard him, as she often did. It was comforting to know that he visited her, that he had not forgotten their love. Tonight his tone, as she perceived it, was different.

"Marfal. Come with me."

She was puzzled. Had she really heard him asking her to go with him?

He repeated himself: "Come with me!"

But it was Peter, there was no doubt in her mind. She felt his presence, his loving embrace. Reluctantly, she got up from bed and left the room, walking through a hallway, as he encouraged her to with subtle thoughts and gestures. As she was opening the front door to leave the house, Halfene came up behind her, startling her.

"Where are you going?" whispered Halfene anxiously.

Marfal hesitated. "Peter has drawn me out here," she said awkwardly. "I don't know why."

They stepped outside so that their voices would not be heard by the family.

"Marfal, are you sure you aren't imagining this?"

"No, I am not sure."

Halfene looked up at the sky. What she saw terrified her. She could not move her lips to form the words to speak,

Chapter 23

but merely stared, frozen where she stood. Marfal looked up too and was equally astonished. They saw what looked like a fireball, far up in the night sky. They could not tell where it was headed, yet they knew it would cause immense damage, should it come their way.

"Let's wake the others," Marfal said quickly. She gave Halfene a little push—as her petrification persisted—and Halfene finally blinked her eyes and shut her gaping mouth. They ran indoors, clumsily knocking about in the dimly lit entrance, and shouted to Morok's family: "Wake up!"

It wasn't long before Perchant and her parents appeared, bleary-eyed and confused, wondering what was the matter. Halfene led them outside. Marfal was there waiting for them, pointing at the thing that had caused them alarm.

"What is it?" Perchant asked, squinting to focus her eyes.

"I don't like the look of it!" exclaimed Elbarlin, pulling his wife close to him.

"What shall we do?" she cried.

Nobody moved. In the silence Marfal felt Peter's touch once again. It was comforting. She listened.

"Go underground," he whispered. "Take all that you can with you."

She looked at Halfene. She could only see the whites of her eyes. "Halfene—Peter says to go underground."

"Where?" she asked. She turned to Morok's parents. "Is there anywhere in this town where we can get underground?" There was panic in her voice.

"The tower where the weapons are kept goes underground at its base," Elbarlin said. He looked startled. "It is locked. It is always locked. We have never yet had to use them."

"Where is the key?" asked Marfal.

"The man who tends the tower has it. He lives in the

254

house next to the tower."

As they looked up they could see that the object of their fear had grown brighter still and appeared—to them—larger.

Halfene was desperate. "Can you take us there? We have to go!"

"And we will need food and clothes and supplies," Marfal added.

Perchant pulled her into the house and lit a candle so that they could see.

"Surely we're not in danger?" she asked Marfal.

"I fear the worst," said Marfal. "That fireball is moving fast."

Halfene rushed past them and into the bedroom. She grabbed her pack and Dentino's shirt and then headed to the kitchen to see what food she could find. Perchant followed her with the candle and handed another one to her mother.

"Marfal, hurry!" called Halfene. Marfal quickly rounded the corner into the bedroom and picked up her dress and shoes and a warm blanket. She stuffed the clothes into her pack, added the blanket on top of it, and searched the house for flasks that she could fill from the well.

By this time more and more townspeople had woken up and gone outside. Perhaps it was the family's yelling that had awoken them; perhaps it was their own inner sense of impending doom that called them to action. There was a certain measure of chaos in that otherwise-orderly town. No one understood what was happening, nor what to do about the situation. They knew that this thing was out of place, unusual—that it didn't *belong*; yet they were powerless against it. It hurled toward the land, growing brighter and fiercer-looking. The shrapnel that was projected from the object created blasts of light all over the sky.

Marfal was beginning to panic. She pulled Halfene aside and said, "We *have* to get to the tower!"

Chapter 23

Halfene agreed and asked Elbarlin to show them the way. "Please come with us," she said to the other women.

They scurried about, gathering this and that in a frenzy, and then rushed back outside to check the sky. There was a brightness to the sky that had not been evident earlier: now they could see each other clearly. The thing was closer and seemed to be accelerating.

"Here!" called Elbarlin. He was pointing to the far side of town, where they could now see the tower, looming above the other buildings. As a group, they bustled through the streets, pausing, on occasion, to glance up at the sky. Those who were in the streets were shouting and running this way and that, unsure of which direction to go in. There was a roar in the sky, an ominous sound that brought everyone there from the state of thinking man to that of an animal, poised to use its instincts for survival.

As they approached the tower, Elbarlin called to the man with the key, who was standing in front of his house. "The key!" he yelled. "We need the key to the tower!"

The man seemed affronted by this request and questioned Elbarlin: "What could you possibly need from the weapons stores on this occasion?!"

Elbarlin's wife spoke up. "We want to be underground. There is nowhere else. It might be safest there."

The man then turned and ran inside, re-emerging moments later with the coveted keys dangling from his fingers. "I will go with you," he said.

Marfal looked at the keys in horror, remembering her dreams.

The keeper of the tower fumbled at the front door to the tower; the key hole was obscured by shadow. It was dark inside, and dusty. There was little room for them to pass in between the rows of shelving, where swords and chain mail lay piled. They followed him through the room to the far side, where a heavy wooden door blocked the entrance to the stairs. The man used a second key to open this door, again fumbling with the lock in the darkness. With a hard pull he heaved it open, and the group cautiously followed him down the stairs to the underground chamber. There he lit a torch, allowing them to acquaint themselves with this room that few people had ever set foot in.

"Now what?" Perchant asked Marfal and Halfene.

"I don't know," whispered Marfal. Her voice was shaky.

Once again she could hear Peter's soft voice in her ear: "Stay."

"I'm going to stay here," she said firmly.

Halfene sat down on the floor. The man with the keys was looking at her. "Where are you from?" he asked. "I have not seen you before. These people—" he gestured to the family— "I know."

"We—my sister and I—are from Tanlar."

He nodded, although he had never heard of the place.

Morok's mother, Monseta, was pacing the room nervously. They could faintly hear screams and shouts outside, but without windows, they could not see what was happening.

"I will go up and look," said the keeper of the tower. He clomped up the stairs and closed the door behind him. They could hear his footsteps on the wooden floorboards above; then he left the tower.

Perchant's nerves had gotten the better of her, and she clutched her father's arm for security. He was looking at the objects in the room, trying to distract his mind from the overwhelming terror that was brewing within him. There were papers and statues, boxes of trinkets; important items to the history of the town. He saw, on the wall, a tapestry depicting the founding family—people he had known only from the tales his grandmother had told him. He pointed this out to his daughter and was beginning to relay one of the old

Chapter 23

stories to her, when the keeper returned, accompanied by his daughter and his mother. They were wide-eyed and horror-struck, unable to speak.

"What is happening?" asked Marfal.

The man himself could barely speak. "It's coming."

The terror of what happened next could only be surpassed by the terror of its outcome. The fireball struck the earth as far away from Gate-Town as ten weeks' ride could take a person. It shattered the ground, blasting a gigantic hole into the landscape. From there a wave of destruction was initiated: death in all directions. By the time this wave hit Gate-Town it was much diminished from its original magnitude, yet its power was great indeed. Those in the streets of Gate-Town did not survive the thunderous onslaught of noise, wind, and upheaval of the land. They were thrown from where they stood, with their screams still idling in their throats. Most of them died immediately.

The tower collapsed. It toppled over, crushing the weapons it had so faithfully preserved for many years. Down below, in the underground chamber, life persisted. With most of the rubble thrown sideways, torn off by the force of the wave, those hiding below were not crushed, but rather suffered the fate of being covered in dust and soil and whatever else had been blown in through a great breach in the floor above. Coughing and sputtering, half-deaf from its roaring noise, the survivors floundered about, gasping for air and grasping for each other. Marfal could hardly see, for the torch had blown out and the sky above was a wall of black dust that no moon could shine through. Peter held her hand, although she was not aware of his presence.

The others slowly came to life, speaking at last in raspy voices through their coughing and retching. The keeper, who was most familiar with the layout of the building, found the stairs for them. The hole in the floor was close to the stairs, and he managed, one by one, to hoist them up through it into the open—and more breathable—air above. No one who had been downstairs was physically injured. It was truly miraculous, considering the force of the wave. Halfene collapsed on top of the rubble, exhausted and unwilling to face the reality of yet another unbelievable trauma. She reached out her hand and called to Marfal, seeking comfort and reassurance from the one who had always protected her when she was a child. And Marfal, following the sound of her sister's voice, crawled carefully over to her and curled up beside her.

Morok's family sat together, blinking in the darkness, trying desperately to see what had become of their life-long home. Dawn was hours away, and they could see no farther than their own noses.

The keeper of the tower stumbled about, yelling, "Hello! Is anybody alive?" His mother and daughter sat holding each other, shivering and crying. The anticipation of what would be seen when the light finally came was terrifying.

Dawn ushered in an era of ugliness that stained the land and dampened the spirits of those who were there to witness this drastic change. Marfal was the first to open her eyes. It was like a bad dream, what she saw, yet she knew she was awake. What had been a town—a thriving community, for decades—had been reduced to a barren wasteland over the course of one night. Bodies were strewn everywhere, human and animal alike. No building was left untouched, and there was no gate left in all of Gate-Town. There was nothing in that place that resembled a civilized domain.

Halfene rubbed her eyes and turned over. She had been in a deep sleep, undisturbed by dream or movement. "What?!" she said, as her eyes focussed on her surroundings. Her memory of the night before came back to her suddenly, and she drew in her breath. She scanned the area for Marfal. Her sister was not far away, though, and quickly joined her.

Chapter 23

"I can't believe this," Marfal said. "What has happened to our world?"

Halfene did not reply but continued to scan their surroundings, absorbing the details of the devastated area. It was quiet. The only sounds they heard were the rustling noises made by the other survivors as they awoke and moved around, trying to get their bearings in a place with no more landmarks. Every tree was uprooted; every rock, overturned. The distant mountains were still standing; however, they looked over the destruction around them with indifference.

Marfal stood up. She wanted to scream. What was left to live for? They had nothing, this group of three broken families. Nothing but each other. Marfal swallowed her rage, her frustration. Looking over, now, to the others, she felt compassion and kindness take over. She gave Halfene a hug. "I love you, little sister." Then she walked over to Morok's family, who had been so generous to take them into their home. She hugged each one of them. Finally, she walked over to the keeper of the tower—the tower that no longer was. She held out her hand to him, looked him in the eyes, and said, "Thank you, good man, for saving us!"

He looked at her with tears in his eyes. "You are so welcome." He introduced her to both of the women he had brought into the tower. His mother was named Hanta, and his daughter's name was Briska. Briska was only fourteen years old. Her mother, the keeper's wife, had died during childbirth. Marfal gave the women hugs as well.

"And what is your name?" she asked the keeper.

"Bertholemew."

He was a man of few words. He was not comfortable with the emotions that were trying to surface within him, so he left, promising that he would gather what he could find of their belongings in the underground chamber.

Marfal took Briska's hand. She was very frightened. "You're going to be all right," she said to the girl. "We will take care of you."

Hanta looked at Marfal, but there was not much hope in her eyes.

The air was still that day and hung heavy with dust and the scent of decay. The survivors did no work. They did not try to move the bodies or fix what was broken. It was all beyond repair. They simply sat and looked and thought. *What to do?*

"This is worse than Palador," said Halfene, with disgust. "We couldn't salvage Palador, and there is no point in hoping to rebuild this town."

Morok's parents looked at each other. "This is the only place we've ever lived," said his mother. "Where can we go?"

"I can't imagine there is much left of *any* town. We won't have anything to eat—here or anywhere!" said Elbarlin.

"Well, I brought some food with me last night," Perchant offered. "I'm sure Bertholemew will get it."

It was a while before Bertholemew resurfaced from the hole. He was scratched from the rocks he had been digging under, but he had managed to locate most of what Morok's family and the sisters had brought. "Here," he said, passing over the items. His own house, next door, was in pieces, scattered a ways from its original location. He and Briska dug through the boards, trying to salvage everything precious to them. His mother sat and watched. She would have nothing to do with it. To her, their old life was gone. She wanted no souvenirs.

Briska showed them a cooking pot she had uncovered. It was damaged but still useable. Her smile gave rise to a glimmer of hope in her stoic grandmother.

Nobody wanted to look at or acknowledge the ubiquitous bodies. It was too much to bear, especially for those who had lived in the town and who had shared their lives with these people. Nobody would admit it, but there were things that needed to be done, and getting rid of the

Chapter 23

bodies was one of them.

It took two days before any of them were ready to face the task. They had busied and distracted themselves for as long as they could by searching for food and lost items. Finally, it was Marfal who called the survivors together for what she deemed a "necessary discussion." Once the group had reunited, by the trunk of a fallen tree, she stood up and faced them.

"We had this very same problem in Palador not long ago. Those who survived were faced with the question of what to do with those who did not. We—or, rather, the men—put them into a mass grave. I must admit I did not help. My job was to help care for the wounded. Here we have no wounded, but countless dead. We must care for them as they would have cared for us, with a proper disposal of their bodies and a prayer to guide them onward, into the Realm of Light." She felt Peter nudge her.

"They do not pray, here," she heard him say.

She looked at Monseta and Elbarlin, who were staring at her with concern.

"We do not have this ritual here," Perchant said.

"But how do they know where to go?" Halfene asked.

The keeper answered. "We believe that God does with them as He wishes. The ones who did as they were told and worked hard go into the Light. Those who misbehaved or challenged Him will have that opportunity taken from them."

"They stay with their bodies," Elbarlin added.

Halfene looked at Marfal. Marfal's mouth hung open. She did not know what to say.

It was Briska who broke the silence. "I think they all get to go," she offered sincerely. "Even the disobedient ones. I'm sure God would let them have another chance. I think God is really nice."

"I think so too," Marfal said kindly. "So where shall we dig this hole?"

"As far away from here as possible," grumbled the keeper.

Marfal rolled her eyes. "And who would carry the bodies that far?"

The task seemed overwhelming, and no solution was forthcoming.

"Perhaps we should just leave this town. Leave them where they lie, just as we left Dentino!" Halfene shouted at Marfal. The discussion was bringing up her most painful memory.

Briska started to cry. Her grandmother put her arms around her, trying to shield her, somehow, from their harsh reality. They decided to take a walk and leave the discussion to the others.

"We can't leave here, Halfene; where should we go?" asked Marfal. "What do you think lies beyond this town—in any direction? There are no towns left. That we can be sure of."

Halfene was adamant that they not stay. "I cannot live here!" she screamed. "We are surrounded by death!"

"That is why we need to bury the bodies," said Marfal. "It is the only way. And then we can move on; salvage what is salvageable; rebuild."

"Rebuild our broken lives? So we can grow old and die?" Halfene was furious.

Marfal felt her sister's frustration. It did seem futile—and lonely. She reached out a hand to her sister, but Halfene rejected her gesture. "Don't touch me!"

Marfal could feel Peter's warmth around her. He was trying to console her, trying to let her know that *he* was still with her. "Let her go," he advised her. Peter was right. Halfene needed to work this out for herself. There was nothing Marfal could do to ease her sister's deep pain.

Elbarlin spoke up. "Perhaps we should all give this some thought and meet again later."

Chapter 23

"All right," said Marfal, resigned. She looked around her, at the wreckage and at the poor victims of this greatest of tragedies. Compassion swelled in her. *I must do something,* she thought. She knelt down next to the body of a young man. *I wonder what his name was?*

"It is Bentur," Peter whispered. "He is with me."

The news alarmed Marfal. *Really?* she thought.

"They are all here, Marfal. Lost, confused, grieving. You can help them—*we* can help them," he added.

"What shall we do for them, Peter?"

"Show them the way to the Realm of Light."

Marfal began to cry.

The guilt was overwhelming her. "I don't know how!"

"You must talk to God, Marfal. He will hear you."

She sat down and closed her eyes. The tears continued to fall. "Dear God...are you there? I must ask for your help! All these people here are lost and I don't know how to show them the way home. Can you come and get them? Please?"

She hung her head. Peter's voice called to her again: "Marfal—it's working. There are angels here."

"I can't see anything."

"You can't because you are not in spirit; but I can."

She felt a chill. "What was that?" she asked Peter.

"Someone brushed past you. They are all leaving now."

After a few minutes, Marfal sighed. She felt lighter.

"They are gone," said Peter. "Bury the bodies if you can."

The night seemed to last forever. Autumn's chill had arrived, and they huddled for warmth around a fire the keeper had made from some of the remains of the broken homes. They slept little. Thoughts of the dead inspired nightmares, and those who fell asleep would jolt awake—remembering, in that moment, that their reality was no less horrifying than the dream.

The Wave

Marfal could not shake the thought that there was some reason she had to live; that she should not give up her hope, her will, so easily. Peter was nearly always with her; his companionship gave her strength, despite the fact that she could only hear him whisper and feel his touch—she did not see him.

Halfene was a wreck. She had become desperately depressed. Marfal kept watch over her, determined to prevent further harm; but emotionally, Halfene had distanced herself. She would not talk, nor would she listen.

In the morning they all sat around the fire—reduced now to embers—and began a conversation about their future. The survivors were a little more relaxed with each other now—except for Halfene, who had shut down—and were opening up about their feelings.

"I'm scared," said Perchant. "Winter is coming and we have nothing to harvest and no shelter." Her mother held her hand. She made a valid point.

"The wells are still functioning," mentioned the keeper, "and we could live in the base of the tower if we cleaned out the rubble and made the ceiling into a roof."

Although it was a sensible suggestion, no one relished the thought of spending more time in that suffocating hole in the ground.

There was silence for a moment and then Marfal, frowning, suggested that maybe they *should* leave Gate-Town and start a new life elsewhere.

"But you said all the towns would have been destroyed!" exclaimed Halfene.

"Towns, yes...but maybe not the land. The thing that caused this—this mess, would have hit the earth somewhere. And the farther we travel *away* from that somewhere, the less the damage should be."

They looked around, trying to make sense of the direction. The trees all pointed east.

Chapter 23

"So it looks like it came from the west." Elbarlin was standing up now, gesturing. "If we head east, following the wave, we should eventually reach a better place."

The heads nodded. They were processing this new idea.

"Who is willing to go?" he asked.

The response was unanimous. No one wanted to spend their life drowning in tragic memories.

"When shall we leave?"

"Let us spend today preparing for the journey," suggested Monseta. She added, quietly, "I need to say good-bye."

"Very well," said the keeper. "We leave at dawn."

It was more difficult than they expected, to prepare for their new life, their adventure into the unknown. Not everything that they sought—or required—to bring was accessible. There was little food that they would consider edible, since it had been tainted by the fallout from the blast.

The weather was turning ugly. Harsh winds started up late in the afternoon, and rain came with nightfall. They cowered under the floor of the tower—in the room no one wanted to go into—to stay dry. What a shock it was to them when, in the morning, the dawn of their departure, they awoke to a forceful thunderstorm and rains that began to cause rivers in what had been streets. The water leaked into the underground chamber, dripping upon them and soaking their feet. It was a cold rain, and they got chilled, along with being hungry. Everything was conspiring against them, it seemed. Halfene was half-mad. She could not speak coherently and picked compulsively at her clothes, twisting the cloth into knots with her fingers. Even Marfal, who was of a more steady nature, had her misgivings about their plan, and she found herself on the verge of tears frequently.

They were afraid. If they stayed, it would be rotting corpses facing them each day. But leaving was a huge leap into the unknown. What awaited them to the east? They were at a standstill. Frozen.

Marfal spoke, summoning her courage. "It looks dire. We cannot just stand here, drowning in this hole! Let us go. As we are. With what we can carry. And if a worse fate awaits us..." She did not finish. The survivors looked at each other. They gathered those items they had collected for the journey, covered their heads from the rain, and climbed out of the chamber for the last time.

Chapter 24

The Paths Converge

Morok awoke with a start. In his dream he had been standing on a precipice. Down below he saw the town of his birth, and in it, his family home. The color was gone from it. It was silent and empty; lifeless. *Where is my family?* he wondered. He scanned the countryside, looking for them. He wandered through the town but could not find his house. Everything was disheveled, out of place. For an orderly town, this did not seem right. He left the town and wandered west. Mountains. He circled back to the south and hung back briefly, inspecting the scenery. Devastation. Annihilation. *Where was everyone?* He called to his mother. "There," she said, pointing to a large depression in the ground. He walked over to it. A man stood up and said, "I have your family." The next scene was confusing. He led a group of people, including his family, to a house on a hill. The hill sprung up from a field of green grass, and flowers grew abundantly upon it. Inside the house were two angels. They counted the people and welcomed them into the home, saying that the door to a new realm was open now. "Please come in," they bade them.

It made no sense to Morok, but he told Loobal of it anyway, and she suggested that perhaps they should go looking for his parents.

"And your sisters," he added.

"Do you think they are in Gate-Town?" she asked.

"Perhaps they are. But we must ask God for direction

Chapter 24

now. As much as I yearn to see my family again—and yours—I will only do so if God wills it."

They decided to pray immediately, to settle this question and to ascertain their future direction.

"Dear Father, we come to You in this time of doubt, seeking guidance and direction in our lives. We ask that You bless our families, and keep them in Your care. Where shall we go, Father? And what shall we do? We desire, as always, to follow Your will."

The two of them heard the words simultaneously. It was simple: "Go to Gate-Town. I have a great task ahead for you."

"How do we get to Gate-Town?" Loobal asked silently. "I don't even know where we are!" She felt peaceful, though, and soon had the sense that the path would be shown to them.

Morok was shown a vision of himself leading a group of people toward a mansion on a hill—it was the same as in his dream. He told this to Loobal, and she agreed that this must be their path indeed.

"Was I in the group?" she asked him.

"Yes. And our son, too, of course."

"Then let us prepare for our journey!" She was excited that they had a new mission, a purpose. And the promise of seeing her sisters again—if they were actually part of the group—was compelling.

They packed what they could carry and set off soon after. There was no sadness at having to leave the cabin. They had known it would be a temporary residence, and they had not become attached to it.

The baby seemed at peace, and he was content to be carried on Morok's chest, as before.

The family was guided to head, first, back in the direction of Akenrah. The landscape was different from that which they remembered from their recent journey, and the farther from their cabin they wandered, the worse it became.

The Paths Converge

It was desolate, unwelcoming; disturbing, even. Loobal did not feel comfortable in that landscape and was thankful when they were guided to change course, heading now south. But their worries were not allayed by this new direction. The darkness was pervasive, and no living things did they encounter: no plants and no animals. Loobal was clearly shaken.

"What happened here?!" she wondered, aloud. "I felt *nothing* at the cabin—yet only something immense in power could have done this. Why, there is nothing left!"

"The wave," stated Morok, staring at the bleak remains of a beautiful world. He looked at Loobal. "And He kept us safe from this!" he cried, incredulous. "We felt nothing but His love! Oh, thank You, Father!"

Loobal finally let go of her tense hold of herself and smiled, overwhelmed with joy at the realization of this truth—that God had saved them. From then on they walked their path with confidence and faith. No longer were they afraid of what lay ahead. God was with them. And wherever they went, He would be.

By the time the storm ended the group of survivors from Gate-Town were far from its sad remains. They were cold, hungry, and tired; wet from the relentless rain; and confused. They could not tell where they were going; they just kept moving in what seemed like an easterly direction. And to their surprise—for they had expected differently—the land was just as desolate and disrupted as it was in their home.

"But surely it will get better if we go yet farther," reasoned Marfal, when one of the others criticized her suggestion to come this way.

"What other choice do we have?" asked Briska, who was the most optimistic of the group, next to Marfal.

Chapter 24

Marfal's optimism derived from Peter's. He never seemed discouraged, only loving, and she felt that, from his vantage point—as a spirit—he must be able to see and understand things that she could not. She trusted him completely.

They rested briefly, for there was not much to do while resting except think about their discomfort, and then they began again their slow, but determined, walk to what they hoped was a better place.

Near sunset the clouds broke apart, revealing the sky. It was orange, and added much-needed color to their lifeless world. It shone on their faces, illuminating the once-joyful expressions that now indicated despair and hardship.

As night settled upon them, they lay down their wet packs, gathered as much wood as they could carry from the broken forest around them, and built a huge fire, one that would warm them through the long night.

Halfene slept fitfully and dreamt that she was stranded on a ship at sea. The waves tossed her from bow to stern—she slid every which way upon the slippery deck. No one was there but she alone. The wind picked up and tore at the sails. She could barely keep a grip on the rails, and the threat of being tossed overboard kept her knuckles white with a desperate desire to survive. She held on for but a moment, and with the next great surge she was pulled under water. She felt her will fading. Who could overcome such a powerful force? She began to drift downward, down deep. A voice whispered to her, "Halfene, wake up." She continued to sink. "Halfene, you are asleep. Wake up!" She struggled to let go of the dream, to respond to the voice that called to her.

He called again: "Halfene!" He was shaking her arm.

"Dentino?" she murmured, her eyelids half open. In that drowsy state of semi-consciousness she could see him at her side, his eyes full of love, his expression joyful at her recognition of his presence.

"I'm here, Halfene, and I love you."

The Paths Converge

She felt him touch her cheek—ever so gently.

"Halfene, I want to speak with you." His voice was insistent, desperate.

She mumbled an affirmation and tried to focus her attention and fully leave the sleep state.

"Why haven't you acknowledged me?" he asked.

She closed her eyes again, backing away from his question.

"I am here with you often. I see everything you do, and I know your thoughts. Did you know I can hear your thoughts?"

She opened one eye. She could see him looking at her with that charming expression she used to love.

"I know you miss me. I also know that you are suffering terribly."

She closed her eye, trying to barricade off an avalanche of tears. She felt him place his hand upon her heart, slowing its rapid beating. It felt good, and she allowed his love to sink in, to penetrate the wall she had built there.

"I'm going to help you get out of this mess—if you will let me."

She merely nodded, for no words could escape her lips.

"You must follow me, for I know of a safe place where all of you can go. Peter is with me. He has been a great help to me—a great friend."

"Where do we go?" she finally asked.

"You must continue east for a little while, and then you will see what I mean. Be strong, Halfene."

She took a deep breath and opened her eyes fully. He was gone. She looked from side to side, up and down, but could not catch sight of him. Immediately she jumped up and went over to where Marfal lay, curled up in a ball.

She gave her sister a gentle shake and whispered, "Marfal! Wake up!"

When Marfal was sufficiently conscious to recognize

Chapter 24

her sister, Halfene asked her to come for a walk, explaining that she had something important to tell her. Marfal was impressed by Halfene's clarity and attentiveness and did as she asked. They ventured forward a ways to a sufficiently sheltered spot that afforded them some privacy.

"He was here!" Halfene said excitedly. "Dentino!"

"You could see him?"

"Yes—and I heard him also."

"What did he say?" Marfal asked.

"Well, that we should follow him—and Peter—because they know of a safe place for us to go."

Marfal gave Halfene a big hug and beamed at her. "I'm so happy that you finally reconnected with him. Do you feel better now?"

"Well, somewhat, I suppose," she admitted. "But it isn't the same. I miss his body, his touch. I want him here like he was before. We never had enough time together. It was too short, too sudden. And I don't think I'm ready to accept that we can't have that—ever."

"I know, Halfene. I know exactly how you feel."

Halfene looked up at Marfal. How selfish she had been, to have forgotten that Marfal's loss was just as great as hers.

"We were going to be married," said Marfal, with a sad smile.

Halfene took her hand. There was nothing to say. They walked back to the others, who were slowly getting up and organizing themselves to carry on with their dreary journey. But Halfene's demeanor had changed drastically, and the others noticed. No longer was she fretful and aloof; the Halfene they saw now was grounded and determined.

"Let us go east!" she declared with confidence. And soon enough, with no reason to stay there, the group fell into line behind the sisters. The sun had risen into a clear sky, and it looked like today would provide some hope and, maybe, some answers.

The Paths Converge

Morok and Loobal were well on their way to Gate-Town before the group had begun their exodus, and by the time Halfene received the guidance to continue east, the couple was already surveying the wreckage of Morok's birth place.

Although they were shocked—to a degree—by the scene in front of them, it was not unexpected. Morok shuddered when he saw the bodies. The storm had not left them in a state where they could be recognized as people who he had known and with whom he had spent most of his life.

Loobal averted her eyes and covered her nose and the baby's. The stench was overwhelmingly foul. "Let us leave here, Morok," she begged. "Surely there is no one left alive in this place."

"I know," he replied. "But give me a moment, my dear. I must make peace in my soul with what has happened here. Many of these people I took for granted. I was uncooperative and unappreciative. And now they are gone. I would have loved to have spoken with them...made right those wrongs of old. I have changed so much since I first left here those few years ago. If only I could share with them what I learned."

"Say your good-byes then, Morok," she said softly. "I pray that they have been carried safely to that eternal place of rest and redemption that our Father provides for mankind."

"I believe they are there already. I feel no presence here."

Morok was puzzled. Where were his parents? His sister? He thought he would find them here—alive. He remembered his dream. In it, there had been a man who said he had Morok's family. Morok looked around for a hole such as he had seen in the dream. It wasn't long before he came

Chapter 24

across the ruins of the tower. He felt drawn to go over there. Indeed, there was a hole in the ground and some signs that people had been there recently—alive.

"Look at this!" he called to Loobal. She rushed over, following the direction of his pointed finger. "Someone had a fire here!" Near the fallen tower he had found the washed-out remains of a campfire—wet ash and soggy burned ends of boards.

"Where did they go?" Loobal wondered.

Morok closed his eyes. He focussed his attention on his family members...feeling his concern for them reaching out into the world. He could sense them slightly...but could not grasp their thoughts.

"Oh God, please lead us to our beloved family," he prayed.

He felt a gentle nudge, a soft internal push, to head east. He took Loobal by the hand, faced the ruins of his home town one last time, and said good-bye. He asked God to bless those who had gone before him and expressed his gratitude for all he had been given and all he had learned from them. And then he quickly led his wife and son away.

It was not long before they reached the site at which the group from Gate-Town had camped, for the storm had slowed the progress of those people, while the young couple travelled swiftly and with ease, in better weather, fueled by the love of God and the desire to do His will. They stopped to rest there and to feed the baby. Then they were on the move again.

※

Halfene was becoming more perceptive and open to Dentino's presence and to his gentle coaxing. She felt drawn to him, as she had been when he was alive. The attraction persisted. She shared this with Marfal and asked her opinion. "Is it wrong to love so deeply one who has gone on? I ask

The Paths Converge

because he comforts me by being here, but I don't want to impose on his time so much that he will get bored with following me around and want to go away."

Marfal was amused by her sister's thought process and had to stifle a giggle. "Halfene, really!" she sighed.

But Halfene would not be put off. "I want to know what you think, Marfal. This means a lot to me. I love him...but I don't like the thought of him feeling bound to me."

"Oh, I see what you mean," said Marfal. "No, I don't think he would feel that way. He loves you too, and he obviously wants to help you—help us," she added.

"I know. But when he is done helping, will he go away?"

"I cannot say, Halfene. Be thankful that you have this opportunity to feel his presence, his love...and when he goes, wish him well. Let him leave with no guilt or regret. You will always be connected through your love. I am sure of that."

"Thank you, Marfal." They continued walking in silence, each one lost in her own thoughts. Peter was with Marfal, giving her his love and encouragement, as always. And Dentino was with Halfene, making up for lost time.

How it was that the two parties—the refugees from Gate-Town and the young family in God's service—should cross paths that day was a mystery to both parties. The intricate details and plans required to intersect the two groups at a precise location at a precise time were beyond anyone's comprehension. But it happened, just as God willed it. A deviation to the south for Halfene's group to circumnavigate a rough area and an acceleration of Morok and Loobal's pace along their God-guided course led to an abrupt meeting in a grove of damaged trees near a quiet, empty lake.

The shrieks and cries of recognition from both parties filled the barren landscape and began one of the most joyful reunions any of them had ever experienced. Halfene dropped

Chapter 24

to her knees at the sight of Loobal, who looked like a radiant angel with a baby in her arms. Morok, too, beamed brightly. It was Perchant who ran to him first and threw her arms around his neck.

"Oh, my brother! You found us!" She sighed with great relief, and their parents crowded close to take in the sight of him, to prove to themselves that he had, in fact, returned to them.

Loobal reached out to her sisters, passing her son to Marfal immediately. Marfal eagerly took the newborn into her arms and wept as he looked up at her, his face shining with an innocence and grace that was so out of place in the ravaged land.

"What is his name?" she asked Loobal.

"Sol," she replied.

"He's perfect! Here, Halfene, you take him." Marfal tenderly passed him to Halfene, who had never held a baby before. She looked almost fearful of the task, and Loobal laughed. How wonderful it was to hear that laugh again, to see her little sister again, and now to hold her son. She smiled at the baby, looking into his beautiful blue eyes. He seemed to stare right into her soul. Halfene was mesmerized. Her longing to be anywhere else, for her life to be anything other than what it was, fell away. It was a moment, but it seemed timeless. She looked up at Morok. There he stood, his family at his side, looking so much more a man than when she and her sisters had first encountered him by the river in Palador. He was sure of himself now. And he had brought Loobal—and their precious baby—safely back to her family. Halfene smiled at him, feeling immense gratitude for this gift. *I am an aunt,* she thought, with pure joy.

After Morok had introduced his wife to his mother, father, and sister, they were keen to see the baby. Halfene reluctantly handed Sol over to Perchant, who cradled him and cooed as he burbled back at her.

Throughout these loving interchanges, the keeper and

The Paths Converge

his mother and Briska hung back and spoke amongst themselves. They were eager to speak with Morok, as he was known to them, but respectfully waited their turn, vicariously enjoying the happy reunions.

Eventually, Loobal noticed their presence and introduced herself. She was interested in hearing the story of their last days in Gate-Town. Since she was not the only one who wanted to share stories, everyone agreed to make camp and spend some leisure time together before making a decision about their future course. The sky remained clear that night, and the group of survivors, now eleven strong, gathered around a crackling fire. Morok had a long story to tell, for the last his family in Gate-Town had seen of him was before he had married Loobal—and the sisters had not seen him since before Palador's fall. The news of Gotsro and their birth city of Tanlar was a shock; however, they had never liked it there—compared to Palador—and they were glad he and Loobal had safely escaped from it.

The stories went on until well after midnight. Each one told his tale, adding a new perspective to the picture of what had occurred in the world those last months. They all shed tears of pain and regret mixed with those of joyful awakening. They opened themselves on many levels as they listened to each other—and especially to Morok and Loobal. How was it that the couple had come out of all of their trials unscathed? They were glowing with happiness despite their material destitution. It comforted the others to see them thus, to know that it was possible to survive these times and to be confident that the future looked bright. Briska, especially, took on their hopeful outlook. As they fell asleep that night, warmed by the glowing fire, reassured by the comforting presence of their kin, the survivors were attuned to the holy presence of angels in their midst, blessing and healing them. It was heavenly.

The morning brought a new beginning for each of them. During the night they had each received a vision, or

Chapter 24

dream, in which they were shown the future of their world. Some saw the regrowth of the forests and edible plants. Others were shown the remolding of the landscape that would occur over time. Halfene saw that the veil between those in the flesh and those in spirit would be thinned. Marfal saw herself caring for many children as the world repopulated itself. And Loobal was given another vision that reinforced the prophecy that she would be a leader of the people.

Morok was told, by God, of the plan God had for him, a special mission. "You are to lead these people to My house," He said. "There they will be safe while the world heals itself."

Morok stood up then and looked around him. All about, the landscape had begun to change. Where they lay, grass grew up around and between them. He saw a path, lined with flowers, that led through a grove of trees. The trees were upright and undamaged. He blinked. Could this be real? Or was it a mere vision of what was to come?

He woke the others. They saw it too. *How can this be?* they thought. They looked at Morok. He smiled, sincere and bright. "I will lead you to where God wishes us to be. The way is before us." He indicated the beautiful path.

Marveling at this unexpected start to their day, they stood up and stretched. They found that they were much less stiff and tired than they had been the previous morning. Smiles were exchanged in abundance.

"Shall we?" Morok asked his wife. She passed the baby to him, linked arms with his other arm, and strode forward into the light of a brilliant new day on the rebirthing world.

The group moved forth slowly, seemingly in no rush to reach their destination. For here were beautiful things—living, vibrant things—for which their hearts ached to look at and touch, to smell and taste. There were fruits in these trees and fragrant flowers grew nearby. They hungered, and they were

The Paths Converge

fed. God had provided bountifully. Loobal and Morok prayed as they walked, delivering a constant flow of gratitude and love through their words to their Creator. The others followed, finally realizing the truth of the couple's devotion and the fruits that such reverence and obedience had brought to them. When the path opened up from trees into a meadow, a stunning sight met their eyes: there, perched on a hill, was a large dwelling. It was unlike anything they had seen: not in Tanlar, or Gate-Town, or fair Palador. Trellises flowing with greenery and bright flowers adorned its alabaster walls. The roof shone golden in the sunlight. Its grounds were dotted with small ponds and fountains, trees of gold, and decorative hedges. The scents of large blossoms wafted down the hill to the eager noses of Morok's followers. Ethereal music emanated from the mansion, calming and rejuvenating all who were attuned to it.

Loobal took a deep breath. She closed her eyes and allowed the strain and worry underlying those last months of homelessness to finally fall away, leaving her in a simple state of joy and gratitude. She knew what lay before them: a life lived in God's loving care—always and forever. She took Morok's hand and hastened, with anticipation, to the foot of that glorious hill upon which the house was built. Halfene followed closely behind.

The ascent through the grounds was delightful. Up close the features of the gardens and the plants themselves were even more stunning and enticed their senses in all ways. It was distracting, but eventually, they continued on to the front door.

There was no need to knock. The door opened. An angel greeted them, majestic and ethereal. All of them were able to see him—just as clearly as if he were one of their own. He smiled, and love—pure love—emanated from his entire being. It was uplifting—and, for some, intimidating—to be in his presence. For, next to that purity, one's darkness stood out in stark contrast. Many of this group did not know, or

Chapter 24

seek to know, their Heavenly Creator. His loving touch, His healing grace, had not yet found a way into their hearts, for it had not been sought or invited. Therefore, much in them was yet unhealed. They became aware of this now and felt shame. Yet there was no judgment directed toward them by the angel. He said, simply, "Welcome."

The group filed through the door after Morok, Sol, and Loobal, crossing the threshold into an even more beautiful place than the grounds preceding it. Inside were many angels and, surprisingly, many people. The house was much larger than it had appeared from outside. They recognized no one, for these people were not from Gate-Town, nor Palador, nor Akenrah; yet they felt at ease, and even happy. They were greeted with smiles and kind words. It was truly overwhelming, for many of the group, to go from a desperate struggle for survival to *this* in under a week.

"What *is* this place?" asked Marfal, sidling up to Loobal. "Can I believe what I am seeing?"

Loobal laughed. "I know. I was expecting something pleasant, but this is truly beyond my imaginings. We are safe, Marfal," she added. "There will be no need to ever go back to what was."

A tear fell from Marfal's eye. The weight of what had been—the memories, the trauma—had been crushing her. She did not know how to let go of it. And then she saw Peter. He was standing up ahead in the hall, staring at her. She gasped. Loobal followed her gaze and gasped as well. She could see him too. Marfal ran to him, and his face broke into a huge smile. They embraced, and Marfal was trembling all over.

"I can *feel* you," she whispered excitedly. He was warm and alive and vibrant. "How is this possible? Am I dreaming?"

"A veil has parted, my love. Here, in this place, this portal, we may be with each other, for a time. I do not live here, nor may I stay; but, by the grace of God, here I am for now."

The Paths Converge

Tears were streaming down her cheeks now. She could not let go of him. But she did feel the weight lifting—the burden of fear and grief and despair. She was melting into him and he into her. And that wonderful love was a deep wellspring of healing for them both.

"W-why did you have to die?" Marfal sniffled.

"I chose it, Marfal. Not consciously, of course. But as soon as it happened, I remembered that it was what I had planned. I am sorry for what you endured, alone. It is unforgivable, I know, to leave you like that. I wanted to tell you, so that you would know you couldn't have prevented my death. It was not your fault. Something compelled me to take that walk into the meadow. I did not feel pain. It was quick. And when I realized I was dead I felt at peace with that. My regret is seeing your anguish. I have been with you as much as I could. I wanted to make sure you would be all right, that you would fulfill *your* destiny."

"And what is my destiny, Peter? What could there possibly be that would interest me now, in a life without you?"

"That is for you to discover."

She was not satisfied with his answer but laid her head against his chest, still clinging to the hope that he would stay.

"Be with your sisters, Marfal. There are still many joys for you to experience in this life. And seek God. Above all else, seek God. Of all I have learned, since beginning my new life, the most important thing is that we should be ever close to Him."

"I know, Peter. I sense this too. And I see in my sister, Loobal, the outcome of such seeking and praying. She is glorious to behold. She always was kind and gentle, but the love that pours from her now is of a quality that does not seem human."

"To my eyes, she—and Morok—appears very different than the rest of you. I see them as light, and they are brighter than you and more refined. They are more alike to the

Chapter 24

angels."

She leaned in close to him and whispered in his ear, "I would like to be that way too."

All the time they were talking, Halfene was scouring the room for Dentino. She was astounded to see Peter and Marfal embracing, and that inspired her thinking that Dentino must also be near—and visible. But he was not. Sorely disappointed and disheartened, she walked over to Morok and Loobal and shared with them her feelings.

"Why is it that I can see Peter, but Dentino is not here?" she asked, pouting.

The two looked at each other, silently negotiating who would break the news to her.

Loobal took her hand. "Halfene, this place we are in is a doorway to Heaven. There is an angelic presence here that allows us to see beyond our normal senses into the Realm of Light. Although Dentino is in the light, he is not so exalted that he can manifest in here."

"What do you mean? Was he not a good person?"

"Of course he was, Halfene. It's just that he still has some things to reconcile with himself—some healing to do. This is what I perceive, at least. Peter, to me, seems more at peace and attuned to God's will."

Halfene was not pacified. "It's not fair! I want to see him!" she complained. Despite the peaceful environment of the mansion, she was restless, and her mind was disturbed.

Loobal put a hand on her shoulder. "Perhaps you should take some time to rest. There is an angel there who is taking an interest in our conversation. Perhaps he will help you to resolve your emotions."

Halfene looked over to where Loobal was gesturing. The angel stared at her intently. It was not disconcerting, however, to be gazed at in this way; she felt only love and kindness from him. She approached him humbly. Something in her knew that Loobal was right, that she *did* need help—and rest.

The Paths Converge

The angel reached out to her. "Come with me," he said kindly. He led her down a quiet corridor, past many closed doors. She was curious to know what was behind those doors, but she followed him obediently. At the end of the hall he opened one and bade her enter. Inside was a bed and a table. The table was laden with delicious-looking fresh food and a warm drink, and the bed was adorned with intricate carvings of flowers and foliage; its cover was soft and white. A small window overlooked the gardens.

"Please," he said, "take some time to yourself. Eat. Rest. Be at peace. I will return in a while to check on you, and we may talk then, if you like."

Halfene was speechless but grateful for the special care offered to her. She nodded, with a smile, and sat down on the bed. The angel left and closed the door behind him.

Chapter 25

The Light

And so it was that the survivors of Earth's great transformation were nurtured and cared for during the transition period of her God-guided healing process. While she regained her vitality, grew and blossomed and reshaped her many glorious features, the humans in God's care, who lived in God's house, followed a healing program of their own, that they could shed the stains of lives lived in ignorance of God's laws and learn anew the ways of harmony and peace. Their bodies changed, for it was crucial that they adapt to live in a less dense environment. They lost weight, and they ate less. It did not take much food to enliven them each day, for love was plentiful, and it was like food to them: they absorbed it joyously. Gone were the days of struggling for survival. Now their days were spent exploring and learning, planning and talking. They became acquainted with the many other inhabitants with whom they shared their home, and beyond this dwelling they were brought into contact with others still. The group split up. Morok and Loobal, along with Sol, were almost always in counsel with the angels. If the new world was to thrive, it would need superb leadership. Sol grew rapidly and was introduced to playmates of similar age. He was very happy.

Marfal and Peter were permitted but a few days together, to work out their unfinished business. For Marfal, it was bittersweet; for as much as she was growing closer to

Chapter 25

Peter during this time, she knew they would soon be apart. It saddened her, although she did feel stronger and more settled than she had been. Peter reassured her that their years apart would seem like days, in the span of eternity, and that he would visit her, on occasion, as he had after he died. She would not likely be able to see him, but she would know he was there and feel the love that he had for her. He asked her if she would like to be married to someone, that her days be less lonely. At first she was shocked by the question, but after some careful reflection, she agreed that it would be nice. Still, she could not imagine anyone being as wonderful as he. He smiled.

Morok's family got to know some new people at the house, and Perchant soon fell in love with one of them. Morok presided over the wedding. Soon she was with child, as were many other women there.

Over the years that followed, the population grew in the places that God held his wondrous creations in safe keeping. And when the earth was ready to host human life once again, there was an even greater explosion of the human population. God asked for a promise from those he had saved from the world-as-it-was, from that place of despair and chaos that had once been perfect; it was a promise to remember what had passed and to teach the generations to come what had happened to the world, that they may uphold her good health and longevity and respect His laws. His laws were simple and, with the help of the angels, became well-integrated into the consciousness of each individual on Earth: to love each other as brothers and sisters; to treat all living things with kindness and respect; and to love God above all else. These were His commands.

The angels supervised the rebirth of the nations, guiding the construction of cities, for there were as of yet no cities, or even towns, in the new world. They helped integrate the survivors of the old world into the new world and to teach them how to provide sustenance for their

The Light

bodies in this new environment. As the sun shone, and the plants blossomed, and the animals roamed, the new earth was beautiful to behold, and God was pleased—very pleased. He asked Loobal one day, in her meditation, if she was ready to fulfill her role as leader of the people. The angels were preparing to leave the domain, to allow the people to try things on their own, to live and be and create for themselves that which they desired to manifest. Loobal agreed. For now Sol, her only child, was seventeen years old and a man in his own right. God's request was perfectly timed. She agreed happily. And when the angels announced to the people of that domain that God had decreed her to be their leader, there was a peaceful acceptance of this proclamation, and she was received into the position with love. Morok stood at her side, second in command, beloved of God and of the people. His wisdom and goodness had assisted many in making the great transition from the old world. Together, Loobal and Morok embraced the populace with the love of God blazing in their hearts, with His will informing their every action. Their first request of the people was simply to pray.

Epilogue

Many years later, as the sun was setting over a pristine lake at the edge of the town that Morok and Loobal called home, the couple asked God a question. They wanted to know why He had given them the opportunity to assist with the resettlement of the world. Why, when so many people had perished, had they been guided through the storm to this place of peace and perfection? The answer was simple: because they had permitted Him to guide their lives.

Pronunciation Guide

Akenrah = A-ken-raw
Alemara = a-LE-mer-uh
Ana = A-nuh
Ansera = AN-sir-uh
Aplan = a-PLAN
Astnor = AST-ner
Bekren = BECK-ren
Benshed = BEN-shed
Bentur = BEN-ter
Bertholemew = ber-TALL-e-mew
Briska = BRISS-kuh
Cerba = SIR-buh
Dentino = den-TI-no
Elbarlin = EL-bar-lin
Farentina = Fah-REN-tih-nuh
Fazpen = FAZ-pen
Fordon = FOR-dun
Frantair = fran-TARE
Gartener = GAR-te-ner
Geminus = JE-mi-nuss
Gotsro = GOT-srow
Halfene = hall-FEEN
Hanta = HAUNT-uh
Josephus = joe-SEE-fuss
Loobal = loo-BALL
Marfal = mar-FALL
Mar-hook = mar-HOOK

Meana = mee-AH-nuh
Menzoneal = men-ZOH-nee-uhl
Monseta = mon-SET-uh
Morok = moe-ROCK
Mortin = MORE-tin
nanchun = nahn-CHUN
Olner = ALL-ner
Palador = puh-LA-dore
Perchant = PER-chant
Peter = PEE-ter
Portshead = PORTS-head
Saminelle = sa-mee-NEL
Samso = SAM-soh
Senelka = se-NEL-kuh
Serbrena = sir-BRE-nuh
Sinwela = sin-WAY-luh
Sol = SALL (rhymes with TALL)
Sulfan = sul-FAN
Tanlar = tan-LAR
Yulert = YOO-lert
Zev-ran = Ze-VRAN